The Darlington Grammar School

From Pease to Peter

The Darlington Grammar School

From Pease to Peter

Dennis Perkins

JANUS PUBLISHING COMPANY LTD
Cambridge, England

First published in Great Britain 2016
by Janus Publishing Company Ltd
The Studio
High Green
Great Shelford
Cambridge CB22 5EG

www.januspublishing.co.uk

British Library Cataloguing-in-Publication Data
A catalogue record for this book is available from the British Library

ISBN   978-1-85756-852-9

Cover design: Janus Publishing Company Ltd

Cover image supplied by the author

Printed and bound in the UK by PublishPoint
from KnowledgePoint Limited, Reading.

Contents

Foreword

I first came to Darlington a fortnight after fire had destroyed the classrooms, library and quadrangle of the Queen Elizabeth Sixth Form College.

As I was a trainee journalist, I quickly learned from my sensationalist elders that what happened on 13 December 1987 was, in fact, a £750,000 inferno that had raged through the heart of the historic former grammar school.

Then the Darlington MP, Michael Fallon, weighed into the hyperbole, calling the college 'the jewel in the town's crown'.

This gave my seniors carte blanche to pun-up the headlines, so we had things like 'MP says college is class act', and 'Fire-hit college is on top form'.

Many of these were my stories because, as office junior, I was given the task of reporting on every penny raised by the £50,000 fire fundraising appeal. I was surprised by the number of raffles, bring-and-buys and disco nights that were quickly organised, and, as a newcomer, I began to realise how much this place meant to the town.

To understand it further, I looked into its past, tracing it back to 1291, although, of course, it was Queen Elizabeth who granted it its charter in 1563 – for centuries, as a grammar school, it was central to the education of Darlingtonians.

I'll leave the proper history to Dennis, except to say that I remember being taken by the Reverend Thomas Cooke, who was headmaster in the 1750s. I came across his obituary in the *Newcastle Courant* of 1783, which spoke of his religious eccentricities. 'He actually supported his doctrine of the necessity of circumcision by practising it upon himself,' it said. While in Darlington, he tried to fast for forty days, but after seventeen days was tempted by the delights of bread and water, on which he dined for twelve more days until he tucked into something more substantial. Anyway, the school governors considered him mad, discharged him after two years, and he ended up in the Bedlam asylum.

I had physics teachers like that.

My reporting role also enabled me to have a look round the charred remains – the fire starter was never traced but the fire's seat was found to be in the library, where it consumed 12,000 books. As I was shown inside the fantastically grand facade dating from the mid 1870s, my interest in the architect was ignited. It turned out to be my first encounter with a masterpiece by G.G. Hoskins, whose architectural style is to be found in everything from the Technical College, the Edward Pease Memorial Library, the King's Head Hotel, many mansions and even small Hurworth village hall – he shaped the face of Darlington with his splendid designs. I have since become a big fan of his work, so it is true that lots of learning begins in a school library – even in a burnt-out one.

After only two and a half years, I was able to report that the fire appeal had hit its £50,000 target. Although the insurance covered all the rebuilding costs, the appeal was to fund extras, like books and computers. The first book was a leather-bound volume containing the names of all the donors, with the Queen Mother's name at the head of the first page.

And still the money kept on coming. The fund eventually topped £60,000, which allowed the Victorian clock, designed by Hoskins but which had not worked for a decade, to be restored.

Such was the enthusiasm from former pupils and the wider town for fundraising that it was clear that the MP had been right all along: this educational institution has for generations been regarded as the jewel in Darlington's crown.

Chris Lloyd
Chief Feature Writer, *Northern Echo*

Introduction

I was a pupil at the Queen Elizabeth Grammar School, Darlington from 1954 to 1961 and, whilst there, had no great fondness for the place. However, I gradually became more appreciative of the benefits that it gave to those of us who were educated there. Then, more recently, I began to feel that the school's considerable influence upon Darlington was in danger of being forgotten and, in an attempt to record its legacy to the town, I took it upon myself to write an updated history up to the end of its existence in 1970.

The only earlier narrative history of the school goes back to 1963. The author was Norman Sunderland, my old history master, and it was published in conjunction with the school's 400th anniversary celebrations. Because the school's time at Vane Terrace occupied only a small proportion of that period, much of Mr Sunderland's book is devoted to the school's lengthy previous existence.

As it is my view that the school established in Vane Terrace had little real connection with its predecessor, apart from its name, I have deliberately focused on the period from 1874 when the old school closed. I have therefore provided only one chapter summarising the first three hundred or so years of the school by way of background, and in doing so, I freely acknowledge Mr Sunderland as the source of the information contained in it. Back in 1963, he expressed the belief that he had probably uncovered all of the available information about the school over those centuries before its time at Vane Terrace. I am sure that he was right.

I have attempted to record, as accurately as possible, the way the school developed, presenting events within the context of the time. Its failures, as well as its achievements, are mentioned and I have tried to avoid indulging in nostalgia. I have also tried, particularly with contentious issues such as the Peter Plan, to be objective.

To those readers who had hoped for large numbers of references to former pupils, I apologise. I have not attempted to count the number of boys who passed through the school whilst it existed at Vane Terrace, but the figure must be near ten thousand, so pupils are named only where there is a specific reason for doing so. To avoid having many lists in the text, similar considerations have had to apply to the reporting of sporting events.

In producing this history, I have received assistance from many quarters. In particular I would like to thank Katherine Williamson and Mandy Fay at the Local Studies Centre, Crown Street, Darlington; Linda Chadd, who was responsible for the Queen Elizabeth Sixth Form College Archive until its closure; and also the staff at the Durham County Records Office. In addition, I would like to thank the many people who agreed to be interviewed by me. I cannot mention them all, but amongst them were Tom Pearson, Hector Parr, Colin Dean, Arthur Hare Junior, Brian Johnson, David Hogg and Ian Dougill.

I must also mention the considerable assistance given by David Howlett, who, with Roger Butterworth, when they were both students at the Sixth Form College, produced the superb *Architectural History of the Darlington Grammar School.* To anyone who is interested in this topic I commend the book. I believe that the only copy not in private hands is the one in the Local Studies Centre at Darlington, so it warrants careful handling!

Finally, I thank my wife Linda for her constant encouragement and advice during the lengthy gestation of this book. I must stress that any errors in the text are my own.

Dennis Perkins 2016

Note:

The many references in this book to amounts of money are straightforward as far as pounds are concerned, but fractions of a pound are expressed in pre-decimal currency. With smaller sums of money, I have also shown the decimal equivalent, but with larger amounts I have not done so. Hopefully, it is sufficient for readers unfamiliar with shillings and old pence to be aware that the sum shown includes a fraction of a pound.

Three Centuries

In December 1874, the Free Grammar School of Queen Elizabeth in Darlington, with its teaching staff of two, closed and its pupils dispersed. The two-roomed school building, located in the Leadyard adjacent to the River Skerne, was sold and was later occupied by what was popularly known as 'the Ragged School', officially the Railway Jubilee School.

The Grammar School's Headmaster, the Rev. John Marshall, a man destined to see the number of his pupils decline from ninety-four to about thirty, had been induced to retire. An annual pension of £84 had been offered, conditional upon his departure, but he did not enjoy it for long, for he died in October 1875. His assistant, known as the usher, was also retired.

For more than three years after the closure, there was no functioning grammar school in Darlington, and the intended replacement, although claiming to continue the ancient traditions of the old school, was to be very different, both in scale and in concept.

In 1963 the Grammar School celebrated the four hundredth anniversary of its founding and Her Majesty Queen Elizabeth, the Queen Mother was the guest of honour at the celebrations. The event commemorated was the charter granted to the school in 1563 by Queen Elizabeth I, but it was not founded then, for it had already been there for around thirty years and possibly for much longer. Indeed, a historical exhibition in the Darlington Art Gallery in December 1954 attempted to show that such a school might have existed back in 1291.

Be that as it may, what is clear is that in 1530 Robert Marshall, a wealthy cleric from Cockerton, endowed a chapel situated in the north transept of St. Cuthbert's Church with the rents from land and buildings owned by him. The income produced was to enable the chapel priest, amongst his other duties, to keep 'a free school of grammar for all manner of children'. The purpose of the school, teaching Latin grammar, was to recruit minor clergy and it was initially housed in a one-roomed thatched building, situated between the River Skerne and the church.

The principal function of a chantry was to enable masses to be said for the souls of the dead. One consequence of the Reformation was their dissolution in 1548, for to early Protestants the practice was anathema. The chantries' assets were then taken over by the Crown, but the value of the grammar schools attached to many of them was recognised and, to keep them going, the Crown funded them. As a result, a fixed annual salary of £4 0s 8d (£4.03 in decimal currency) was allocated to the Master of the school at Darlington.

Unfortunately, because of high inflation, the salary was soon insufficient for the support of a master, and recruitment problems resulted. The consequence was that in 1563 the Earl of Westmorland and James Pilkington, the Bishop of Durham, petitioned Queen Elizabeth I, requesting that the assets of the former chantry be directly transferred to the school.

Their petition was successful, and the resultant Charter, granted at Westminster on 15 June 1563, resulted in the re-endowment of the assets for the direct benefit of the school. They comprised land at Heighington, Thornaby and in Darlington at High Row and Tubwell Row.

What the Charter did, particularly as inflation had increased the value of the endowments, was to rescue the school from financial disaster and secure its future. It also put the school's affairs on a more formal footing, by providing for it to be governed by the four churchwardens of St. Cuthbert's. They would have the power to appoint and dismiss masters and ushers. The need for replacing a warden who died or was removed was also recognised with suitable powers being given to the leading parishioners.

By the Charter, the Free Grammar School of Darlington was to be 'forever established for the perpetual education, erudition and instruction of boys and youths of that town'. Despite its name, nothing was free other than the teaching of Latin and Greek and up to 1874 the school relied upon fees for all of its pupils.

The Earl and the Bishop are still commemorated, together with Queen Elizabeth I, in the War Memorial windows in what is now the Sixth Form College Hall. They were also remembered in the School Prayer.

Little is known of the first school building except that it had a yard and that the Head's study had two fireplaces. It was demolished in 1647 at a cost of 5/6d ($27^{1/2}$p). Damage caused to it during the Scottish occupation of Darlington during the Civil War possibly contributed to its end. The replacement building was constructed of stone with a thatched roof and had a walled garden. It was erected in the same location as its predecessor.

In 1813 the burial ground at the church needed to be extended and the site of the school was required for the purpose. The second building was therefore demolished and its replacement was opened three years later in the Leadyard, a road which, more or less, lay on the line of the present road running between St. Cuthbert's Church and the Town Hall. The new building was situated at the end, by the river, close to the footbridge leading to the Ring Road. A commemorative stone inserted in the wall by the footbridge across the river shows the location.

The new school, constructed of brick, initially comprised one room only and had a small walled playground. One description says that it was:

> ... a long one-storeyed building with the Headmaster occupying a wooden erection like a huge reading desk at the north-west corner; the Second Master a much smaller one at the south-eastern corner. The boys occupied seats round the School, not unlike the stalls in a chancel.

A second storey was added in 1846 and after the closure of the school, the building survived for seventy-five years or so. Long abandoned by the 'Ragged School' and largely forgotten, it was demolished in the middle of the twentieth century. Even when the Grammar School used it, the building was seen as being unworthy of the town. To the local historian Longstaffe it was a 'mean building' and an inspector of the Charity Commission reported that the school was in a 'low and scarcely healthy situation'.

There was a portrait of Queen Elizabeth I on the east wall of the building, donated by George Allen of Blackwell Grange in the late . eighteenth century. It seems likely that the portrait now in the main corridor of the Sixth Form College (formerly in the school hall) is the same one. If so, it is probably the only remaining tangible link with the school at the Leadyard, apart from the Charter itself. The portrait is fortunate to have survived. In 1878 it was repaired at a cost of one guinea (£1.05), so there may well have been damage during storage after the closure of the old school, or in transit to its new location. Then in the days of the college it was discovered in a skip and retrieved!

The Grammar School's fortunes over the 311 years from the granting of the Charter to the closure in 1874 varied enormously. The churchwardens, as governors, were of variable quality and the endowments provided under the Charter were not always used wisely.

Financial difficulties were common and there were often insufficient funds to support the salaries of the schoolmaster and usher or to cover repairs. It was not uncommon for the vicar of St. Cuthbert's or his curate to be schoolmaster and sometimes it was necessary for the services of the usher, effectively the assistant teacher, to be dispensed with. The schoolmaster would often supplement his income by charging for extras or by taking in boarders. The majority of the schoolmasters, even if not vicar or curate at St. Cuthbert's, were clergymen.

For most of the time, the standard of education was rudimentary and, with a few exceptions, there was no attempt to teach to university level. By 1800 the school was giving little more than an elementary education to thirty-five pupils and, despite the terms of the Charter, eighteen of these were girls. There was, by then, little Latin teaching. Both pupils and teachers were expected to attend church,

After some recovery, there came, in 1836, the disastrous appointment as Headmaster of the Rev. George Wray, a 29-year-old graduate of St. John's College, Cambridge. His annual salary was £150, whilst his usher received £50. After four years there were only twelve pupils left and the few remaining parents were even being charged extra for the heating and cleaning of the school. Wray was accused of making the school his sinecure and the governors dismissed him, accusing him of gross mismanagement and dereliction of duty. He responded by refusing to hand over the keys and the usher was forced to teach the remaining pupils from temporary premises. The Darlington Grammar School had reached its lowest point.

Wray's refusal to accept his dismissal led to a lawsuit being instigated by him. He lost, but appealed. The appeal was heard in 1844 by the Lord Chief Justice and no fewer than five other judges, and was dismissed.

The replacement Headmaster, the Rev. John Marshall, was to be the last at the old premises. By 1855, when an inspection was carried out, numbers were up to fifty, the boys being described as mainly 'the sons of respectable tradesmen'. The school, however, was providing little more than an elementary education and the inspector was critical of the neglect of their duties by the churchwardens. In particular they were failing to maximise the school's income from its endowments.

At one point the numbers reached ninety-four, but there was then a continuous decline and a report of the wardens in December 1869 stated that the school had only thirty-seven pupils on its books, with ages ranging from 8 to 14. Ten were studying Latin and two Greek. Average attendance was thirty-three, the fees were £2 per annum, and Mr Marshall was fighting a losing battle. The school's decline was reflected in his personal circumstances, in that he passed from living on spacious Harewood Hill to a small rented house in Regent Street, off Northgate.

There were two fundamental problems. First, to the middle classes, the school's location close to a river now polluted as a result of industrial development was seen as being unhealthy and the developing working-class area around Park Place, across the river, was seen as being undesirable.

The second problem was that by the nineteenth century the system of government for the school was totally inappropriate. The Charter of 1563 had placed the school's government in the hands of the churchwardens. Although perhaps well fitted for performing their parochial duties, they were not necessarily equipped for also administering a grammar school. They were, by definition, Anglicans responsible for an Anglican school in a town increasingly dominated by wealthy and influential nonconformists, Quakers in particular. These new men were unable to exercise any control and were therefore unsympathetic to the plight of the school. There was little effort to teach anyone to university level and there were no additional financial resources available to effect any improvement.

The school had failed to keep pace with the expansion of the town, which had grown rapidly in size during the first half of the century. Then, in the twenty years from 1851, the population almost doubled, reaching 27,729 at the time of the 1871 census. Darlington had changed from a being a small market town, manufacturing textiles at a modest level, to a town with a substantial and growing engineering industry.

For such a town, the existing Grammar School was clearly inadequate and the consequence was that it faced competition from a considerable number of private or voluntary schools. Large numbers of parents must have concluded that there was no point in paying fees for their sons to attend the Grammar School when they could pay for an education in schools, located in more attractive areas, that were not fettered by the constraints placed upon the old school. For a town of such a size, the number of boys at the Grammar School was derisory.

The problems caused by long-obsolete charters were not peculiar to the Darlington Grammar School. Many other ancient grammar schools were in similar predicaments and the Endowed Schools Act, passed in 1869, was intended to permit the making of radical changes to their organisation. The influential citizens of Darlington soon realised that new opportunities were now available to them.

New Beginnings

During those final years at the Leadyard, the governors were not complacent about the school's difficulties, but they had little confidence in their ability to make any changes for the better. It was thought that the arrangements imposed by the Charter were so restrictive as to exclude from appointment as governors the churchwardens of the new Anglican parishes created in the expanding town, such as Holy Trinity and St. Johns. Even the number of churchwardens for St. Cuthbert's had been reduced to three as a result of the creation of a separate parish for Cockerton.

Three years before the new legislation the governors had written to the Charity Commission, the body supervising the charitable status of the school, about their concerns. The letter conceded that matters needed to be improved, and expressed the hope that a new scheme, altering the terms of the Charter, could be drawn up. In response, the Commissioners sent a copy of a plan for the reorganisation of Denbigh Grammar School as a model to work from.

Then, in April 1867, George Grace, at the time a warden but later the first Clerk to the Governors of the new school, wrote asking whether the existing Charter precluded increasing the number of trustees, i.e. governors, and whether the trustees had to be members of the Church of England. Although they were equivocal as to whether the trustees had to be Anglicans, the Commissioners ruled that the co-option of governors who were not churchwardens of St. Cuthbert's was possible. The possibility of a more broadly based governing body than had earlier been thought permissible therefore existed.

Two months later the governors submitted a draft scheme to the Charity Commission. They wanted a wider body of trustees and stressed the need to raise funds for new schoolrooms in a better part of town, thus raising a new issue, the need to remove their restraints on fund-raising. In November, after a reminder had been sent, a reply from the Commissioners was obtained. They responded cautiously, suggesting that, in the first place, action should be limited to the appointment of a suitable body of trustees.

The governors must have decided to be bold, for when the list of proposed trustees was published at the beginning of January 1868 it was seen – despite the reluctance of the Commissioners to commit themselves about trustees who were not Anglicans – to include Quakers. In response, a solicitor called Willan lodged objections, claiming that the appointment of Quakers as trustees of an Anglican charity was contrary to decided legal cases. Fortunately, after much wrangling, a compromise was reached and a new draft scheme was ready in January 1869. The new proposed governing body was wider than before and Quakers were still included.

Shortly afterwards the Endowed Schools Act came into operation and, under its terms, the Endowed Schools Commission was set up. The function of the new Commission was to facilitate the reorganisation of schools like the Grammar School, and to enable them to find additional funding. All proposed schemes would now have to be approved by this new body.

Unfortunately, large numbers of schools requested schemes, causing lengthy delays, and the result was that for three years nothing happened to the Darlington proposals. Eventually, in February 1872, its proponents were driven to involve J. Backhouse, the town's MP. His intervention proved effective and a Mr Stanton from the Commission came to Darlington at the beginning of May to investigate the situation and to report to the Commissioners.

Stanton's view was clear. A new school building was undoubtedly necessary and the existing governing body needed to be dissolved and replaced, but he also had to consider the nature of the education to be provided at the reconstituted school.

The recent legislation had categorised secondary schools into three grades and Stanton's conclusion was that a second-grade school, intended to give a 'useful and practical' education to the age of 17, was sufficient for the town. This grade envisaged pupils going into commerce or the professions and would be of more value to the professional and mercantile classes of the town than a first-grade school. The classical education up to the age of 18, intended to lead to university, normally provided by a first-grade school was not necessary for Darlington. The possibility of having the third grade, with a leaving age of only 14 and with pupils intended for commercial or industrial life, was not considered.

It should be remembered that, although compulsory education had recently been introduced, the great majority would receive an elementary education only. Secondary education, not necessarily beginning at age 11, was for the few.

The proposed grading of the school was controversial. Darlington was not keen on making do with a second-grade school and Stanton reported that the governors hoped to raise the character of the school, preferring, in their conservatism, a classical education to a scientific one. However, the Commissioners agreed with Stanton and the new school would start life as a second-grade one, but the issue about its status would be revived a few years later.

Stanton had also to consider the tricky matter of the appointment of the governing body and, in February 1873, when his draft scheme was published, there was again controversy. The proposal was for a governing body of twelve, comprising the local MP (or his nominee), two town councillors, two of the St. Cuthbert's churchwardens, two members of the School Board, and five co-opted members. Although the local School Board, a product of the Education Act 1870, controlled elementary schools only, Stanton felt it should be represented.

The *Northern Echo* and the local nonconformist ministers objected to the churchwardens' inclusion, saying it offended against religious equality, whilst, for its part, the council wanted to concentrate power in the hands of itself and the School Board. It proposed having the Mayor, the MP, the Chairman of the School Board, and three co-opted members from it, plus six nominees representing the council and the Board.

The School Board's views were similar to those of the council, but it wanted the exclusion of the Mayor. The Burgesses disagreed with everyone else, contending that all of the trustees should be elected. They also wanted a reduction in the proposed fees at the school.

After considering the responses, Stanton conceded that his inclusion of the churchwardens had been for, what he called, 'sentimental' reasons only and, despite their objections, they were dropped. Ultimately the twelve governors were to be the town's MP, the Mayor, the Chairman of the School Board, three co-opted members, three council nominees and three School Board nominees. One of the co-opted members had to live in, or be a ratepayer of, Archdeacon Newton or Cockerton. Although the School Board was independent of the town council, many of its members were also council members.

The first twelve trustees appointed included Edmund Backhouse MP, Henry Pease, the then Mayor of Darlington, and David Dale, Chairman of the School Board for the borough. The presence of at least five Quakers on the Board was partially offset by that of a Mr Plews, who traded as a wine merchant.

The numerous local private schools had benefited by the decline of the Grammar School, and, unsurprisingly, their staff joined in the debate about the nature of its replacement, presenting arguments to protect their own positions. They demanded a school that would provide 'an incentive to raising talent without being a direct rival to the private educational establishments of the town and district'. They also argued that the courses offered should not exceed those available in the 'higher class' schools in the town i.e. their own. The Grammar School Headmaster should not necessarily be a graduate and the new school should be for day boys only. So far as their observations were specific, they were disregarded.

At last, on 7 July 1874, the 'New Scheme for the Management of the Free Grammar School of Queen Elizabeth in Darlington' was approved by the Charity Commission. (As the Endowed School Commission was seen as being merely a temporary body the Charity Commission had resumed responsibility for the supervision of endowed secondary schools.) The Scheme directed the governors to sell the existing site and buy a new one, upon which a new building accommodating 150 boys was to be erected. It also directed that, without the Commissioners' sanction, no more than £2,000 of the trust funds, plus the sale proceeds of the old school, could be applied towards the new site and its buildings. The intended size of the new school would therefore necessitate raising substantial funds by a public subscription.

The school was intended to be mainly a day school, but the governors could permit the Head or other masters to receive boarders into their homes upon agreed terms. In the event, the school building itself was designed to accommodate boarders. Although subsequent changes became necessary, the 1874 Scheme proved to be the basis of the school's organisation for the next forty years.

The Entry of the Peases

At its first meeting, the new Board elected David Dale chairman, and appointed George Grace, the former churchwarden, as its clerk. It resolved that the press would be free to attend meetings, unless expressly excluded. A critical decision was then made, for it was decided to inform the existing Headmaster and his assistant that the school would close at the end of term in December and that, when it did, they would no longer be needed. The pension for Marshall, the outgoing Headmaster, was dependent upon his willingness to resign. Parents would have less than three months in which to make fresh arrangements for their sons' education.

Three and a half years later, at the opening of the new school, Dale said that but for 'the situation and character of the old school building, and, more especially, the health and age of the late Headmaster ... the old school might, with advantage, have been carried on till the new school could be provided'. Given that the town was without its Grammar School for three years and that its pupils were forced to look elsewhere for their education, it seems clear that the new governors placed little value on the old school.

At the second Board meeting, on 9 October 1874, the Charter and the School Seal were handed over by the former trustees, and the clerk was asked to inspect the school with a view to advising on the best method of disposal. Of greater significance was an announcement made by Henry Pease. He promised, for himself and for various members of his family, a gift of £5,000 for the school, provided it was matched by £2,500 found elsewhere.

A special committee was immediately set up to organise the appeal. In the resultant publicity, great stress was placed upon the value of having a good school in the town and it was argued that it would stimulate trade by encouraging persons to take up residence in Darlington or to have their sons board there. The response was immediate. Within ten days no less than £3,059 had been promised for general purposes, plus a further £2,000 for special ones. At the next governors' meeting, Arthur Pease reported that he had secured a site for the new school at Vane Terrace and, by the end of November, its suitability had been approved by the Commissioners.

At the meeting on 6 November, the governors were told that £3,660 had now been raised for general purposes, so the decision was made that the school would now provide for 200 boys, including 40 possible boarders, overriding the 150 recommended by the Commissioners. There would be dining accommodation for 60–70. The school would include a principal room, i.e. a hall, for 200 boys, together with 5 or 6 classrooms and a house for the Headmaster.

The Pease family's initiative had transformed the situation. When the churchwardens had first submitted their proposed scheme, they had merely envisaged replacement schoolrooms, presumably similar to those in the Leadyard. The funds now available would permit a development on a much grander scale than had been previously expected and the new Grammar School would be very different from the one it replaced. There was to be nothing remaining of the old regime, except for the charitable trusts.

By the end of 1874 the old school had closed and the town would be without a grammar school until a new school had been built, a new Headmaster and staff recruited and pupils found.

The Pease family (Sir Joseph W. Pease and his four brothers) responded to the initial success of the appeal by raising their gift to £6,250, thus encouraging further donations from the public. Although subscribers were keen to offer payments, they were less enthusiastic about making them and the governors were obliged to send out reminder letters over a considerable length of time. Indeed, a decision to send yet another circular pressing for payment of outstanding subscriptions was made as late as October 1877.

There is a mystery, given the immediate success of the appeal, in the form of a letter published in the *Northern Echo* of 26 February 1875. A Mr John Bowman of 'Belle Vue', Darlington stated that a gentleman, whose identity he was not yet at liberty to disclose, was concerned about 'the efficiency of the building being interfered with through lack of funds'. He had therefore authorised the writer to say that he would give £500 if another £1,500 could at once be raised. Alderman Luck, or Bowman himself, would be happy to take charge of the £1,500. These sums were, of course, modest compared with those arising from the governors' appeal. It remains unclear whether Bowman was involved with a rival and less ambitious scheme. The letter appears to have provoked no response of any kind.

In April the governors delegated three of their number to wait upon the Duke of Cleveland, the owner of the land upon which the school was to be built, to request a subscription from him. He indicated that he would consider the matter, but the published subscription list does not contain his name.

Having the offers of financial support to rely on, the governors proposed a competition intended to find a suitable architect to design the new school. They arranged for their clerk to write to various local architects on 11 January 1875 inviting them to enter. The closing date for entries was 27 February, later extended to 15 March. The school would have five classrooms, the cost was not to exceed £8,000, and consideration should be given as to how parts of the building could be omitted to keep the cost down to £6,000, if necessary. The entrants to the competition were to use pseudonyms.

It had been decided that the celebrated Alfred Waterhouse, designer of Darlington's Town Hall and clock tower and of what became Barclay's Bank on High Row, should be asked to advise on the rules for the competition and to supervise its operation. However, when it transpired that Waterhouse would not be in Darlington for some time, a Mr Giles was found as an alternative.

On 25 March, Giles reported to the trustees that in his opinion, of the seven designs submitted, the one from 'Economy and Efficiency' was far superior to the others. He did, however, express doubts about whether any of the designs could be built within the cost limits and perhaps this prompted his observation that the design he preferred was also better for curtailment than the others were. This proved to be significant.

The governors resolved to accept the recommended design. The identity of the architect was then revealed as George Gordon Hoskins and he was offered the contract. At the same time, the governors specified certain alterations to be suggested to the architect, including provision of a carriage drive to the Headmaster's house.

Hoskins, a godson of the Duchess of Gordon, was born in October 1837 and first came to Darlington in 1862 as Clerk of Works on a development at Croft. Waterhouse was the architect and, thanks to him, Hoskins then became Clerk of Works for the building of Backhouse's (later Barclay's) Bank on High Row. He stayed in Darlington for the rest of his life with a house at Thornbeck Hill on the corner of Woodland Road and Carmel Road. Later, he was a councillor and JP.

Hoskins' most notable design is perhaps Middlesbrough Town Hall, but he has left his mark upon Darlington. Amongst his designs were the Technical College on the corner of Northgate and Gladstone Street, the Edward Pease Public Library, the North of England School Furnishing Company's shop (until recently Lloyds Bank) at the bottom of Coniscliffe Road and the now demolished Greenbank Hospital. The architect's fondness for pitch pine, which had earned him the nickname of 'Pitch Pine' Hoskins, was evident in the design of the school, it being featured in wall panelling and in the hammer beam roof of the hall.

As early as 30 April 1875 the *Building News* published a drawing of the selected design. It shows the school substantially as it was built, but changes to the original design were soon made. The hall is shown on the drawing as being of slightly greater length than the finished product and it has a rounded end. The main entrance has two arches instead of the one actually provided and is approached by a sloping ramp rather than by steps. The tower is lower and appears to have a chimney stack at one side. In the background, in the playground, what looks like a child's swing is visible – a frivolous touch perhaps. Another modification, decided upon in October 1876, was the inclusion of a life-sized bust of Queen Elizabeth at the front of the tower, at a cost of £25. It was copied from the effigy on her tomb.

By the time of Hoskins' appointment, the old school had realised £390 at auction, but, for reasons which are not clear, the balance of the sale proceeds was not paid into the school's bank account until April 1878, three years later.

Giles' reservations about the costs proved to be well founded, for on 5 May Hoskins was asked to sketch out a curtailment of his designs. Having done so, he attended the governors' meeting on 12 July, when it was agreed that two classrooms were to be omitted. The Charity Commission quickly sanctioned the proposed alterations.

On 16 August 1875 the Chairman of the Governors was asked to see the Duke of Cleveland to get possession of the site for the school and it was agreed that the subscribers should be asked to pay the balances due before 1 January 1876. Others who had not offered anything would now be asked whether they would be prepared to donate.

Arthur Pease had already obtained an option on the intended site and by an indenture dated 9 September 1875, the Duke sold the land to him. By the same indenture, Pease immediately vested it in the twelve governors of the Free Grammar School of Queen Elizabeth as trustees for the school under the terms of the 1874 Scheme. The site, which has remained unchanged in size to the present time, cost £1,636 5s 0d plus £141 8s 4d to cover the expense of road and drainage construction. It comprised just over 2 acres and had its frontage on Vane Terrace, then at the very edge of the town. Open country lay behind it. The area across Vane Terrace would not be laid out as Stanhope Park until 1879. In 1880, £298 12s 10d had to be paid in respect of the school's share of the cost of making the road in Vane Terrace.

The site was adjacent to a plot of similar size already purchased by the British and Foreign Schools Society for its Training College for Elementary School Mistresses. It was to move there from temporary premises at Woodside Terrace on Grange Road. Perhaps the governors were aware that their older pupils might develop an interest in the young ladies next door, for they had suggested to the architects entering their competition that the Headmaster's house should be located at the end of the site nearest to the Training College. The house, with its grounds, would therefore form a barrier.

In the indenture the governors covenanted that no manufacture, trade or business, which might be a public or private nuisance, would be carried on. They would, within a time limit which was never specified, commence the erection of the buildings having had (if required) the plans approved by the Duke's surveyors. There were also fencing obligations imposed on the new owners.

What is odd, in view of the completion date for the purchase, is that the cheque for the balance of the price was not drawn until 10 November 1875. It seems unlikely that the Duke was prevailed upon to wait for his money, particularly as he had, in executing the indenture, already acknowledged receipt of it! More likely Arthur Pease, as the direct purchaser from the Duke, made payment, trusting the governors, many of whom were his close relatives, to reimburse him later. Although there had been other governors' meetings since the completion of the purchase on 9 September, the first report of it taking place was not given to a meeting until 17 January 1876. At the same meeting it was resolved to publish advertisements for tenders.

The Charity Commissioners' approval was required before any building work could be started, and, on 15 September 1875, they consented to the proposals, but with a condition. An assurance had to be given by the trustees that all of the costs over and above the £2,000 coming from the endowments together with the £390 from the Leadyard sale were available. Costs were increasing and many subscribers had yet to pay the money promised by them. The trustees were therefore uneasy about giving the required assurance, and they decided to defer the matter till tenders had been obtained and a response obtained from the defaulting donors.

Any delay in starting the building work would involve the setting aside of tenders and more time would be lost before the new school was available, so on 28 February 1876 a further appeal for subscriptions was made. The printed document listed subscribers with a total of £8,937 4s 0d pledged, including the five Peases with their £1,000 apiece. There was also a supplementary list with £2,100, including £1,550 from the Peases. In addition, there were donations to fund scholarships and £105 (one hundred guineas) was received from J. Marley in aid of masters' salaries.

In the appeal letter, the background to the making of the appeal was set out, and reference was made, perhaps unfairly, to delays on the part of the Charity Commission in approving the plans. The conditional nature of the approval, given in the previous September, was also referred to. The costs would now not be less than £15,000.

Available was the £2,390, comprising the permitted sum from the endowments plus the Leadyard sale proceeds, the £8,937 already promised, if not received, plus accrued interest of £250. There was therefore a deficiency of £3,423, so the required assurance as to the available funds could still not be given to the Commissioners.

The hope was that sufficient could still be raised not only to meet the shortfall, but also to avoid using the £2,000 from the endowment. Henry Pease promised that, if this could be done, he would give an extra £250. He must have been satisfied, for he made his promised payment at the end of December.

Different sources quote the sum eventually raised by public subscription as £11,000 or £13,316. To this must be added approximately £2,600, comprising the endowments of £2,000, the sale proceeds of the old school of £390, and the accrued interest on the donations received. If the total cost was indeed about £15,000, over £12,000 must have been raised by public subscription.

By March 1876 the trustees were sufficiently confident to award the first building contracts and work started. As the aim was to complete the school within eighteen months, the contractors were subject to penalties for delays. In the same month Hoskins successfully asked for £200 in part payment of his commission. In July it was decided not to have a foundation stone and in March of the following year the hanging of the bells was arranged at a price of £1 7s 0d (£1.35) per bell. As there were still recalcitrant subscribers another circular had to be sent, reminding them of the amounts still due.

Progress with the building work was not always smooth and when, in the summer of 1877, time was lost because of a strike, several contractors were given notice that the penalty clauses in their contracts were to be enforced. During the building of the school there were frequent complaints to one of the main contractors, Messrs Hornsey, about delays and shortages of bricks.

By May 1877 fire cover of £5,000 on the partly completed building had been arranged with Liverpool and London and Globe Insurance Company. Cover was not increased until March 1879 – over a year after the building was finished. It was then for £7,500, plus £200 for outbuildings, at an annual premium of £6.

Viewed from Vane Terrace, the new school, built in a style described by Hoskins as 'Scholastic Gothic', looked similar to the structure today. The main differences are that the hall is now longer and has rooms under it, and that, at the north end, the turret with the pinnacle over it has gone, demolished in 1971, when the newly formed Sixth Form College constructed the first of its many extensions on the site.

It was undoubtedly impressive set against the mean little structure in the Leadyard. Yet the reality is that, despite the successful fund-raising, the new building had only three classrooms, one more than its predecessor. It remained the intention of the trustees to build additional classrooms when more money was available.

The new building had two projecting rear wings running at right angles from the frontage. One ran from behind the entrance hall, whilst the other was at the north or Trinity Road end. The area between the two wings formed a courtyard, open at the rear.

What seems surprising now is how the space in the school was distributed; and, to present-day readers, the governors' sense of priorities, given the need to cut back on the original design, may seem questionable.

The entire north wing comprised the Headmaster's house with its own front door. On the ground floor a dining room, sitting room and study were provided. There were also a kitchen and a serving room. These catered for the needs of the boarders as well as those of the Head and his family, but the serving room was also the servants' dining hall. At first-floor level, there were no fewer than five bedrooms plus two dressing rooms and two servants' dormitories.

In addition, there was a basement at the rear of the house and here were located the Head's wine and beer cellars. This was where the pottery shop was located in 1963. The Headmaster was also provided with a large rear garden, with an orchard behind it. The arrangements for laying out this and the school playground were agreed on 21 June 1877.

A covered way ran along the Headmaster's side of the courtyard. It segregated the boys from his kitchen courtyard and provided access to the area behind the house, which included an outbuilding. Outside stairs led from the rear end of the kitchen to that courtyard.

Half of the outbuilding, accessible only from the house, comprised a wash house and bake house. The other half contained the boys' toilets, and a parallel covered way, apparently open on the school courtyard side, gave access.

Within the house lay the library, used variously in later years as the library workshop and as the school secretary's office. It measured 15 feet 6 inches by 17 feet, and access was obtained via the Head's vestibule. The school itself had no library, but whether pupils were allowed to use the Headmaster's is not known.

At ground level, there was a corridor, familiar to later generations of boys as 'the main corridor', connecting the house to the school entrance under the tower and, on the Vane Terrace side, there were two rooms. One, by far the larger, was the dining hall. It was to serve the boarders' needs, but day boys, upon payment, could also eat there. A feature of the room was the baronial chimney-piece at each end. At that time there were two doors to it, the one nearer the house being reserved for the Head's exclusive use. It became successively the gym and the library and is now the recreation area called 'the space'.

Next to it, with its door facing onto the entrance hall, was the sitting room of the Housemaster. He would live in and be responsible for the boarders outside school hours. Across the corridor lay the boot room, 8' deep, and on the hall side of it there was a lavatory.

Directly above his sitting room was the Housemaster's bedroom, remembered by many pupils of later years as the Head's study. Between it and a door on the stairs giving access from the Head's house were two rooms, familiar to later generations of first-year boys as Rooms 23 and 24. These were the dormitories for the junior pupils, each room having beds for eight. Older boys were to be appointed monitors to keep an eye on the younger boarders.

The wing behind the entrance hall and tower contained, at ground-floor level, the three original classrooms. Access to them was via an enclosed corridor. The direct access from the courtyard, sheltered by a veranda and familiar to later pupils, did not appear till much later. The fourth side of the courtyard was completely open to the school yard behind.

On the first floor, above the classrooms, was the senior dormitory, also with space for sixteen. Each pupil had an individual window, a bed, a chest of drawers, a washstand, a chair and space for a trunk. Later there was a physics lab here.

Between the dormitory and the stairs there was a linen room, a bathroom with two baths, WCs and a housemaid's closet. There were, until the school ceased to have boarders, no stairs at the rear of the wing, so, unless the door to the Head's stairs was unlocked, the only staircase available for an escape in the event of fire was the one leading to the entrance hall. Fire regulations belonged to the future. Given the layout of the school, it is difficult to see why, for several decades, day boys should have need to venture upstairs.

There was also a second basement located under the main school entrance area. The heating system was here, together with coal storage. The use of water pipes to heat the entire school was seen as worthy of comment when the building was new. The basement also contained a workshop-cum-lab, but there would be no proper laboratory for some years. The school was lit by gas.

Across the main entrance hall lay the school hall. It was about two-thirds of the length of the current building. Despite the sloping site, it was built on the same level as the rest of the school, but the area beneath it was not utilised for teaching purposes. The hall simply rested on arches, thus providing a covered play area. Entry to and from the school could be gained in wet weather via the steps leading down from the entrance hall. There was no proper stage in the main hall until after it had been extended, but before that, in the early years at least, there was a platform.

There are three shields on the western face of the tower (the yard side), the centre one depicting an owl, representing wisdom. The side shields show the dates of the foundation of the school and of its re-establishment at Vane Terrace.

The lowest level of the tower, later the Natural History Museum part I, originally contained a cistern of 1,500 gallons' capacity to provide for the school's water needs. The next level (part II of the Museum) was a box room and was used for the storage of boarders' trunks. The original intention was to install the school bell in the centre turret or spire of the hall, but it was actually installed in the tower, where it still remains. In 1880 Henry Pease donated a clock for the tower in memory of his wife.

There were initially only two entrances into the school grounds and both were on Vane Terrace. The northernmost one was the drive leading to the Head's house, but a path from it gave access to the main door under the tower. The other led directly to the main entrance, but the stairs below the hall were also available. There was no way in from what was to become Abbey Road until 1881, when, to facilitate access to the cricket field on Abbey Road, an opening (probably the one at the corner of Vane Terrace) was inserted. In later years at least, pupils, other than prefects, were forbidden to use the main entrance.

Admission to the school was to be open to all pupils of good character and good health, provided that they passed the entrance examination set by the Headmaster. As befitted a school starting with no pupils, this examination seems to have been rudimentary in character. The school's grade-two status had the restrictive effect of prohibiting the admission of boys under eight and of requiring pupils to leave by the end of the term in which they attained the age of seventeen.

The governors placed advertisements for a headmaster in various national and local newspapers in May 1877 and by June had been rewarded by no fewer than fifty-five applications. A shortlist of five, including three clergymen, was produced. Those on it were requested to attend for interview in July on the basis that they would have their first-class railway fares paid. One of them was Philip Wood and on 2 August, after the chairman's casting vote had been required, he was appointed Headmaster of the new school. Remarkably, he was to be the first of only four between 1877 and 1970 and would himself serve for thirty-four of those years. Of the four, three were in their early or mid thirties when they were appointed.

Wood, described as a 'muscular Christian', was born in Dunbar in 1846 and was awarded a first-class honours degree in mathematics at Edinburgh University in 1870. Before coming to Darlington he taught at two prestigious Edinburgh schools.

The new Headmaster attended the governors' meeting held on 27 August, when it was agreed that the school would open in the third week of January 1878 and that advertising for pupils would now take place. An entrance fee of £1 per boy was to be payable, but this would be remitted for those enrolling before the school opened. At a later date, the decision was made to remit the fee until the school was full.

The Head's salary, or stipend, was a modest £130 per annum, but, in addition, he would be paid a capitation fee of £4 per year for each boy attending the school. These fees would considerably increase his income and provide a strong incentive to increase the numbers at the school. A roll of only 100 boys would therefore produce an annual income of £530 and an increase of another 100 boys would add a further £400. In addition he was provided with the house.

Wood was to appoint the assistant masters and would pay their salaries from a sum assigned to him for that purpose by the governors. They would also allocate him money for the maintenance of 'plant and apparatus'. Whilst the governors were to prescribe the subjects to be taught, the Headmaster would control the choice of books and the teaching methods, and the arrangement of classes and their hours. He would also be responsible for discipline and management. Before the school opened, Wood was required to sign a declaration that he would discharge his duties to the best of his ability.

The curriculum was to include religious instruction, reading, writing, maths, arithmetic (taught as a separate subject), English grammar, composition and literature, together with history, geography, Latin, French or German, natural science, drawing and vocal music. That, at least, was the expressed intention, but not all of the subjects listed were taught in the immediate period after the school opened. The scheme contained a conscience clause permitting exemption from religious instruction and worship, where appropriate.

The initial advertising of the school referred to the fees payable, but also indicated that nine scholarships tenable at the school were available and that three more would be available to assist boys from the school who had gone on to university.

By December 1877 the Head had appointed the staff, and seventy boys had passed the examination for admission, but the school was not quite finished. On the 10th of that month Hoskins had expressed the hope that it would be ready within two weeks, with the approach to it finished in three. On the same date notice was received from Darlington Corporation requiring the school to flag and repair the road in Vane Terrace. A further notice, requiring it to flag and repair that part of Duke Street (later Abbey Road) onto which the school abutted, was received in the following February.

Surprisingly, the school desks were not ordered until 21 December and at the same time the governors changed their minds about the paling originally intended to run along the boundary between the Headmaster's intended garden and orchard and the school yard. They decided to have a wall, six feet high, in its place. The result would be to shut off, even from sight, the Head's private area. The governors also had the foresight to arrange with Wood that as much of his land as lay within 80 feet of the rear boundary might, at any time, be added to the school playground. It was on this land that the school gym was to be built sixty years later.

Even when the opening was imminent, there were still matters to attend to. On 14 January the Building and Finance Committee instructed Hoskins to form a path for the scholars around the classrooms and to put up temporary rails, posts and steps; and four days later he was asked to design seats for the grandly named science room, i.e. the basement workshop. It was March before Hoskins was asked to prepare plans for levelling and gravelling the remainder of the playground and the specification for laying it out was not approved until three months after the opening.

At about this time the governors received a rating assessment of £300 for the new school. They were not happy, thinking that £250 was sufficient, and after fruitless correspondence, an appeal to the Petty Sessions was lodged, but it failed. Shortly afterwards, in January 1879, the school contributed £166 13s 4d to the open space in front of the school, purchased by the council. It is not clear whether the payment was a contribution towards the price or towards the cost of laying out the park that appeared on the site. As the payment was one third of £500, it looks as if the costs were split three ways.

By January 1878, after three years without a grammar school in the town, everything was ready, apart from the loose ends mentioned. Then, on the 12th, nine days before the official opening, the Mayor and Mayoress, Mr and Mrs Theodore Fry, were hosts at an evening of entertainment at the school. The function was described in the *Darlington and Stockton Times* in an article entitled 'Conversazione' and the account in the paper was so extravagant in its language that the use of French was resorted to on three separate occasions. There were over three hundred guests, including many Peases and Backhouses. Amongst the others were many local worthies whose names are borne by the surviving nineteenth-century streets of Darlington.

A long covered way, crimson carpeted, with plant borders, led from the street to the main entrance. The guests were protected from the chilly night air by screens along the sides. The reception was held in the 'large room' – presumably the school hall – and, on a raised platform, 'a select band of ladies and gentlemen' gave vocal and instrumental performances during the evening. Refreshments were served at intervals in the dining hall. The school was converted into 'a veritable museum' with an *'embarras de riches'* (sic), comprising flags, trophies and antique pottery, and plants and flowers from the Mayor's hothouses · decorated the reception rooms. The rare and costly pottery came from the Mayor's house, 'Woodburn'. Some of it was said to date back to the age of 'Homer's forebears'.

A Mr Lindsay performed scientific experiments and there was a display of microscopes, each with a specimen to view. However, both the orchestra and Mr Lindsay were upstaged by Professor Bell's telephone, the new wonder of the age. A quarter of a mile of wire connected the instrument to the adjacent Training College and guests were permitted to speak one sentence to the operator at the other end. Even though the telephone had five ear-pieces, enabling five people to be present at the same time, it proved to be impossible to satisfy the demand during the evening. Arrangements therefore had to be made to exhibit the telephone again on the following morning, till 11 a.m.

The New School

On Monday 21 January 1878, before a large assembly of guests, the school was officially opened by David Dale, the Chairman of the Governors, and a lengthy article describing the ceremony appeared in the *Darlington and Stockton Times* of 26 January.

Despite its impressive building, the school was starting from scratch and in the early days various limitations were apparent.

At its opening, the school possessed, in addition to Mr Wood, only two full-time masters. They were W.E. Inchbold, described as a tiny man with large side-whiskers, who was invariably accompanied by a large bull terrier, and C.W. Garrard. They received salaries of £200 and £100 respectively, and both had departed within eighteen months. Inchbold taught classics and Garrard English, leaving maths to the Headmaster. There were also three part-time masters who taught music, French and drawing respectively. The rooms deleted from the original design became available in 1881. Until then, the three initial classrooms had to cater for all pupils, but the school hall was available for teaching by the part-time staff. Use was also made of the workshop, which doubled as a lab although it had no proper equipment.

According to L.W. Williamson, one of the original pupils, there was a porter called George. He looked after the furnace, came into the classrooms to stoke up the fires, and was also responsible for ringing the school bell.

The three classes in the school, which sufficed for the entire age range, were simply numbered 1, 2 and 3. On the opening day, the boys were lined up around the walls of the hall; Mr Wood read out their names in turn and allocated each one to his class. For the first term, the number of weekly lessons in each subject would be as follows:

	Class 1	Class 2	Class 3
English	12	8	6
Classics	9	8	9
Maths	7	8	10
French	0	2	2
Drawing	0	2	2
Singing	1	1	0
Scripture	1	1	1

The limited number of subjects initially taught showed little improvement in the breadth of the curriculum over the previous school and fell short of the governors' intentions. At this stage there was no teaching of science (despite the science room), geography or history and there was no kind of physical education. For Dr Muller, the German teacher of French, there was no opportunity for him to teach his native language. There were only four French lessons per week in the entire school in those early days, but by September Muller was teaching French for an extra two hours per week.

The need to put boys of different ages in the same class would have been of much less concern to the Victorians than to us. The choice of class for a pupil was as likely to be determined by attainment as by age and it was common for a pupil who was seen as not having made the grade to be kept in the same class for a further year. Views as to the age when a full grammar school education should begin were variable. It seems that, at this time, the Darlington Grammar School regarded the process as beginning at an early age, whilst, forty or so years later, many pupils at the school, particularly those who were not scholarship boys, were seen as needing pre-grammar school tuition up to age 13.

In July 1879 the practice of awarding class prizes was started and, at the beginning of the next term, the teaching of Greek (as permitted by the Scheme) was introduced, but an extra fee of £3 per annum was charged. By April 1880 fourteen boys were paying it, but, with the growth of the school, the number of Greek scholars increased and by 1884 there were twenty-eight.

The tuition fees had been fixed by the governors and at the time of opening were as follows: for 8–10 years £2, for 10–12 years £2 13s 4d (£2.67), for 12–14 years £3 6s 8d (£3.33) and for those over 14, £4. The charges were per term. In addition, there was the one-off entrance fee of £1, but this would not be charged until the school was up to capacity. Such was the low rate of inflation that the fees in 1914 were not significantly different. Boarders were to pay an extra £16 per term, with washing included, and day boys could lunch at the school for £3 10s per term.

By contrast, Gainford School, which boasted five classrooms, cricket and croquet grounds, a fives court, a library, gymnasium and bathrooms, advertised its fees in guineas. They ranged from 11 guineas per term to 16 guineas.

There were three terms with eleven weeks' holiday per year, i.e. two weeks at Easter, six weeks during the summer and three weeks at Christmas, but there seems to have been no provision for half-term holidays. The school had a five-day week and the hours were 9 a.m. till 4 p.m., but with a generous two-hour lunch break from 12 noon to 2 p.m. The mornings were occupied by four lessons of three-quarters of an hour each, and there would be two, each of one hour, in an afternoon. It will be seen that no time was allocated for breaks. By comparison, the school of 1855 had five more hours in the week with only eight weeks' annual holiday.

There was an assembly each Monday morning in the hall with prayers, including the Lord's Prayer, and the first period in each class on a Monday morning was to be given over to a Bible lesson. This caused one parent to complain to the press in October 1879 about the lack of religious instruction. He said he thought the requirement to buy a Bible for his son indicated that the subject would be taught more frequently than only on Monday mornings.

Sixty-eight boys had been registered for the school by the opening day, although two never turned up. The distinction of being the first pupil to be enrolled had fallen to William Edward Fisher of 16 Kendrew Street, a 10-year-old who had previously been educated at home. He left after six years and was one of the few early pupils to remain at the school for any length of time.

Half a term's notice was required of any parent wishing to withdraw a boy from the school, a stipulation which continued long enough to be set out in the School Lists published by the school in the middle of the twentieth century, although by then surely unenforceable. However, it the early days, parents who failed to give the requisite notice were normally pursued for the outstanding fees. Similarly, where fees had been paid in advance, the school would always refuse to return any part when a pupil was withdrawn without proper notice, unless the cause was the boy's illness.

Hoskins showed faith in the school he had designed, for amongst the first entrants were his two sons. The first entrants were aged from 8 (the youngest permitted by the Scheme) to 15 and, apart from one from Shildon and another from Northallerton, all came from Darlington, Cockerton or Sadberge. Unfortunately, the admissions register does not indicate whether a pupil was a boarder. Only one boy had been previously educated at a Board School; the rest, apart from a few ostensibly educated at home, came from the various small private schools then existing in Darlington.

Starting a school where the pupils, all new, spanned such a wide age range must have presented many problems and by 1880 a substantial proportion of the initial intake had gone, some after only two terms. The oldest pupils would have had only a year or two's schooling left when they arrived, and there were probably many pupils who simply proved to be unsuitable.

By the end of the first month fees for eighty-one boys had been paid, so, even in those early weeks, there was an increase in numbers. A few more pupils arrived during the first couple of months and although a batch of twelve started on 29 April 1878, no fewer than ten of them had gone by 1880. By mid 1879, the number of pupils had increased to 132, but too many boys were still leaving after only a year at the school. Admittedly, some had been aged 14 or 15 when they arrived. The practice of pupils starting at the beginning of the winter or spring terms or entering the school mid term caused the school inconvenience for many years.

Wood expressed himself satisfied with the school's results at the end of the first year, but he conceded that they would have been bad had the school not been new. It does appear that many of the early entrants were backward and not well behaved. There were no prefects until decades later.

The register recorded the 250th entry in May 1881, but about 100 of the earlier pupils had gone by then. Not every pupil lived in the affluent areas of Darlington, for a significant proportion of them came from the streets near the town centre, or from Bank Top, Albert Hill, and Rise Carr.

By the early 1880s an increased proportion of pupils were coming from out of town but it is impossible to identify the boarders. We know that during this period boys living in locations like Shildon and Northallerton were travelling daily to the school. They at least had a rail connection to Darlington, but what about pupils from Sadberge or Denton? Did they, unless they lodged in Darlington during the week, walk every day? The useable bicycle was still a few years off. The proportion coming from Board or Church schools, as distinct from private schools, was also increasing.

Entry number 300 was William Chaytor, son of Sir William Chaytor of Croft Hall. Born in June 1867 he was admitted, mid term, on 14 November 1882 at the age of 15, but he had gone by Easter 1883. He came to the school from no less an institution than Harrow, so one is left wondering what caused such a sudden fall in status.

An early visitor to the school was Cha'en Yuan Chi, the First Secretary to the Chinese Legation. Lessons had ended when he arrived on 28 October 1878, but he spoke to the boarders. He was returning from a visit to Raby and it is not clear whether the school expected him. The pupils at large were no doubt gratified, even though most of them did not set eyes on the visitor, for a half-day's holiday was announced to commemorate the event.

Not surprisingly, the local press always showed interest in the new venture and it was not always uncritical. The *North Eastern Independent* seems to have been a journal priding itself on being outspoken and, in its issue of 22 May 1880, it reprimanded the Head. He had refused a half-holiday on the previous Tuesday even though it had been the custom since time immemorial for Whit Tuesday to be celebrated as a holiday in the town.

Six months later, it was complaining of the clique of wealthy men of 'the dominant class' who kept control of everything in Darlington, including the Grammar School. The school had 'failed to a considerable extent to answer the expectations formed of it'. The cause must be management, it said, going on to claim that, in the previous year, an inspector was far from satisfied with the school's efficiency.

The newspaper, in other issues, was critical of the selection of governors, suggesting that those in control, namely the Pease family and their associates, elected new members from their own ranks. Often those elected had too many commitments elsewhere to give the school proper attention. The poor attendance record at governors' meetings over the years suggests that there was justification for this criticism.

Mr Wood kept a book of press cuttings relating to the school and, to his credit, those articles and letters that were unfavourable were included.

The 1881 census shows the school's residents as being the Head and his wife and two children, together with Wood's sister-in-law Sarah Lawrence, then aged 31. His son could later claim the unusual distinction of having been born on the school premises! Thomas Warne, aged 23, lived in as Housemaster and seventeen boarders, aged from 10 to 17, are also listed, together with five resident servants, all female.

By this time, further fundraising had made the construction of the intended extension possible. The need was desperate, as it had become necessary to use two bedrooms as classrooms. It is not clear whether these were in the Head's house or whether dormitories were used.

The extension, also designed by Hoskins, was of two storeys, and was built at right angles to the south wing, so there was then a 'T' shaped block behind the tower. On the ground floor there were four additional classrooms, served by a passage. The doors for the two end rooms faced onto the ends of the passage so these two rooms were larger than the others.

The intention had been to build the single-storey classroom block only and tenders to a total value of £976 18s 6d had been accepted. Then on 9 May 1881, as an afterthought, the governors decided to add an additional floor to provide more dormitory accommodation at an estimated extra cost of £570. The new block was insured for £1,000.

The upper extension made room for twenty-three senior boarders, so the entire extension at first-floor level was still given over to accommodation. As on the first floor, the end rooms were larger. Two rooms which had fireplaces may have been used to house monitors or sick pupils, but it is possible that one of them was occupied by a matron. The only access to the new rooms was through the existing dormitories. Around this time a doorway was installed in the classroom corridor to give direct access into the yard.

As the existing boarding accommodation was full in 1881, the decision to extend it is understandable, but hindsight shows that it was a mistaken one. There followed a steady fall in the number of pupils who boarded, but there was no reduction in the space allocated for them before 1914.

A couple of years later, in April 1883, one of the masters, Mr Pryce, soon to become Headmaster of Coatham Grammar School, indicated that he wanted to receive a few pupils as boarders, believing that their friends might then be influenced to come to the school. He had apparently incurred preliminary expenses in the belief that the governors had already sanctioned the practice. The governors were unanimous that 'it was inexpedient, at any rate in the present position of the Boarding Department, to authorise the taking of Boarders by assistant masters and others'.

However, because of the special circumstances, Pryce was allowed four boarders, provided that their identities, and the payment terms, were reported to the governors. He complied, charging the same fees as the school. The wording of the governors' response suggests that, even by then, the school's boarding capacity was far from full.

The additional classrooms enabled the Head to double the number of forms to six and, as a result, a tender from the North of England School Furnishing Company of Darlington was accepted in November

1881. It was for the supply of four masters' desks with two chairs, two slate blackboards, plus sixteen desks for pupils. As the desks were to be seven and a half feet long and would be supplied with five inkwells each, it appears that a mere eighteen inches was allocated to each pupil! The total price was £69 15s 0d.

As there were now seven rooms, the governors took the opportunity to provide themselves with a meeting room and Mr Hoskins was instructed to provide fire irons and twelve chairs for their use. Soon afterwards, the Head was asked to provide them with a table. The location of the original room is not known, but by the beginning of the next century, one of the junior dormitories, no longer needed for its original purpose, was being used by the governors.

The increasing number of pupils had made it possible to increase the number of staff, and, within two years of opening – even before the construction of the additional classrooms – there were five full-time members, in addition to Wood.

Alfred Massingham on a salary of £200, increased to £250 by May 1880, had replaced Inchbold. Known as 'Massey', he became the Head's 'right-hand man' and he served the school for thirty-three years until his sudden death in 1910 at the very end of Wood's regime. He was on sufficiently close terms with the Headmaster to play golf with him at Seaton Carew. Garrard's successor was W.C. Anderson at a salary of £130.

The three additional masters were T.W. Barker, T.J.C. Warne (otherwise Cleeve-Warne) and A.C. Tofts. Warne, as, the Housemaster, lived in and presumably had free board and accommodation, so had to make do with a salary of £80, whilst Tofts was paid £100. In January 1880 these salaries were increased to £90 and £120.

Because Barker had a qualification in drawing, he was initially paid £120 and the services of the part-time drawing teacher Samuel Elton were dispensed with. However, when his two contemporaries had their salaries raised, the governors declined Barker's request for an increase.

There was another addition in September 1881, when, as there were now six forms, Edward Bowman came as the First Form Master. Whether there were doubts about the cost involved or whether the Headmaster had a strong desire to keep Bowman is not known, but in November he offered to contribute £40 towards the new master's total salary of £120, as from January 1883. The governors accepted the offer, but Bowman resigned in December, after one term. He was replaced by W.B. Woollam. He received the same pay, but is not clear whether Wood's offer also applied to him.

All teachers, on appointment, were given a copy of the Scheme that regulated the operation of the school. During this period, it was the practice for First-Formers to go to Mr Wood on a Friday for reading.

The governors seem to have regretted offering Wood a capitation fee of £4 per pupil, for in September 1879, when there were more than 130 in the school, the amount was reduced to £3 per annum on each boy in excess of 120. Despite the adverse change to the capitation fee, Wood could, on current admission levels, expect an annual income well in excess of £600, plus free accommodation. At the same time the entrance fee for boys over twelve was doubled to £2, but the increase would not apply to boys coming from the local elementary schools.

Speech Days, held at the end of the school year in late July, were a regular event from the beginning. No attempts were made to find a distinguished speaker, but a local MP would often be in attendance. The proceedings were interspersed by recitations from pupils. For instance, at the 1885 Speech Day no fewer than eleven separate recitations were given by pupils, including a scene from *Les Femmes Savantes* presented by three boys. Despite the *Northern Standard's* denigration of the recitations, the practice continued for many years.

The report of the 1880 Speech Day in the *Darlington and Stockton Times* indicated that the annual exams were held under the auspices of the Cambridge Syndicate for Local Examinations and were entirely in writing for the Upper School, but were partly oral in the lower forms. Unfortunately, the results had not been received by Speech Day.

On 4 September 1880 the same newspaper indicated the latest Syndicate report was before the governors. It stated that there had been a marked improvement since the previous year, with an advance in both the range and quality of the work. The standard of handwriting in the school was criticised, but in other respects the school 'was in the highest degree satisfactory'. New subjects had been added and the extra class had allowed the Sixth Form to produce some creditable work.

Discipline had also improved. The examiner stated that 'the somewhat rough set of lads whom I then found having, either disappeared from the School, or having fallen gracefully into habits of good order, so that a most gentlemanly tone appears to pervade the whole School'. He went on to mention that some marks had been lost through boys writing on both sides of the paper. The criticism about handwriting was endorsed in letters to the local press.

The Cambridge examiner's report for 1882 was a favourable one and the teaching of French and German was singled out for praise. Wood must have been gratified, as, shortly before, he had established what he called 'the Modern Side', enabling boys to study French and German in preference to Latin and Greek.

By this time pupils who had left the new school were beginning to have successes. The first exhibitioner, James Brown, was a medical student at Edinburgh. Another was C.G. Glover, who unfortunately died at twenty-three. Other former pupils had passed the preliminary examinations of the Law Society or of the Pharmaceutical Society. Another pupil, R.B. Dixon, entered the Royal Naval College at Greenwich after leaving the school in 1885. He ended his career as Vice-Admiral Sir Robert Bland Dixon, Engineer-in-Chief to the Fleet.

By 1884 there were eight boys in the Sixth Form studying Greek and, doubtless to the relief of those who had expressed their concerns, the handwriting of pupils was reported to be much improved.

For the financial year ending on 31 December 1879 the school's total income of £1,997 0s 8d was nearly matched by its expenditure of £1,910 9s 7d. The payments to the Head accounted for almost one third of this figure. Fees, including entrance fees where charged, produced £1,264 6s 8d, the Bellasses Charity (of which more later) provided £110 14s 0d and the remaining income came from the endowments and interest. The school was responsible for repairs to the Headmaster's house and for the rates due on it and during the year paid out £33 15s 9d. There is nothing in the published summaries of the accounts to suggest that they were ever audited before 1908.

The 1879 accounts are significant in that they are the last not to show any income from public sources. Even then there were public grants to be had, and an application for funds for science teaching was made to the Science and Art Department of the Committee of the Council on Education, a predecessor of the Board of Education.

Anderson was promised that he would receive half of any teaching grant received, so the implication is that, although engaged as an English teacher, he was paid to teach science too. If so, Anderson was successful, because in addition to his receiving £25 per year from the funds, the school regularly received payments from the Department for its science examination results, starting with £44 in 1880. By November 1882, the payment had increased to £61, and in subsequent years, payments of a similar size were received. As the Cambridge board did not examine science subjects, the examinations of the Department of Science and were taken. In 1880, twenty-nine out of thirty-five candidates passed in magnetism and electricity, with ten out of fourteen successful in inorganic chemistry. Unfortunately, only seven out of twenty-nine passed physiography, described as 'a kind of rationalised geography'.

The school also decided that drawing would, in future, be taught in accordance with the same Department's requirements. The decision proved to be justified, for it too led to payments being received.

It may be that the school failed to keep pace with the Department's requirements, for by the late 1880s the payments fell. In 1888 the amount received was £30, and after some fluctuations was down to £13 in 1892 and £17 6s 0d in 1893.

The school's first concert took place in the hall on 2 April 1880. The purpose was to raise funds for the new cricket field and tickets were priced at 4/- (20p) for reserved ones, and at 2/- (10p) for the others; substantial prices for the time. J.W. Marshall, the part-time music teacher, was the accompanist and reserved tickets could be purchased from his music rooms in Northumberland Street. The performers were described as 'Amateurs' and Dr Muller was amongst their number. The school Glee Club also performed.

A second concert, this time in aid of School Sports, followed on Friday 8 April 1881. This time all tickets were 2/6d (12½p) and the Glee Club again performed. The concerts then became established as an annual event in April or late March every year. By 1882 the school

Glee Club was said to have about forty members, but thereafter their numbers declined.

The school was not without adverse publicity during its early years at Vane Terrace. The behaviour of pupils led to correspondence in the *North Star* in February 1880. A correspondent describing himself as 'A Resident' referred to the barbarism of those 'young rebels' attending the Darlington Grammar School, saying there was a continued nuisance of snowballing in the Duke Street and Winston Street area. He wrote:

> For the last month, scarcely a day passed without a regular row in those streets and I am sorry to say that, in every case, it has been commenced by boys from the Grammar School. Some people living in these streets have had to fasten their doors, being quite alarmed by the noise of one or two hundred boys in a row. As I write these lines, there are about six squares of glass broken in the Wesleyan Chapel windows facing Winston Street. The police would have no difficulty in seeing these young rebels between four and five o'clock every afternoon.

The boys did not take this criticism lying down. They responded in graphic terms, saying:

> A volley of stones always awaits us going along Duke Street and if 'a resident' thinks they [sic] will not retaliate, we beg to differ with him. The young beggars from other schools stop some of the Grammar School boys on their way home to the town, and, of course, we can't see them slaughtered in cold blood without coming to the rescue.

They alleged that they were greatly outnumbered and claimed that most of the broken windows resulted from their adversaries' stones. The pupils' account was backed by a letter from 'Another Resident'. The police do not seem to have ever intervened.

Four years later, it was much worse. There was considerable press publicity, not only in local newspapers, about discipline at the school.

It concerned Arnold Davison, a 10-year-old pupil. His gravestone at Grangetown, Sunderland records that he died on 7 May 1885 'of injuries sustained whilst attending to his duties at the Grammar School, Darlington'. The boy, described as delicate, was the son of David and Esther Davison of Lieben Lodge, Coniscliffe Road. The father was said to be of independent means. The death was of sufficient concern to justify the calling of an emergency meeting of the governors on the same day. It also justified no fewer than five governors attending the inquest to represent the school.

On 21 April, the boy had complained on his return from school that he had been pulled about and trodden on by other boys. No complaint was made to the school, but after a short time Arnold developed a pain in his leg and eventually was barely able to walk. He was seen by two doctors, but then died.

At the inquest Mr Davison complained that his son had been subjected to attacks almost every day and that there had been a lack of care on the part of the school. He insisted that his son had come home after the final incident harassed and distressed and with clothes sodden. The allegation was that boys in the Fifth and Sixth Forms were responsible and that one George Gardner Peacock was the worst offender. Peacock gave evidence, saying that he had got hold of several boys by the hand and pulled them down three steps to make way 'for his entrance to a courtyard'. When he was pulled, the deceased might have fallen. The Coroner was somewhat dismissive about the allegation, suggesting to Arnold's father that boys tended to be rough.

The two doctors concurred as to the cause of death. They suspected 'an internal inflammatory fever caused by some deep-seated mischief'. A verdict of accidental death was recorded, the Coroner stating that there was no blame on the Headmaster, the staff or on the general discipline of the school, although the jury thought that there needed to be more watchfulness when boys were at play. At this point in time, it is, of course, impossible to know whether Arnold Davison's experiences were typical.

There were allegations of a 'cover-up' in some other newspapers according to the *Darlington and Stockton Times*, but it was supportive of the school. Someone using the nom de plume 'A Graduate' wrote to the *Sheffield Evening Star* to the effect that he had taught at the Darlington Grammar School, going out of his way to praise it. Similarly Arthur Pryce, now at Coatham Grammar School, wrote to the *Christian World* in defence of his old school.

Anxiety at the school continued into June, for Sir William Harcourt, the Home Secretary, had referred the matter to the Public Prosecutor for investigation. In consequence, the clerk to Darlington Magistrates' attended the school in early June and took written statements from twenty boys. Fortunately, no prosecutions resulted.

There had been another crisis a couple of years earlier, leading to an extraordinary meeting of the governors being called on 16 February 1883. A boarder was suffering from typhoid fever and the school had been surveyed by the town surveyor and the splendidly named Inspector of Nuisances. As a result, it had been closed as a precautionary measure. The governors were keen to reopen, but the doctors thought otherwise, so hasty arrangements were made to inspect the town's Drill Shed, rooms at the Central Hall and premises in Victoria Road as possible temporary school sites.

To keep the school going, arrangements were made on the following day to rent Walbrook House in Victoria Road at £2 per week, and, remarkably, the school was able to start operating from there four days after the crisis began. On 3 March, the school was permitted to reopen at Vane Terrace and arrangements were made to return there from the 6th.

On a happier note, through the involvement of two members of staff, Messrs Pryce and Warne, a meeting was held at the school on 20 July 1883 to elect a committee to found Darlington Football Club. Another master, Tofts, was one of the early team players.

The improvements made to the Grammar School during those early years led to the demise of many of those local private schools that had benefited from the decline of the old school in the Leadyard. One was Cleveland College, located at the top of Milbank Road. At its peak, it had four resident masters, including a 'foreigner' to teach German, French and music, but it closed in the 1880s.

Consolidation

For a few years the school continued to grow. In March 1885 it was reported that there were 154 fee-paying pupils, to which number the 'scholars', who will be referred to shortly, should be added. The proportion of older pupils was also increasing. Unfortunately, after allowing for fluctuations, there would, for the next thirty years, be no significant increase in the number of pupils attending the school, notwithstanding the continued growth of the town.

The six full-time masters at this time were Massingham, Anderson, Gregoire, Warne, Smith and Rogerson. They, together with the two remaining part-time teachers from 1878, Dr Muller and Mr Marshall, shared £320 amongst themselves for one term's salary. Tofts had gone to Coatham Grammar School with Pryce as his Second Master.

The examinations of the Cambridge Local Syndicate were originally set individually for different schools, but from December 1884 they became common to all schools, so the achievements of boys at the Grammar School could now be compared with those of candidates elsewhere. Overall, only 33 per cent of candidates passed with Honours, but 59 per cent from Darlington Grammar School did so. Furthermore, the school had an 86 per cent pass rate against a national average of 74 per cent, so Philip Wood had reason to be pleased.

The results were better in the following year with a 92 per cent pass rate for the school, but only 44 per cent gained Honours. In was then usual in subsequent years for the school's results to be better than the average. The Head pointed out at a number of Speech Days that

Darlington's results were actually better than they appeared, because the majority of schools only entered selected pupils for the examinations, whereas the practice at Darlington was to enter every boy in the Fifth and Sixth Forms. The entry fees were normally met by the pupils, so were additional to the tuition fees.

Wood seems to have had reservations about the system in that a candidate could be awarded a certificate, despite failing in French, Latin or mathematics. However, failures in arithmetic, reading, spelling, dictation, grammar or religious knowledge would prevent the award of a certificate.

At the beginning of 1886, there was concern because, in the previous year, the school's expenditure had exceeded income by £117. Part of the deficit was said to relate to a payment due during the year being received too late to be included in the accounts and the governors were confident that rising pupil numbers would prevent the need to reduce staff. However, to assist the situation, the Head offered to forgo any income due to him in excess of £680 10s 0d and this led to him making a special contribution of £27 10s 0d in 1887. Wood also offered an annual sum of £30 to be applied towards the salary of the First Form Master. The governors, although claiming to be satisfied that no further action was needed because of the deficit, still accepted the offer. The situation was almost identical to when Bowman was taken on some years earlier.

Science teaching remained the poor relation. The claim at the time of opening that the subject was taught seems to have been optimistic, despite the provision of the basement room for 'scientific experiments'. Later, as already mentioned, the incentive of grants had led to the Fifth and Sixth Forms studying basic scientific topics, but there were still no labs and there were no funds for any. The Department of Science and Art science exams seem to have been rudimentary, with, for instance, a separate certificate awarded for a pass in the magnetism exam.

The Head reported at one Speech Day, in rather defensive terms, that the school could congratulate itself on at the results of some of its scientific experiments. He tried to argue that if science lessons were illustrated by experiments, rather than by reference to a textbook, they would become one of the most interesting and mentally stimulating lessons of the week.

In 1885 Wood admitted that because the subject was not examined at all by the Cambridge examiners the time devoted to it was apt to be overlooked. He would be sorry to see science teaching cease, or to have less time devoted to it, but he had to concede that when the Cambridge Locals were drawing near there was a strong temptation to steal time from science subjects to concentrate upon the ones that were examined. The Head acknowledged that the teaching of science at the school was elementary, but claimed that it enabled boys to read further with ease and intelligence.

At the 1888 Speech Day the reported figure of 139 pupils in the school, including 21 boarders, showed a decline in numbers. The Headmaster gave a summary of the first ten years at Vane Terrace. That the numbers of university graduates and of pupils awarded certificates was low compared with later years is a reflection on both the times and the small size of the school, but the achievements of the old school in the Leadyard were negligible in comparison

There was, in one respect, an immediate difference between the new school at Vane Terrace and its predecessor, in that scholarships were available to pay for, or at least subsidise, the cost of education for those who won them.

The process started with the Bellasses Charity, founded in 1636. Over time, its objectives had become obsolete and in 1870 its trustees and those of the old Grammar School had agreed to apply to have £50 from its endowment used for the advancement of education. Nothing was achieved until the 1874 Scheme for the new school was operative. Then, £50 per annum was allocated to the school for the provision of scholarships.

There were to be six Bellasses Scholarships, with an age limit for application of 14. Three elementary scholarships would be open to existing pupils at public elementary schools, whilst three entrance scholarships were to be available to boys who applied for admission to the school in the ordinary way. One scholarship from each group was to be open for competition each year and initially the winners would have their tuition fees remitted for three years. However, from 1880 three entrance scholarships were provided in September of each year, but each was then tenable for one year only. Apparently, the object was to induce boys to enter the school only in September, but the large number of admissions during the school year persisted.

In addition, Mr Wood personally funded three scholarships, to be known as the Queen Elizabeth Annual Scholarships. He met the cost by forgoing the capitation fees for the six Bellasses Scholarships. These scholarships would be competed for by boys who had been in the school for three terms. They would be tenable for one year, and were open to those aged under 14, 15 and 16 respectively.

Other benefactors soon came forward. In 1880 Mr S.R.C. Ward of Neasham Hill donated £1,000 to fund the 'Mrs Chapman Ward Memorial Scholarships'. The Head then responded by creating a fourth Queen Elizabeth Scholarship by forgoing the relevant capitation fees due to him for the winner.

There was also the George Stephenson Memorial Scholarship. Its creator, although not the George Stephenson, had been the Passenger and Goods Manager of the Darlington section of the North Eastern Railway. He died in 1881 and in his will had stipulated that the scholarship was to be competed for by boys not exceeding 11 years of age whose fathers were employed by the railway company. Whilst the governors recommended acceptance to the Charity Commissioners, they added a rider. They wanted to record that although they accepted Stephenson's offer, they did not want to be seen creating a precedent for the acceptance of further scholarships limited to a particular group of boys.

Then the Head offered to bear the cost of two additional scholarships – open to boys who had applied for admission – providing for the remission of entrance and tuition fees for one year.

Finally there were six scholarships from an existing charity, to be known as 'The Thomas Richardson Entrance Scholarships', made available by H. Fell Pease. These were open by competition to boys educated in elementary schools in South Durham, Cleveland and areas of North Yorkshire within five miles of the school.

The result was that, within five years, the school had over twenty entrance scholarships, including thirteen restricted to boys from elementary schools, but with the limitation that many were tenable for one year only. There were instances when an entrance scholarship was not awarded because no candidate of sufficient standard had presented himself.

Soon after the opening of the school, leaving exhibitions had also been created. These were intended to give financial assistance to selected pupils in preparing the way for university and further education. As the school was still a second-grade one, an exhibition might enable its recipient to go to a first-grade school for a year so as to qualify for a university place.

Initially, two leaving exhibitions were established, each open to boys aged 16 or over who had been at the school for two years. They were the William Barningham Exhibition, founded by the ironmaster of that name, and the Edward Pease Memorial Exhibition, given by Henry Pease in memory of his father. Each scholarship was worth £40 per annum, tenable for three years at a university, college of science or other place of study approved by the governors. As each would therefore be awarded only once every three years, permission was obtained from the Charity Commissioners to introduce a Bellasses Exhibition upon the same terms as the others, so that one exhibition could be awarded annually. In later years the terms of all three were varied to meet changing conditions.

As the school was new when the facility became available, it was provided that until boys reached the Upper School and could qualify for an exhibition, the surplus income from the charity was to be made available towards the general funds of the school.

At the 1885 Speech Day, the number of boys from outside the town who were competing for the school's scholarships was cited as evidence of the Grammar School's growing reputation, although a year later when J.H. Bowman was chairing the proceedings, he expressed the view that too many successful scholarship candidates lived in the surrounding villages, rather than in Darlington. He was, however, pleased that half of the scholarships had gone to boys from elementary schools.

As soon as the school's standards started to improve there were fresh concerns about the second-grade status imposed upon the school by the 1874 Scheme. The grading carried with it a compulsory leaving age of 17, so any pupil wishing to go to university had to leave the school without being properly prepared and would then normally have to spend a year at a 'crammer'. The appearance of the exhibitions assisted by providing funding for such a year, but it also exacerbated the situation as the prospect of financial support for former pupils encouraged more candidates.

By 1880 Philip Wood was arguing for an amendment to the Scheme. He wanted the power to permit up to 5 per cent of pupils, as recommended by him, to stay on to the age of 18. In January 1882, when the school had its intended number of classrooms, the governors asked the Charity Commissioners to allow such boys as the Headmaster might recommend to remain in the school up to the term in which they attained eighteen, subject to the consent of the governing body. On 28 April 1882, the Commission consented and another supplemental scheme was prepared. The school then became a genuine grammar school with first-grade status and pupils could now aim to go to university directly from the school.

The procedure for being allowed to stay on was a ponderous one. Every application had to be approved at a governors' meeting, but there were only a handful of them during the first few years. The reasons behind the applications were varied, but in most cases the pupil needed more study to obtain some form of higher qualification. A more unusual application was discussed on 24 September 1883. A boy called Jones had not found employment and his mother was concerned about the effects of idleness upon him if he did nothing until something was found. As Wood believed that he could be taught with other existing pupils, he was allowed to stay until he was eighteen. In practice, if the Headmaster favoured the application, the governors always supported it.

However, the 5 per cent restriction persisted for many years and was not removed until further amendments to the Scheme were made in 1905. Boys were then permitted, in special cases, to stay on till they were nineteen, but the requirement to refer applications to the governors ceased to be necessary.

At the governors' meeting on 28 July 1887, the Head reported that there were few boys in the school aged under 10. He believed that there were advantages in entering younger boys on the books and he asked for a room in the building to be made available for a class for boys under 8. When they reached that age, they would go into the main school. The class would be taught by Sarah Lawrence LLA, who, conveniently, was Wood's sister-in-law. The proposals and a draft of the proposed curriculum were approved.

LLA was an abbreviation for 'Lady Literate in Arts'. This, in an age before the granting of degrees to women, was an award available to them from St. Andrew's University.

Wood must have expected a favourable response from the governing body, because the establishment of the Preparatory Department was announced a mere four days after the meeting. It would open in September and was to cater for boys under eight at an annual fee of four guineas, a figure significantly less than the fee for an 8-year-old in the main school. Payment could be made in instalments at £1 8s 0d (£1–40) per term. The hours were merely 9.30 to11.45 a.m. and 2.30 to 3.30 p.m.

The prospectus stated that, 'Mr Wood has the permission of the governors to announce that a class for boys under 8 years of age, specially intended to prepare for the Grammar School course, will begin in September next. While the work of the class will not form part of the course of education for which the governors take responsibility, they have consented to its formation in the expectation that boys would be thus better prepared than they are now for the ordinary school work.'

The department was not an integral part of the school, nor was it within the governors' control. They merely provided a room. By its nature, the department could not fulfil the requirements of the Endowed Schools Commission's Scheme for the Grammar School. The Grammar School admissions register does not contain entries for boys under eight and Sarah Lawrence and her successor were not paid from Grammar School funds. Although it was described as the Preparatory Department and used a room within the school, the new institution was effectively a private venture of Philip Wood, possibly in partnership with his sister-in-law.

The situation is further complicated because the school proper was itself used as a prep school. Many pupils aged eight or over entered the

Grammar School, for five years or so, to be prepared for a grammar school or public school education.

There were continuing signs of financial pressure during this period and to save costs, the Headmaster suggested that the Modern Side Master could be given additional work teaching the boys in the lower classes. The school could then dispense with one master and also reduce Muller's teaching time from six hours to three, thus saving the Junior Master's annual salary of £110 and half of Muller's salary of £30. The governors were happy to leave the matter with Mr Wood. He acted upon his proposal and the number of full-time assistant masters fell to five. It looks as if Mr Rogerson was the one who had to go. Wood also repeated his offer of 1886 to contribute towards a master's salary and again the offer was gratefully accepted. The practice then continued into the 1890s.

Early in 1887 the Head conferred with Capt. Barron of the Darlington Fire Brigade about suitable appliances for the school, but the outcome was not reported. Around the same time Lindsley Pratt resigned as Clerk. He had succeeded George Grace who had died in January 1885. Joseph Forster, a local solicitor with an office on High Row, was elected as Pratt's replacement. The salary for the part-time appointment was £25 9s 6d.

In 1888 consideration was given to teaching drill. A Mr Cartwright, who operated a local gymnasium, was engaged to drill those boys whose parents were prepared to pay 5/- per term over and above the standard fees. By 1902 a gym at the YMCA in Woodland Road was being used and the facility was available to day boys as well as boarders.

The governors had to call a special meeting on 11 October 1889. Mr Wood reported to them that Ashton Morgan, a boarder, had on Wednesday, the 2nd, let himself out of the school via a window at night and did not return until Friday morning, having been at Stockton and elsewhere. In consequence, the Head had expelled him and the governors saw no reason to question the decision. No explanation as to what lay behind young Morgan's escapade was given.

This is the only reference in the minutes to a punishment, although, for reasons not stated, a sub-committee had been set up in the previous year to consider with the Head the general discipline and punishment of scholars.

It was decided in 1891 that certain rooms in the Head's house, no longer used by servants, should be converted into an isolation hospital and a sketch was obtained from a Mr McKenzie showing how new attics for the servants could be provided. In April an estimate for £59 6s 2d from McKenzie was accepted and the work was done satisfactorily by the end of July. Plans for the conversion have not been traced, so it remains unclear where the attics were.

There was no quorum at either of the governors' meetings that authorised this work. Similar failures arose on a number of occasions and those present were happy to make decisions on the assumption that they would be retrospectively approved at the first subsequent meeting with a sufficient number of members present! In 1890, there were three successive meetings without a quorum.

Issues relating to the endowment lands occupied much of the time at governors' meetings. Amongst matters to be considered were changes of tenant, rent arrears, and the need for fencing work and for alterations to shops in Skinnergate. On one occasion, work to drains at Mr Sayers' farmyard at Heighington had to be authorised after service of a Sanitary Notice.

In May 1890 there were 156 boys in the school of which 13 were boarders. The respective figures were the highest and lowest yet, but the number of boarders jumped to twenty-three in September of the following year. Back in 1889, because the number boarding had continued to fall, it had been decided to spend £6 advertising further afield for them, so the expenditure may have produced an eventual benefit. Although the number fell again after the peak of twenty-three, the overall numbers of boarders in the school remained relatively stable till the Great War. There were still many boys aged 13 or more when they started at the school and many entrants were still leaving after a year or so.

In 1890 two long-serving masters resigned. One was Dr Muller, the part-time teacher of French and German who had been at Vane Terrace from the beginning, and who had had his hours cut as part of the Headmaster's economy measures; the other was W.C. Anderson, who had come in 1879. He left to take up the practice of medicine. At the end of 1890 the assistant masters were Massingham, Coleman, Bannerman, Newman, E.C. Watson, who had replaced Anderson at £40 per term, and Marshall, the part-time singing master and organist at St. Cuthbert's Church.

The Glee Club seems to have provided the only out-of-school non-sporting activity in those early days and, in time, as with the Speech Day recitations, it died. Much later, in 1911, Mr F.M. Smith, a master, attempted without success to revive it. There was, in 1886, a brief appearance – for one night only – of the 'Grammar School String Band'. After that it was heard of no more.

An Old Boys' Dinner was held in 1891. Attendance was limited to those who had been pupils at the new school, so the oldest present must have been aged about thirty. Because of its success, a repeat event was decided upon, but, this time, Old Leadyard Boys were invited and two of their number were invited on to the committee. The Headmaster and Massingham were also to serve on it. Their meetings were held in the governors' board room at the school.

The event was advertised in the *Northern Echo* and the *North Star* and 180 invitations were sent out, using printed pre-paid postcards. There were forty-nine acceptances, but of those who did not attend, an impressive 104 took the trouble to say they would not be coming.

The 1892 Dinner was held at 6.45 p.m. on 9 April at the Imperial Hotel on the corner of Grange Road and Coniscliffe Road. The cost, exclusive of wine, was 6/6d ($32^{1/2}$p). As well as musical entertainments, there were toasts to the Queen, masters past and present, the school and athletics. The proposer of the final toast was Tom Watson, who had attended the Leadyard School. He would, many years later, achieve local celebrity as a very active longest-surviving Old Boy. The Dinner was preceded by a football match between the 'Past School' and the 'Present School', the Past winning. Despite the success of the event, there is no evidence of any attempt to organise another one.

Around 1895 a school magazine called *The Sixth Form Gazette* was established. There is an example of it in the County Record Office at Durham. It has been duplicated from a handwritten original and runs to ten pages. It has no date or price indicated and gives no indication of its author(s). The editorial notes refer to the necessity of raising the price to 1½d and mentions that the issue is a special number containing a record of the School Sports. A large proportion of the magazine, which is difficult to read, relates to the sports, described as being the school's fifteenth. It mentions that the local Volunteers' Band played and that Mrs Wood distributed the prizes. There is also a half-page devoted to cricket, with reference to matches against such schools as Coatham Grammar and Stockton.

One page contains jokes, some in the form of mock advertisements. One example will give some idea of the standard: 'For sale. A pony for a little boy with a long tail.' Another page contained the fourth chapter of a cowboy and Indian story.

Attached to the magazine is a typewritten note to the effect that the issue is dated 1895. Later editions became scurrilous and attacked members of the staff. It was therefore suppressed. The school would have to wait until 1912 for the reappearance of a school magazine.

At the 1890 Speech Day Wood questioned the idea of free elementary education. He said that no doubt it would come as a relief to the working man 'with a quiver full of children', but the middle classes on 'whose broad backs was laid the burden of the rates' would experience no relief from the change. In that year the Headmaster earned £710 10s 0d, before his voluntary deductions, the combined income of the rest of the staff being £790.

Early Sport

There seems to be no evidence that the pupils at the old school in the Leadyard participated in any sporting events with other schools or organisations. It was different with the new school, although it seems to have taken about a year after its opening to get sporting activities under way.

The first recorded athletic event was a 'Hare and Hounds' reported in the *D&S Times* on 8 March 1879. Percy Snaith and H. Hoskins were the hares and were given a seven-minute start. There were between fifty and sixty hounds, a high proportion of the pupils at the school. The route took in Low Coniscliffe and Cleasby, before following the line of the Merrybent Railway – the route now followed by the Durham motorway – in the direction of Barton Quarry, before heading towards Manfield and Aldborough. The hounds won and the exhausted competitors returned to the school five hours after leaving. One had to be carried to bed after his bath!

Wood was a member of Seaton Carew Golf Club, and at one time was its second captain. It may be due to his connection with the place that the second recorded sporting event, a cricket match, took place there on 12 June 1879. Four members of staff played for the school, and, although the school won, 86 of the 108 runs scored for it were obtained by Mr Massingham! The Head contributed a further six and there were five extras, so the pupils provided a mere eleven. The first football match was played against a Mr Meek's XI on 22 November at 'the School Ground'. The school won 5–1. In the following month, the school played Gainford School at home. Only association football (i.e. soccer) was played. Several decades would pass before rugby football put in an appearance.

There were some odd formations in those early days. In one match there were three forwards, two right sides, two left, two half backs, one full back and the keeper. At another game seven forwards were sent out! As with cricket, staff members could be found in the school football team. According to several press reports around 1880 the team included the Headmaster and Messrs Massingham, Warne and Tofts.

The lack of a school field was a problem and early football games had to be played on land rented in Polam Park, but there seems to be some uncertainty as to whether some matches were played elsewhere. There exists a photograph taken in the early 1880s showing the football team in action, with a caption referring to 'the New Field', but it is not clear whether the game was taking place on a school pitch, at Feethams or at North Lodge Park. Another photograph of the 'New Field' taken at about the same time shows a primitive pavilion erected on it.

L.W. Williamson, one of the original entrants of January 1878, writing nearly seventy years later, said that the first cricket field was situated behind West Lodge on what is now part of West Crescent. Then, he stated, a field beside the Skerne, later incorporated into the South Park, was used. Probably this was the land in Polam Park, already referred to. In March 1879 the Clerk to the Governors was instructed to arrange a cricket field tenancy from October, and in July £9 was paid for a cricket pavilion, but no mention was made of an intended location.

The letting must have been a short-term one, for in December 1879, a public subscription was opened to raise funds to acquire a permanent field for the school. It was aided by the school's first concert already referred to. During 1880, when cricket was still being played at Polam, sufficient money had been raised to enable the renting of land in Abbey Road from Lord Barnard and in May the Clerk to the Governors was instructed to sign a lease. Nevertheless, there exists a press report referring to the contractors starting work in March 1880. Then, in March 1881, the Head was authorised to spend £15 to remove and repair the cricket pavilion. Presumably, it was moved to Abbey Road from one or other of the temporary sites.

It is difficult to determine the exact annual rent for the field. In 1880 £17 was paid, but for the next twenty years the figure fluctuated from £16 10s 1d to £19 8s 5d. Then, from 1902 till 1910 a consistent annual sum of £20 was paid.

During 1883–6 the school played football against the County School at Barnard Castle. Darlington won the first game 13–0, but after winning again in 1882, lost the 1883 game 11–1. Thereafter, normal scores were said to apply, although, when Stockton High School's team visited in 1885, it was beaten by the Darlington school 13 to love [sic]. At that time, the *North Star* thought that the school held the premier position in the district for football.

The field was always referred to as the Cricket Field, and as sheep were grazed on it outside the cricket season, until at least 1891, it appears that football continued to be played elsewhere. The accounts for 1880 record an income of £4 received for grazing on the field. The original site is still used by the Sixth Form College as its sports field, but the field did not extend across to Cleveland Terrace until much later.

The opening of the ground enabled the school to increase its activities. The first athletics sports day, aided by another School Concert, took place on 2 April 1881. The flat races were all handicaps and were open to all pupils in the school and for other boys aged under 13. There were four events that disappeared a long time ago. These were throwing a cricket ball, a three-legged race, a sack race and a dribbling football race, involving a course 100 feet long and 12 feet wide. Anderson, Cleeve-Warne and Tofts were the judges and Barker was the starter.

The sports day became an annual event and the Sons of Temperance Brass Band played at the 1884 sports. From 1886 the Cockerton Brass Band performed, although in the 1887 report the Cockerton Saxhorn Band was described as providing music. Mrs Wood customarily awarded the trophies. Athletics and games developed from these beginnings, but there was no House system to foster competition within the school.

By 1886 the playing of cricket had developed sufficiently to justify the employment of a professional by the name of Watton, but he was soon replaced by George Spence. He continued till 1915 when failing eyesight compelled him to give up.

Although there was no school uniform, those in the school teams were entitled to wear school colours in the form of a jacket and cap. Photographic evidence suggests that the jackets had piping around the edge and also round the sleeve, a few inches from the cuff. There was a badge on the breast pocket with a similar one on the cap. It comprised a large letter 'D' and entwined in it were the smaller letters 'G' and 'S'.

At the beginning the school football team played in knickerbockers with long socks and hats. On an 1881 photograph of the team the hats appear as a kind of cross between a 'beany' hat and a nightcap. By 1888 the players were depicted as having a Maltese Cross on the left breast of their shirts, but in 1890 this had disappeared, replaced by a design which, with modifications, was to last for very many years.

The new shirt was in two colours. The left half was in white or a pale colour, as was the right sleeve and the right half of the collar. By way of contrast, the right half of the shirt, with the left sleeve and left half of the collar were in a darker colour. The right-side breast pocket was in the light colour. The players were still in knickerbockers and long stockings. However, by the time the 1892 team had its official photograph taken, some of its members had taken to wearing shorts, admittedly virtually knee length.

By the 1896 team photograph the lighter colour on the shirt appeared to be darker than it had been, so it may be that the shirt was by then in the two shades of blue familiar to many later generations of school football players. The shirt also now had a badge on the breast pocket. It contained the letters 'DGS' in the style used by the cricket players, but was flanked by the small letters 'F' and 'C'. By 1901 the small letters were in the bottom corners of the pocket in the manner of the letters on the breast pockets of school blazers in later years denoting membership of a House team.

Apparently, around 1890 it was the custom of Mr Wood to present caps, paid for by himself, to the three boys who had been the most outstanding during the football season.

Although there was then no Old Boys' Association, former pupils were obviously in touch with each other, for an Old Boys' football team existed in the mid 1890s. The team shirt displayed the Maltese Cross used by the school team a few years earlier.

In his 1895 Speech Day report, the Head asserted that the lack of a swimming pool and a gym at the school did not indicate an absence of gymnastic exercises or swimming. During the two (sic) winter terms the boarders went every week to a Mr Cartwright's gym and in summer had season tickets for the Town Baths in Kendrew Street. Nothing was said about the day boys, so they presumably made their own arrangements outside school hours. Mr Wood said that he regarded cricket and football as being more important because of the element of moral training involved. Boys learned to co-operate, to check their tempers, to obey without question the orders of their captains, to be brave, to struggle for victory to the last moment, to win without offensive jubilation and to lose with good humour.

At around this time there were concerns about the future of the Cricket Field on Abbey Road. It was still rented on a short-term basis from Lord Barnard, but, as new housing was being built in and around the bottom of Abbey Road, there was a fear of Barnard selling the land for development. Accordingly, early in 1898, it was arranged that Sir David Dale would communicate with him.

In contrast to the 16 acres later occupied by the school, only 4 to 6 acres was wanted by the school and terms were eventually agreed, at least in principle. In December it was decided to raise funds to buy, level and fence the field. Yet, a month later, the chairman and the Head went to see Lord Barnard to try to obtain a modification of the terms. It seems that the governors had, after further consideration, decided that the owner's terms were too rigorous. The school did not have the funds for an outright purchase and, as an alternative, terms for a twenty-one-year lease were agreed. However, an option to purchase the freehold for £375 per acre was also obtained. By late March 1899 a draft lease for the field had been produced and the formalities were completed soon afterwards. The school agreed to pay Barnard's legal fees and was obliged to fence the site. The area occupied by the school was 4.005 acres according to the 1913 Ordnance Survey Map.

Fencing the field at a cost of £262 14s 5½d was carried out, as was some levelling work. Water was laid on and a proper pavilion was built. By April 1900 a total of £463 18s 0d had been raised for the field and a fund-raising concert, suggested by Wood, then raised a further £25. Unfortunately, this fund-raising was not sufficient to cover all of the costs and in July 1900 it was announced that here was a £50 deficit in respect of the Cricket Field.

It looks as if there was some further fund-raising, for there exists a circular letter dated 1901 from the Headmaster to Old Boys telling them that although the estimated costs had risen from £500 to £560, the money had been raised in full. He added that a large proportion had been given by Old Boys and that each was to receive a list showing all of the contributors, arranged in the order of their starting at the school. Wood hoped that this would revive pleasant memories and perhaps encourage contact amongst former pupils. A list, showing about 120 names was attached to the letter.

There were evidently still hopes that the freehold of the field could be purchased, for a year later the Headmaster was proposing to hold a bazaar to raise funds for the purpose. The governors, however, decided to defer the matter for a year and nothing more was heard of the idea.

It may be appropriate at this point to mention a mystery about the land actually owned or occupied by the Grammar School at this period. The 1898 25-inch Ordnance Survey map for the area shows the land at the rear of the school, extending to what was to become Cleveland Avenue, as being in the occupation of the Grammar School. The same indication is given on the reprint of the same map available commercially a few years ago.

It was always understood that the land behind the school yard, or what was left of it after Abbey Road and Cleveland Avenue were developed, was the playing field for the Training College, although one informant wonders whether it was the field for Arthur Pease School on Trinity Road. It was apparently the practice school for the college.

The author has to conclude that the Ordnance Survey was in error. If the Grammar School owned the land, and no evidence has been found that it ever did, it had an asset of such value, given the development potential of the area, that it is inconceivable that it would have suffered the financial problems that befell it. The school may have had temporary use of the field immediately after it opened, but all the evidence indicates that it continuously used the field beyond Cleveland Avenue from 1880.

One final piece of evidence perhaps confirms the position. In July 1898 a request was received from the Training College for the erection of an unclimbable fence on top of the wall on the west of the school yard. The intention was to deter trespassers. The matter was left to the Head, the Chairman of the Governors and the Clerk. Although the outcome is not known, it is obvious that the college was, at that time, in possession of the field behind.

External Pressures

In the beginning at Vane Terrace, the governors were, effectively, answerable only to the Charity Commissioners for the operation of the school. Then, as they began to look to other bodies for funding, they began to realise that those providing money would have an interest in how it was spent.

As has been mentioned, the school had been in receipt of some public money in the shape of the grants obtained from the Department of Science and Art from 1879 onwards. Gradually, the Department, by its system of examinations, grants and prizes to pupils, exercised a growing influence on the curriculum and teaching methods at the school.

Soon, a further organisation would show an interest in the way the school was conducted, for in 1888 a second tier of local government was introduced in the shape of the county councils. In the following year the Technical Instruction Act 1889 permitted the new councils to spend a 1d rate on technical education. This development was of interest to the Grammar School for it was anxious to improve the quality of its science education.

Under the 1874 Scheme it was supposed to place an emphasis on science teaching, but, despite the grants received from the Department of Science and Art, the school's teaching remained basic. In particular, there was still no proper science laboratory or qualified science teacher. There was, therefore, an obvious attraction in obtaining some money from Durham County Council.

Accordingly, late in 1891 the school contacted the council about funding for technical instruction. The step was a small one, but it led to developments that would have a considerable effect on the school's future by the early years of the next century. The council's initial response was encouraging, so a grant of £200 was requested to enable the school to add a fully qualified science master to its staff. Then, in May 1892, to satisfy the council's requirements, the amount was reduced to £150.

In its application, the school referred to its teaching of freehand and model drawing, physiography, electricity, magnetism, theoretical mechanics and inorganic chemistry. It also stated its intention to introduce practical chemistry and to double the time allocated for teaching science to the Fifth and Sixth Forms. It would also extend science teaching to the Fourth Form.

The council's Technical Instruction Committee responded, indicating that it would recommend that the grant be made, but it wanted to know what the school would give in return. The grant would cover the salary, but the committee stipulated that a practical chemistry laboratory would have to be constructed, warning that the county council was not prepared to meet the cost. In September, Wood contacted Hoskins about the construction of a lab and an estimate of £345 was given on the basis that the lab would be built within the open arched area under the hall.

The next governors' meeting approved the general scheme and the Headmaster was asked to seek a county council grant at a suitable time. Unfortunately the application had to be resubmitted because the school had failed to use the proper form.

In April 1893 the Charity Commissioners authorised the building work, but the school had no funds to meet the costs. By the following January, however, it had managed to obtain an order from the Commissioners enabling it to borrow £430 17s 2d from the Bellasses Charity to cover those costs. The loan was to be for fifteen years, with interest, and repayment would be at £24 per year. Although there was no money from the county for the building work, the school did, in March 1894, manage to extract a grant from it to cover half the cost of the fixtures and fittings.

The current financial pressures also compelled the school to sell some of its endowment land at Heighington in April 1893. When it was built, the new lab did, at least, produce a small income for the school, as the town council was permitted to use the lab on evenings for a night class for a charge of £5 12s 6d per annum.

The school's application to the county council prompted a further development, for in January 1893, the Technical Instruction Committee enquired about the school's terms for accepting scholarship boys funded by the council. The school was interested and indicated that it would accept £10 per annum per scholar.

Arrangements were quickly put in place and fourteen 'Durham Scholars', including five from outside the town, were soon installed in the school. The boys from out of town came in by train, having railway passes paid for by the county. The number of pupils increased as a result of the new arrangements and the Head's income per term increased from £207 in July 1892 to £239 6s 8d in December 1893. The Cambridge Local Examination fees for the Durham Scholars were initially paid by the school and refunded by the council.

An early recipient of one of these scholarships was David Carrick. Later he gained a county council Leaving Scholarship worth £60 per year and went to the College of Science at Newcastle. He returned to the school in 1903 as the science master and, in time, was the school's Second Master. Long after his retirement in 1946 he remained an officer of the Old Boys' Association. So close was his connection to the school that he even lived in Vane Terrace!

On 26 July 1893, Mr Wood reported favourably to the governors on the conduct and studiousness of the Durham Scholars. But by the following year, there was one aspect of the scholarship arrangements that was concerning him. He reported to the governors on 20 June that, because the Durham Scholars received free books and (where applicable) free rail passes, their scholarships were more valuable than the school ones. They were also normally available for the holder's entire Grammar School career, not limited to a year or so.

Both scholarship exams were held around the same time in July and candidates normally sat both. The best, Carrick amongst them, would, if successful in both, elect for the Durham Scholarship, so the Grammar School was then left to confer its scholarships on those who had failed to obtain a Durham one. A perception was therefore developing that the school scholarships were inferior.

The Head suggested that the school scholarships should also provide free books. It would cost about £18 per annum, but adjustments to the rules for the scholarships could provide the sum. The governors agreed.

The scholarship arrangements with Durham were gradually extended and by January 1895, out of 169 pupils, including 17 boarders, no fewer than 39 were county scholars. The county paid the science master's salary for one year only, but, from 1894, it provided the school with a capitation fee based upon the number of pupils attending. In consequence, for 1894 the school received, in addition to the payments for the scholars, £165 3s 4d for the capitation grant. No records have come to light to show how the grant was calculated, but by 1897 it had increased to £231 4s 8d.

As a result of these developments, the school was, by 1900, dependent on the county for about a quarter of its income. Not surprisingly, the increasing payments made by the county's ratepayers to the school led to an increasing interest by the council in its management and standards. The first intervention was as early as January 1894, when the council, backed by the Department of Science and Art, suggested that the Modern Side (i.e. modern languages) be reorganised as a science school.

Reference has already been made to the falling off of the income received from the Department, but the possession of the lab provided an opportunity to restore the situation. In consequence, an application was made in 1894 to the Science and Art Department for the Upper School to be recognised as an Organised Science School. The application was successful, but there was a stipulation. A drawing master with 'special qualifications' had to be appointed as part of the requirements and, in consequence, the school had to appoint A.B. Dresser to teach part-time at £25 per annum.

The school's new status produced results. In 1894 grants of £67 17s 0d were received from the Department, but the figure jumped to £142 15s 0d in the following year and to £234 18s 1d in 1896.

In 1895, armed with its new status, the school decided to have a practical physics laboratory and by the end of the year steps were in hand. But there was a limitation. The Science and Art Department stipulated that no more than twenty-four boys would be permitted to participate at any one time, apparently because of space considerations.

The Preparatory room was the proper size for a lab, so the decision was made to move Miss Lawrence and her pupils into the governors' room. It is not clear which room the Preparatory Department originally used or whether the governors lost their room to Miss Lawrence. All we know is that by 1902 her class was occupying Room 1, one of the original rooms facing onto the quad, and that the governors had the use of a former junior dormitory. It was hoped that the county would meet half of the cost of the lab. It refused, but it did provide a grant for apparatus.

On 21 January 1896 it was reported that the physics lab was practically complete, but a year later, Wood was worried about the requirements of the Science and Art Department and was hoping that strict compliance with them would not be insisted upon.

It looks as if the Department was making its requirements more stringent for everyone, for the problem was discussed by the Headmasters' Association, which made representations about them. There was some benefit, for shortly afterwards, the Department gave exemption from its requirements for manual instruction, limited to the current term only. Thereafter, increased accommodation, both for that subject and for practical physics, had to be provided. Unfortunately, there is no further indication as to the nature of the requirements. At least possession of the new lab enabled the school to increase its annual income from Darlington Council for accommodating night classes to £23 19s 0d.

In the summer of 1895 the county council wanted an instructor of woodwork at the school and had engaged one who was offered to the school on a part-time basis. The school complied, but it had to provide a woodwork room and procure the necessary benches and tools. The estimated cost was £40, but it would be partially refundable. Control over the woodwork instructor remained with the county, and in January

1899 it, not the governors, terminated his employment. The Science and Art Department also maintained a continuing interest and in 1900 it was pressing the school for further woodworking accommodation. The school's insurance cover had to be increased from £8,500 to £9,200 because of the lab and woodwork room.

By this time the school's expenditure was exceeding its income. It had an overdraft and it had been agreed with the National Provincial Bank that interest at 3 per cent per annum should be paid on the basis that the liability was guaranteed by Sir David Dale, the Chairman of the Governors.

There were changes amongst the staff during the decade. The engagement of H.J. Staines as the school's first science master brought the number of full-time assistants back to six after an interval of five years, but he lasted only six months. His successors did not stay long either and there were four science masters in five years. At this time Bannerman was replaced as junior maths master by F.J. Widdowson, who later taught French and German, whilst Newman's salary was increased from £115 to £126 per year. These changes did not provide stability and, by December 1894, after further departures, the assistant masters were the long-standing Massingham, together with Widdowson, Shaw, Hogg, Newman, Blain and Marshall, the part-timer.

Then, within a month, Shaw and Newman both left and had to be replaced. At this time, full-time members of staff were invariably Oxford or Cambridge graduates, apart from the occasional one from a Scottish university or from Trinity College, Dublin, but the younger universities would be represented within a few years.

In May 1895 the governors decided to add £25 to Massingham's salary in view of his long and excellent service. A couple of months later, the salary of Hogg, the then science master, was increased from £150 to £200 because of the extra work arising from the requirements being imposed upon the school. He left soon afterwards. The giving of these increases may well have reflected an anxiety to encourage members of staff to stay.

The departures of staff did not stop and other replacements had to be recruited including N.E. Dangerfield at £120 per year. Soon he too resigned, after having obtained £3 compensation from the school for the theft of an overcoat. This time the Headmaster suggested that he not be replaced, so the number of full-time assistant masters fell back to five. Early in 1896 Marshall, the part-time singing master, died and was replaced by Thomas Henderson at £15 per annum. Mercifully, there were then no staff changes for about four years.

The number of pupils still fluctuated considerably, creating difficulties for the organisation of the school as well as making the Headmaster's income uncertain. As an example the number on the roll in May 1897 was an impressive 175, yet the number had plummeted to 128 by September.

The school was not viable with such numbers and, in an effort to relieve the situation, Wood successfully proposed a combined boarding and education fee of £48 for under 12s, with £54 payable for older boys. He vainly hoped that this would increase the number of boarders. There were still pupils from diverse places at the school and amongst the 1900 admissions were boys from Hartlepool, Carnoustie, Norfolk, Southampton and Hungary. Perhaps the most exotic entrant to the school was one Antonio Gavidia. He came from the Lycée Bordeaux in September 1903, leaving in July 1905, aged 17.

The arrangement whereby the Head contributed £40 each year towards the salary of the First Year Master had continued from 1883 till this time, but he now asked to be released from his agreement and the governors agreed. The loss of Wood's payment to the school would further damage its financial position, but equally the fall in pupil numbers had reduced the Head's own income. The small numbers in the school were reflected in the number of candidates in the Cambridge Local Examinations. In 1890 twenty-four out of twenty-eight candidates passed the Seniors Exam and twenty out of twenty-one the one for Juniors.

The staff at the Grammar School were seen as being poorly remunerated but, by way of comparison, male teachers in Board Schools in the locality were being paid up to £105 per annum, compared with a maximum of £75 for women. The Headmaster of Beaumont Street Elementary School received £250, little more than one third of Philip Wood's usual income, yet he ran a school with about 700 pupils in it.

In April 1897 it was agreed that a tablet commemorating the Queen's Diamond Jubilee be placed in the school with the cost being met by the Darlington Jubilee Committee. Two years later, honours boards commemorating the recipients of the various awards were placed in the hall.

Durham County Council still wished to extend its control over those schools it was assisting and on 22 March 1899 a letter was sent to the secondary schools within the county. The council proposed to institute a scheme of inspection for secondary schools and each school was invited to co-operate. Forster, the clerk, responded in rather stiff terms on behalf of the Darlington governors. His letter emphasised the control exercised by the Charity Commissioners under the 1874 Scheme and the obligations of the governors. He also mentioned that, in addition, the school also appointed its own annual examiner.

The response of other schools may well have been negative too, for the Grammar School heard nothing more for a couple of years. Then, although changes were expected under pending legislation, the county revived the issue in July 1901. Again the proposal was stillborn and on 19 March 1902 the school had, for the first time, to submit itself to the attentions of the inspectors appointed by the newly established Board of Education.

Durham County was also keen to have a uniform system of exams for those secondary schools that it assisted and in May 1899, by way of response, the governors had a discussion about the school's July examinations. These were unconnected with the Cambridge Locals, which were sat in December of each year. It was agreed that Wood would ask Durham University to appoint an examiner for the July exams and to report on the school for the year. The pattern was then established that in summer the Durham Locals were sat by senior boys, whilst the rest of the school were examined by Durham University examiners. The Cambridge Local junior exams were taken in December by Form IV and part of V whilst the Senior Exam was taken by the remaining boys in Form V and by those in Form VI.

By 1899 there was a further anxiety about finances, for the county was proposing new regulations intended to halve the capitation fee paid by it to independent schools. The Head was directed to write to the authority giving reasons why the school should secure exceptional treatment. Mr A.F. Pease was to deliver the letter – but only at his discretion.

In November of that year the Head, with other parties concerned about the proposal, attended a conference at West Lodge in Darlington and as a result, a deputation attended the county. The representations seem to have had a beneficial effect.

At some point, the flat-rate system of payment was replaced by a progressive one. We know that in 1912, for schools in the Darlington Grammar School's category, the county paid £1 for each 12 to14-year-old, £1 10s 0d for 14- to 15-year-olds, £2 for pupils aged 15 or 16 and no less than £3 for those over 16. Unfortunately, it is not clear when the new system was introduced. It looks as if no capitation fee was then payable for any boy aged under 12, presumably because such boys were considered too young for a secondary education.

The extent of the involvement of the county council with the school is demonstrated by the regular attendance at governors' meetings, despite his lack of status, of Robson, the Higher Education Committee's secretary. This practice continued from mid 1900 till the spring of the following year.

Payments were still being received from the Science and Art Department, justifying its continuing involvement with the school. Soon the Department would be part of the newly formed Board of Education and Whitehall's interest in the school would vastly increase. That other schools were similarly affected was scant consolation.

There was now a third external pressure for the Charity Commissioners were starting to take a close interest in the school's financial situation. In 1881 there had been a credit balance of £126 at the bank, but from then onwards the school was overdrawn. By 1896 the bank overdraft amounted to £924 and the governors had to apply to the Charity Commissioners to be allowed to take another loan from the Bellasses milch cow. The purpose was to enable the governors to improve the properties forming part of the school's endowment and to discharge the bank liability.

In the summer term of 1881 there had been 154 pupils and a fee income of £549, but in the corresponding term in 1900 the respective figures had fallen to 132 and £490.

The governors, nevertheless, laid much of the blame for their situation on the cost of the laboratories provided for the school.

The furthest that the Commissioners were prepared to go was to make an Order allowing £369 to be borrowed on the security of the endowment properties. The school governors refused to mortgage them, and, as the Commissioners were insistent, the loan was never taken up. The school met the repairs expenditure out of income but, by the end of 1900, the overdraft was £300 greater.

In 1899, three years after the unsatisfactory application, the school managed to pay the sixth instalment of the original loan for the lab, but the financial problems continued. The Chairman of the Governors was obliged to write to the Commissioners fully explaining the financial position of the school. An interview with the secretary to the Charity Commissioners followed and this time the Commissioners were more receptive.

It was suggested that the school take a consolidated loan of £1,200 to clear off its existing debts and, once again, the Bellasses Charity was suggested as the source of the borrowing. The sum would be raised by the sale of Consols, a kind of British government bond, held by the charity and repayment by the school would be over twenty years. The proposed alterations to the fund were publicised, a meeting between Mr Leach, Assistant Charity Commissioner, and the governors took place in November 1900, and by the following March the school had the order for the loan.

By the following July the £1,200 was in the school's bank and the overdraft was cleared off, but not for long.

Early in 1902 the school received a slight amelioration to its financial position. The Charity Commission, in reviewing the old charities in Darlington, had realised that about six acres of land at Brankin Moor, known as Poor Moor, actually formed part of the assets of the Bellasses Trust and not of the Middleton Charity as previously supposed. The school governors saw their opportunity and pressed their case. Because there was a presumption that over half of the Middleton endowment formed part of the Bellasses Charity, the Commissioners decreed that a proportion of the rental income from it would become one of the subsidiary endowments of the Grammar School.

A couple of years later, as a result of the Board of Education Act 1899, the overseeing of the Grammar School was transferred from the Charity Commission to the Board of Education.

The New Century

At the beginning of the twentieth century, Philip Wood had been Headmaster for almost a quarter of a century. In that time he had created, from scratch, a respected and established Grammar School, serving a genuine need in the local community. During the previous ten years, thanks to public funding, the number of scholarship places had been increased and the school's science teaching facilities improved. Nobody could possibly doubt that the school in Vane Terrace was a huge improvement upon its predecessor

But perhaps all was not as it might be. Despite the continuing growth of Darlington the number of pupils was, after allowing for fluctuations, no greater than it had been twenty years earlier and the financial deficit persisted. Furthermore, it could be that the Headmaster was less dynamic than in the early years. The school lacked many of the features that characterised grammar schools, such as a uniform, a House system, prefects, a magazine and school societies. There were no dramatic performances, and the School Concerts had ceased.

However, there is nothing to suggest that anyone, amongst the public at least, was worried unduly about these considerations. The town was proud of its Grammar School.

In 1902 a young Alfred Smith arrived at the school as successor to F.J. Widdowson. Thirty-six years later, when he retired as Senior Classics Master, he left his impressions of the school as it was when he came to it. They provide a useful snapshot of it as it was at the beginning of the century.

By the time of his arrival one of the junior dormitories had become the governors' committee room, but the adjoining room still accommodated some of the remaining twenty boarders. Years later, after their departure, it became a further Preparatory Department classroom. In later years, then numbered 23 and 24, the rooms housed two of the Shell (i.e. first-year) forms. The remaining boarders resided in part of the upper west wing, but the rest of the wing was merely used for storage.

By 1902 the Housemaster had to put up with his sitting room being used during the day as the school staff room, whilst the hall had to be used for the singing and drawing lessons given by the two part-time staff members. The Head taught maths in the room at the north end of the 1881 extension and kept what Smith described as the Black Book in his desk in this room. Many years later, when the extension at the rear of the court was built, the room was used to provide the lower stairwell and the remaining area became a cloakroom. Smith also recalled that two masters, Blain and Ferguson, taught woodwork, free of charge, out of hours to a limited number of boys in the workshop by the boiler room under the main entrance.

There was also a reminiscence about this period in issue 130 of the school magazine, the *Elizabethan* (October 1967), from a Mr T. Gilchrist who had been in the school cricket team in 1902. He said that younger boys in the school wore Eton jackets, but the older ones were permitted lounge suits. He also claimed that all boys, as well as masters, wore mortar boards. Photographs of the time suggest otherwise, but, according to another source, boarders wore them when they attended the Sunday morning service at St. Cuthbert's.

The impressions of two pupils of their Headmaster around this time have also survived and it is appropriate, at this point, to record them too. One of them, Richard Healey, set out his recollections of Wood in 1963. He had first seen him in 1902 when Wood was in his mid fifties with white hair and beard carefully trimmed. He was well over six feet tall and was broad shouldered and upright. He maintained this stance to the end of his life and moved easily, gracefully and quickly.

Wood had a slightly aquiline nose with shrewd blue-grey eyes. They could twinkle or 'harden and glitter' most disturbingly, should the occasion arise, and he used them to enforce discipline. He had a slight Edinburgh accent and in his manner he was quiet and composed, but if he were solving a maths problem on the blackboard, he would, with his left hand, turn end for end a seal carried on his gold watch chain.

Richard Healey said that in school the Head wore dark striped trousers with a dark jacket and waistcoat. However, a solar topi (pith helmet) and a light waistcoat were signs of the onset of summer. He would ride into town on a tricycle wearing a green tweed Norfolk jacket with similar knickerbockers. He incessantly smoked pungent cigars, lighting one from the stub of its predecessor. Often Wood umpired the last hour or so of the Wednesday cricket match, when he would sit on a shooting stick. Afterwards, the location was marked by a ring of cigar stubs.

The Head, nicknamed 'Nix', had been a notable footballer. He was also a keen fly fisherman for trout and kept a house near Grinton in Swaledale for this activity. The pupils felt a fear of his displeasure, yet they felt he was their friend and, in modern (1963) jargon, he was 'the complete father figure'.

A pupil called R.W. Goldsborough told two stories about Wood. He said that the Head's advice to pupils was to always carry three items: a sixpenny coin, a piece of string and a penknife. He also related that he was once walking behind the Head in the quad when a crow 'bombed' his mortar board. Wood shook the deposit off, turned to the boys behind him and said, 'It's a jolly good job that pigs don't fly, isn't it?'

Goldsborough provides an excellent example of how someone facing the most difficult circumstances could benefit from an education at the Grammar School. He was born in 1890 at Hurworth and his father died when he was young, leaving his mother destitute. She had married beneath herself and her family rejected all of her pleas for help. As a result she and her infant son entered East Haven, the Workhouse on Yarm Road. There the sexes were kept separate, as were children and parents, and the boy was allowed to see his mother only once a week. She died when he was eleven.

He attended St. John's Church of England School nearby and was entered, with nine other pupils at the school, for scholarships at the Grammar School, but young Goldsborough was the only successful candidate. Later the Workhouse Guardians placed him with a local family. In 1905 the cost of his school books was being met from school funds. After school Goldsborough graduated in 1912 with a First Class Honours degree awarded by the University of London. Then he became a classics teacher, but after the Great War, he returned to university and became a doctor.

Some insights into the composition of the school at this time can be obtained from a report prepared in 1901 about the local charities, including the school.

Of the 136 boys in the school, 14 were boarders and, of the total, only 21 pupils were aged between 8 and 12, so the numbers in the junior part of the school were low. Similarly there were few pupils at the top end of the school, with nine aged 16 to 17 and a mere three aged 17 to 18. The great bulk were in the 12 to 16 age group. No fewer than thirty of the pupils came from outside the borough, the largest contingents being five from Shildon and five from tiny Denton. Most of the remainder came from the villages surrounding Darlington. Over 30 per cent of the pupils held scholarships.

According to the report about 16 per cent of the pupils were the sons of professional men, whilst most of the remainder came from the commercial and trading classes. There were still only six classes to cover an age range of ten years and the Sixth Form had an average age of only 15.3 years. The first year had an average age of nine.

Latin was taught throughout the three lower forms; thereafter Greek was an alternative and was studied by seventeen pupils. French and Bible instruction were taught throughout, as was drawing, except for those taking Greek. Physics and chemistry were studied in the three highest forms only. The Lower School was still examined annually by the University of Durham and everyone in the Fifth and Sixth Forms was routinely entered for the Cambridge Locals. Many pupils, however, never reached the Fifth Form.

A study of a sample of ninety pupils on the admissions registers for the period suggests that the majority of entrants had not come from fee-paying schools. The breakdown, where the source is traceable, is as follows:

Private school	14 (including 3 from Polam Girls' School)
Grammar School Preparatory Class	11
Other grammar schools	3
Educated at home	2
Local church schools	35
Elementary schools	20 (including 2 from Teacher Training School)

The Teacher Training School mentioned was a practice school for the Training College next door.

About half of the sample appear to have been exempt from fees for at least part of their careers at the school, but it must be remembered that many of the private scholarships were tenable for one year only. Even the county scholarships were subject to review, so, in theory at least, a county scholar could have his award revoked for poor performance.

The sample is small; the information provided is not always clear and it may not be representative of a longer period. At best only a very general picture is shown.

No less than thirty former pupils of the school served in the South African War and at the end of 1902 the decision was made to erect a memorial to the five who had died. A subscription fund was started, one of the subscribers being the Old Boys' Football Club. On Monday 22 June 1903 a memorial tablet was unveiled by Major H. Bowes. Made of brass, it measured 27 inches by 20 inches and was located under the Queen's portrait on the wall of the large hall just above the entrance door. It is now in the Local Studies Centre at Darlington Public Library.

A little while earlier, Bowes had formed a cadet corps at the school on an experimental basis and in the middle of 1903 it was announced that the corps was to be continued. However, no further reference to it has been found.

In late January 1903 all of the elementary schools in the town were closed for a fortnight because of an epidemic of measles and diphtheria. The Grammar School, following the local authority's advice, followed suit.

The number of candidates sitting the Cambridge Locals at this time was still small. On 1 April 1903 it was reported that eight seniors had sat the exam. Four had gained 2nd class, three 3rd class and one failed. However, twenty-four juniors sat and six had gained a 1st class award, but five had failed.

There was now a much lower turnover in staff, but in July 1903 Dodds resigned because of illness. By the next term, following upon a temporary replacement, David Carrick was appointed the new science master and commenced a very long career at the school. He also became Housemaster, so his apparently low salary of £100 was justified by the free accommodation provided.

At the beginning of 1905 the full-time assistant masters were Massingham, Blain, Smith, Ferguson and Carrick, but in the spring Ferguson, the modern languages master, left to take the headship of Bideford Grammar School. Back in July 1902 a grant of £10 had been made by the governors to enable him to spend one month in Germany so that he might obtain a better knowledge of colloquial German.

In 1905 the old restriction on the percentage of boys permitted to stay till they were eighteen was lifted. In special cases they were allowed to remain to the end of the year in which they attained nineteen. That pupil numbers were down is shown by the reduced size of the Head's income for the first term. It was £192 13s 4d.

The lack of proper facilities for physical exercise remained a concern, but in December 1904 Wood reported to the governors that he could arrange for the use of the Drill Hall in Larchfield Street for physical exercise. The estimated cost for the hire was about £20 per year, but, a couple of months later, it was stated that the expected cost would be £15 per annum. These arrangements presumably made the use of the YMCA unnecessary. Only two references to payments have been found. In 1905 £12 6s 0d was paid to the CO of the 1st Volunteer Battalion Durham Light Infantry, but in 1907 the amount had increased significantly to £21 15s 6d.

From 1906 the school benefited for a time from another scholarship when a successful application was made by the vicar of Sadberge to send a scholar to the school at £10 per annum under the Bucks Charity which dated back about two hundred years. It appears that the intention was to benefit one pupil from Sadberge every three years. Regrettably, in early 1915 the trustees of the charity had to admit that they were unable to meet the full fee of the boy sent to the school from the village. The governors left the Headmaster to deal with the matter as he thought best.

Unfortunately Mrs Wood died in late 1905 and at about the same time her sister, Sarah Lawrence, resigned as the teacher in the Preparatory Department. Later she assisted the Headmaster's daughter in the care of the boarders and died in 1928 at the Woods' family cottage at Grinton. The replacement Preparatory teacher was Ada Williams.

Looming Threats

The official correspondence received by Mr Wood and the governors now referred to 'School Number 2745' and thus provided them with a constant reminder of how both central and local government were increasingly intruding upon their world. Unfortunately for them new legislation would not only increase the state's involvement in secondary education, but would contain provisions which would present the school with its biggest threat yet.

In 1899 the Department of Science and Art and other existing bodies were combined to form the Board of Education. The new Board aimed to increase the control of education by local authorities and one result was the Education Act of 1902 which, amongst its objects, increased the financial aid permitted for secondary schools. County councils could, for this purpose, now levy a rate not exceeding 2d in the pound, but with government consent could exceed this figure.

The Act also gave county councils the power to maintain a secondary school rather than merely aid it. An aided school was given financial assistance but, subject to inspection and approval of the curriculum and timetable by the county, it remained independent. By contrast, a maintained school was completely controlled by the council which accordingly appointed all governors. As the authority would be totally responsible for such a school, it was likely that the cost to the ratepayer would be higher.

It must be remembered that at least one quarter of the boys in the school (excluding those in the Preparatory Department) were on scholarships at this time and many were funded by the county. In addition, as mentioned already, it was now also providing capitation grants to the school and, overall, was contributing about one quarter of the school's income. Given its increased spending powers, the council's attitude to future funding would therefore be critical.

One concern arising from the 1902 Act was that, if increasing amounts of ratepayers' money were to be given to independent schools, the ratepayers' representatives should be better represented on the managerial bodies. By 1897 the county council had obtained representation for three of its councillors on the governing body, but in 1905, the composition of the Grammar School's governing body was again revised. The increased involvement of the county was recognised by increasing the number of its representative governors to four, to equal the representation of the borough council. The total number then on the board was fifteen, of whom two, the Mayor and the borough's MP, were ex-officio. Another was nominated by the Durham University Senate and the remaining four were co-opted.

On 27 February 1903 the school underwent its first Board of Education inspection and afterwards, a special meeting of the governors was held. It was necessary to discuss the finances of the school and its management in view of the concerns raised and no fewer than four inspectors, together with J.A. Robson from the county council, attended the meeting. The inspection had led to a recommendation for an additional master. Also, it had concluded that the Head was spending too much time teaching and there was inadequate cover in the event of staff illness. The inspectors had also objected to the three-guinea fee paid for Greek teaching and were unhappy about the continuing lack of games and physical training facilities.

A further topic arose. The advance from the Bellasses Fund had not been used to clear off the outstanding loan for the chemistry lab, so the annual payments of £24 were still being made. The needs of the school would have made the inspectors all too aware of its financial problems and they suggested that it should apply to the Board of Education asking to be allowed to forgo repayment of the remainder of the loan. The implication is that the inspectors already knew the likely response, for, on 29 July, after receiving the school's request, the Board remitted the further annual payments due to the fund.

In December 1904 Sir David Dale, as Chairman of the Governors, wrote what amounted to a begging letter to Darlington Borough Council. He referred to its powers under the Technical Instruction Act 1889, reminding it that his school had never made any application because of the amounts needed by the council to fund evening classes in the town. Dale contended that the new Education Act had modified the situation in two ways. Firstly, general secondary education had taken the place of technical instruction and, secondly, financial responsibility for such education had been transferred to the county council. It was therefore assumed that the borough might now have some money left over. There is no record in the governors' minute book of any response from the borough council, but the school's continuing problems suggest that, if there was one, it was negative.

Nevertheless, the school managed to fund the employment of a sixth full-time master as recommended by the inspectors. On 29 September 1905, the Headmaster was authorised to get an additional master, if a satisfactory candidate was available 'at this late stage'. By the end of the year the extra master, Mr E. Ballantine Baker, had been engaged. He was to receive £135 salary for the first year, and £150 in subsequent years. The governors also found the means to pay additional salaries to the existing staff for the one term on account of the extra work they had had to undertake. The amounts ranged from 3 to 5 guineas, but in the following spring, Blain, who had received the same salary for 15 years, was awarded a £15 increase.

In 1906 the school faced two crises. The first was triggered by the death of Sir David Dale in May. He had, except for one year, been Chairman of the Governors since 1876 and had also, for many years, guaranteed the school's overdraft. It will be remembered that in 1901 a loan of £1,200 had been obtained from the Bellasses Charity and that this had cleared off the overdraft which on 1 January 1901 had stood at £1,224 16s 2d. Unfortunately, by the time of Dale's death, the school not only owed the bulk of the Bellasses loan, but was in overdraft again.

The National Provincial Bank was unsettled by Dale's death, regarding the overdraft as being unsustainable without his guarantee. In consequence the school was notified that the overdraft facility was withdrawn and the bank wanted to know what the school proposed. A meeting between the Clerk to the Governors and the bank manager had produced the alarming information that the bank would not honour any cheques after 11 July.

Two days before the deadline the governors met to decide what to do and it looks as if the Quakers on the board exerted their influence, for Sir J.C. Backhouse of Barclays Bank, with whom Backhouses Bank had amalgamated some years earlier, was present. The governors agreed to transfer the account to Barclay and Co., provided that the Chairman and Clerk could arrange satisfactory terms. Ironically, National Provincial Bank had made a donation of one hundred guineas (£105) to the fund for the construction of the school thirty years earlier.

At the next meeting (held without a quorum) C.H. Backhouse was appointed Treasurer for the purpose of receiving county council payments in place of Mr Pearson at the National Provincial Bank. Barclays had indicated that they would allow an overdraft of £500, if secured, and Dale's son had agreed to provide a short-term guarantee. Sir David had, on his death, provided the school with one benefit in the shape of a legacy of £1,000. He had expressed the wish that a scholarship be created with it. However, the new bankers required an undertaking that the legacy would not be handed over until the school's finances were put in order. The immediate crisis was resolved but the underlying financial problems were not and, within a few years, there was again a substantial overdraft.

The poor income from fees had been a source of anxiety for years. At their existing levels, the school could not survive without outside assistance, but the market would not stand any increase. By 1906 there were only 14 boarders out of 138 pupils and the space occupied by them was out of proportion to the financial benefit of their boarding fees. Yet, even if boarders were eliminated, the school could not afford the cost of converting the dormitories to the classrooms so badly needed if pupil numbers were to be increased. As it could not increase its fee either, it was caught in a vicious circle.

The disposal of endowments, which provided capital at the expense of future income, had begun in the early 1890s, when land at Heighington had been sold, and the crisis with the overdraft following upon Dale's death emphasised that the school was now dependent upon increased public funding.

The second crisis, in part, related to the level of fees. It would take much longer to resolve than the first, for it struck at the very nature of the school and would, in time, threaten its existence.

The Struggle for Control

Armed with its new-found powers under the 1902 Act, the county council was keen to increase control over the secondary schools within its area. It is clear that its policy was to favour total control by encouraging schools to accept maintained status. The greater expenditure needed for providing better facilities in schools was more easily justified if the Authority had total control. The process started in 1904 and by 1911, eleven schools had become fully maintained, and therefore fully controlled, by the county council. Nine of them had already benefited from new premises. By then there were only four aided schools left, including the Darlington Grammar School. Durham classified those secondary schools as were wholly maintained by it as Division I, whilst those merely aided were classified as Division II.

The county had printed regulations for both Division I and II schools. A Division II school had to have the appointment of a headmaster, but not of other staff, approved by the Committee, likewise its curriculum. It had to submit its accounts and forward a copy of the minutes of governors' meetings within seven days of the meeting.

Amongst the schools in Division I was the Darlington High School for Girls, established in 1885 at 'Claremont' in Trinity Road. It became a county council maintained school in 1906 and, with the benefit of the increased funding made available, it transferred in 1911 to the site in Cleveland Avenue which it occupied till its move to Hummersknott in 1955. Remarkably for the time, all of those maintained schools that gained new or enlarged premises were given facilities for providing school dinners. No one saw anything odd in having schools fully controlled by a local authority charging fees for some pupils.

The statistics for the year ending 31 July 1912 reveal how few children then progressed beyond an elementary education. The Division I schools averaged 2,263 pupils, with 596 in Division II, so, apart from those receiving a technical or commercial education, there were less than 3,000 secondary pupils in the entire county council area. In the four Division II schools there were a mere twenty-five pupils aged between 17 and 18 with seven more aged over 18, yet there were eighty-nine aged under 11.

We have seen already something of the council's attempts to influence the operation of the school and, more recently, in January 1904, it wanted to set up a Commercial Education Department. The school declined the suggestion, but more was to come.

The second crisis of 1906 started with a letter from the county council. It appears that, although the school was receiving payments from the county, it was not yet categorised, for the letter set out the conditions upon which the council would recognise secondary schools within its area. The Grammar School was, of course, financially dependent upon recognition, so would have to elect for either Division I or Division II status.

The county council's preference for having a maintained school was obvious, for it submitted a scheme to this effect for the governors' approval. The county had a set rate of fees for authorised secondary schools of £1 10s 0d (£1.50) per term and its intention was that the fees chargeable by the Darlington Grammar School would be charged at that level – a drastic reduction.

The governors of the Grammar School were less compliant than those of the High School, yet were well aware that they needed to safeguard the grants and fees paid by the council. The death of Dale and the subsequent changes had brought home to them the school's potentially dangerous financial position and they were realistic enough to realise that, even with the present level of fees, their school could not continue without outside financial assistance.

If the county council succeeded in forcing the fees even lower, the school, if independent, would need still more public funds to retain its independence, but if it became a maintained one, those public funds would automatically be available. The school would therefore survive as a maintained one, but could well fail if it remained independent and aided. Nevertheless, the Headmaster and the governors resisted the prospect of having maintained status. As will be seen, their objection to the proposed fee reduction was not merely financial.

The governors therefore sought Division II status and formed a sub-committee to draw up a petition to the council. The few governors present at the meeting decided to be bold and to write to the county resisting a reduction in fees whilst seeking to have to the Education Grant substantially increased.

Five years later, in 1911, when the problem with the county council was still ongoing, Mr Wood took the opportunity, during his address at Speech Day, to summarise the concerns about reduced fees. He said that some people thought it was a hardship if parents could not send a boy to a secondary school for a year or eighteen months after he left elementary school at fourteen, but, in his view, a grammar school education was not designed for this kind of pupil. The school offered a continuous course from age 12 to 17, designed to prepare pupils for a professional or university career. To throw a boy of fourteen, unprepared to tackle new subjects, into a strange environment was to condemn him to failure and to do him a disservice.

Wood went on, 'But it may be said that in other towns in the county that very course is rendered open to parents since the County Education Committee proposes to charge them only 30/- [£1.50] per term for education and books in Division II schools.' The fee had been fixed, but he had yet to see any regulations guarding against abuse and waste. If the regulations were to prescribe a maximum age of entrance of (say) 12 and demand a guarantee that boys take a full four-year course then minimum harm would be done. But Wood thought that if boys could come and go as they pleased, and free use of the privilege was made by parents, the county's grammar schools would cease, within a few years, to be true secondary schools. 'They would fail to prepare boys for university, the professions and the higher walks of commerce.'

In short, Wood's concern was this. Some parents who could not afford the fees over a longer period might manage to pay them over a year or so. The pupil, unprepared for the course and possibly unsuitable for it, could then claim the benefit of a grammar school education. It was believed that the position of poorer children with ability was already protected, given that at least one quarter of the entry was via the school's or the county's scholarships.

There is nothing to indicate that the Headmaster considered that lower fees might encourage poorer parents to finance a child for a full grammar school career, rather than for a mere year or so. He was firm in his belief that the existing fees did not deter parents. In speaking of a continuous course from age 12 to 17, Mr Wood also overlooked the high proportion of boys who left between the ages of 14 and 16.

Meanwhile, back in October 1906, a reply from the Higher Education Committee was still awaited, but the crisis between Durham and the school would always be characterised by a lack of urgency. The county eventually accepted the Division II status and, despite the lack of a formal response from Durham, the governors, now under the chairmanship of Edward Hutchinson, seem to have considered the issue to be concluded. They were wrong.

In July of the following year, the school suffered for its intransigence. The governors, again acting without a quorum, applied to Durham for a grant towards the cost of new woodworking apparatus and for books for a new reference library. Without referring to his committee, Robson bluntly rejected the application. He simply stated that there was no provision for such grants for schools in Division II.

The school's Division II status survived without a serious challenge until 1912. The threat then to be presented was much greater.

Philip Wood's Swansong

Despite the crises of 1906, the school still got by and there were, for some years, fewer comings and goings amongst the teaching staff. There were still achievements to record. In 1905, for instance, Philip Wood could report that four former pupils had been awarded their BAs whilst two more, both at Edinburgh, had gained MAs. Two years later another liability, fortunately a small one, arose. The school now had to meet the requirements of the new Workmen's Compensation Act and had to pay £1 4s 0d to insure the teaching staff against injuries on the premises.

The Headmaster's situation would not have been helped by a school inspection that took place on 25–26 January 1907. It was followed in February by a conference between the Board and the governors. The usual inadequacies were discussed and, as before, the governors' ability to remedy them was circumscribed.

By 1907 there was an increase in the numbers at the school, making it necessary to engage another master, taking the number of full-time staff from six to seven, but the school's finances did not improve. The Board of Education's habit of periodically altering the criteria under which the grants payable to secondary schools were calculated also presented problems. In 1907 such concerns led to the Chairman of the Governors attending a meeting in London with the governors of other schools who shared the same concerns.

The grant was reduced for 1906 and for 1907, despite the increase in pupil numbers, and the school's resultant financial position caused the Head to produce an estimated balance sheet. He prepared it on the footing that there were 150 boys in the school. It showed a projected annual deficit of £130 and resulted in another letter to Durham appealing for increased aid. Specifically the application referred to a grant towards the cost of new woodworking apparatus and for books. The governors also approved a request made by Wood for a new scale of fees. They were all increased by one guinea per year, thus gaining a 5 per cent advantage over an uplift of a mere pound. As an example, the charges for a 10-year-old went from £8 to nine guineas (£9.45).

Some months later the Board of Education wrote to the school. There was a problem. As the maximum fee chargeable under the existing Scheme was £12, the recent increases meant that the fees now payable for the oldest pupils exceeded the limit. To alleviate the situation, the Board suggested that the fee in respect of scholars aged 12 to 14 should be increased to £12, but a new Scheme would be needed. In response, the governors instructed their Clerk to advise the Board that a proposed new Scheme had already been submitted to it, but that nothing had been heard in response.

Three years later the fees were again an issue. The governors wanted to revise them, so the consent of the Board was again required. This time some of the fees were reduced.

In December 1910 the Board of Education intervened again, this time by refusing to accept the school's long-standing practice of compulsory charging for examination fees. The Clerk to the Governors was instructed to tell the Board of the potential loss to the school, but the governors agreed that if the Board persisted, the Head should accept the position. It is not known whether the Board did persist.

At the same time, the Board wanted to clarify the terms under which the Preparatory Class could be continued. The adverse inspectors' reports had not been forgotten and the Board wanted to tighten its requirements. Its suggestion that an application should be made for a new Scheme for the class was agreed, with the class being permitted to continue until a new Scheme came into force.

Happily, in 1908, an increase of £250 was expected in the grant from the Board of Education and, as it was recognised that staff salaries were inadequate, increases were made. Massingham, who had served for thirty years, had his salary increased from £275 to £300, whilst that of Blain, with fourteen years' service, went up from £165 to £190.

Smith and Carrick gained increases of £25, whilst Storry, with only two years' service, was awarded an extra £20. Baker, who had gone by the end of the year, and Turner, a recent arrival, were not awarded increases. A teacher called Drake appears to have replaced Baker, but was replaced in turn by Ronald Mutimer. His annual salary remained at £150.

The salary of Dresser, the part-time teacher of drawing, was increased from £36 to £45. In future, Redpath would undertake all woodwork teaching and would be paid £36 instead of £24.

From 1906 the school benefited slightly, at least in numbers, from the admission of pupil teachers. A Pupil Teachers' Centre, intended for the preliminary training of would-be elementary school teachers, had been established in the town in the late nineteenth century. Its object was to provide a four-year apprenticeship leading to an examination at the age of 18 and those who were successful gained a Training College place. As apprentices, the potential teachers shared their time between lectures at the centre and teaching in local schools.

Then, in 1906 the centre was closed and the county council proposed that the Grammar School and the Darlington High School provide an alternative course of education for the pupil teachers. At that stage free studentships were envisaged and the Grammar School governors were agreeable, 'subject to the numbers not being very large'. The majority of pupils, being girls, were then enrolled at the Darlington High School, but there were eight for the Grammar School.

By 1911 the county was meeting the costs for the pupil teachers, but as usual in its dealings with the Grammar School difficulties arose. The special grant that was available could not be claimed because the pupil teachers comprised less than 5 per cent of the school's population. The county council therefore proposed that the school should accept a purely nominal fee and it also declined to meet the school's claim for the payment of fees for four terms for each pupil teacher.

It appears that the course provided by the Grammar School extended over four terms, as the school considered it advantageous to start courses in January rather than in the following term, when the work really began for the senior Cambridge exam in December. The council evidently thought that three terms' tuition was sufficient. The school protested that no warning had been previously given that the four terms would no longer be paid for. It also made the point that, although it had never had the required proportion of pupil teachers, it had previously received the special grant. The school continued to press for payment of the fourth term's fees previously claimed, but agreed not to claim for the fourth term in future After a couple of months, agreement with the county council was reached, but the terms have not been ascertained.

In the following year a Fire Brigade inspection was arranged to check the safety of the school and two recommendations were made. The hazard to boarders in the west dormitory was at last recognised and the fitting of a rope fire escape to the south window was suggested. Second, it was recommended that a telephone be installed in the school. Whether the ladder was installed is not known, but some years passed before the telephone arrived.

By late 1909 Wood saw a need for an assistant science master and an Old Boy, H. Tiplady, was engaged at a mere £75 per annum. It looks as if the Headmaster met with reluctance on the part of the governors as he had to revert to his earlier days and agree to contribute £30 per annum, soon increased to £40, from his own income.

The year 1910 opened with the good news that the Head had been elected President of the Incorporated Association of Headmasters. Then on 18 March, the newly elected Liberal MP for Darlington, Ignatius Trebitsch Lincoln, was appointed as a governor. He lost the seat at the second General Election of 1910 and it appears that he never attended a meeting, which is probably as well, given his subsequent notoriety. Later in the same year, Forster, the local solicitor who had been part-time Clerk to the Governors for many years, resigned and was replaced by George Todd, at £30 per annum. Forster blamed an increase in correspondence with the Board of Education and the increasing complexity of regulations for his departure.

In the same year, Wood's mainstay, Alfred Massingham, died. He had been Senior Assistant Master rather than Deputy Headmaster and was succeeded as Senior Classics Master by A.J. Smith, the 1902 arrival, at a salary of £195. Confusingly, A.J. Smith's position was filled by F.M. Smith.

Such was the differential between A.J. Smith's new salary and the one received by Massingham that other salary increases could be given without any increase in expenditure. Blain now received £200, Storry £180 and Carrick £130, whilst the underpaid Tiplady had his remuneration increased by no less than 40 per cent. The governors also agreed to relieve Wood of his annual contribution to his salary, but Tiplady died shortly afterwards. His replacement was John Milner, another Old Boy, who had received a special grant of £30 from the school to assist with the costs of his further education. He had, however, to make do with £15 less than Tiplady's augmented salary.

Happily the accounts for the year ending 31 March 1911 showed a better than usual position, with an income of £3,326 1s 6d against expenditure of £3,308 7s 1d. There had also been a reduction in the bank overdraft thanks to a large payment from the Board of Education.

The Coronation of the new king had to be celebrated and the governors recommended that Wood grant at least two days, 22 and 23 June, as holidays. It was left to his discretion as to whether the summer vacation should also be extended.

Although it did not merely benefit Grammar School pupils, it should be mentioned that the medical inspection of schoolchildren began after the 1907 Education Act. By World War I minor-ailment clinics had been set up at North Lodge, including one for dentistry.

During Wood's final years two more leaving exhibitions were provided. One was the Sir David Dale Exhibition, already referred to. It was awarded at four-yearly intervals. The other was the 'William Russell Scholarship', restricted to boys who had entered the school from the public elementary schools of Darlington. The funds, amounting to £800 (£720 net) became available on the death of Alderman Russell's widow in 1911.

The creation of other later awards might be mentioned at this point. In 1936 Lady Starmer founded the 'Sir Charles Starmer Exhibition' in memory of her husband. These awards were tenable for three years and in 1963 were worth £40 per annum.

There were two other leaving scholarships: the 'Middleton Greathead Printers' Scholarship', founded in 1921, open only to the sons of journeymen printers in Darlington and available only as funds permitted; and the 'William Draffan Scholarship', dating from 1936, tenable at Edinburgh University.

From the early years there were variations in the terms of the awards, due to changes in conditions, and up to the 1960s the school could offer at least two major leaving awards each year. There were other bequests for essays or services, such as the F.C. Coleman and the Robert and Anne Teasdale prizes, the last being reserved for the Senior Librarian.

In 1911 the Board of Education suggested that the Bellasses Charity, which had for so long alleviated the financial crises of the school, be merged with it. Between 1901 and 1904 a number of small payments, used to purchase Consols to replace those sold to fund the lending to the school, had been made by the school, but there is no trace of any later payments. That the school readily agreed to the proposal is unsurprising, given that the merger would relieve it of the obligation to discharge the balance of the debt.

The new Scheme provided that Bellasses and the Grammar School would henceforth be one Foundation, administered by the school governors. It was also stipulated that no master at the school could be a governor and that the Head had to be a graduate of a university of the United Kingdom and must reside in the official residence. The power was given to the school to contribute towards masters' pensions.

The governors were to decide upon the general subjects of instruction, the number of boarders and the holidays. There had to be, at least once in every two years, exams for the Upper School under the direction of a university or other examining body and there was to be an internal exam in the Lower School once every year.

As before, no boys under eight could be admitted to the school and there had to be an entrance exam. The school had the power to award maintenance allowances, not exceeding £10 per year, to boys exempted from tuition fees in case of need. The retention of the Preparatory Department for boys only was permitted, as was the education of boys intending to qualify as elementary school teachers. The governors could make, subject to Board of Education approval, variations in the provision relating to their fees, exams and ages.

Most of these provisions presupposed that the school remained independent.

The last development during Wood's headmastership was the introduction of a school magazine. It was an immediate success, the main initial criticism relating to its small size. The Old Boys were pleased by it, and it was expected that future copies would be sent to places as diverse as the Straits Settlements, Canada and the Argentine. The magazine was still being published after the school had ceased to exist.

The title was the *DGS Magazine* and the first issue, although published later, was dated January–April 1912. The printer was the *Northern Echo*. Mr Dresser designed the cover and it contained twenty-eight pages. Contributions for the next issue were requested but writers were warned to avoid using the split infinitive. It was taboo.

The cover design was still used in the early 1930s. The early advertisers included the School Furnishing Company, which had a shop on the corner of Skinnergate and Coniscliffe Road, J.F. Smythe, Gun and Fishing Tackle Makers, and Hodgsons the Chemists on High Row, who offered their own products for photographic developing. Lishmans of Bondgate sold garden tools, including a spade (suitable for a lady) at 2/3d (11p). By the early 1920s, Hodgsons were regularly advertising Kodak film on the back cover.

The first issue reported that on 30 January, the Headmaster ended lessons at 2.45 p.m. to allow the boys to go ice-skating. The bad weather continued and on Friday 2 February there was heavy snow and 'in accordance with established custom' forty or fifty boys lined up inside the gate at lunchtime and threw snowballs at boys coming back from lunch. Some tried to evade the force waiting for them by using the stile, which is believed to have been the Abbey Road side of the yard. Their fate was to be 'scrubbed'. Because of the weather, the first game of football of 1912 took place on 14 February, almost a month after the start of term.

The second magazine, perhaps unsurprisingly as the crisis had re-emerged, contained an editorial expressing concern that the school might be turned over to the county council. In addition to an article by

R.G. Brebner, an Old Boy, about his participation in the recent Olympic Games, there appeared the first English translation from Greek of a recently discovered fragment written by a dramatist of the post-Euripidean school. There is nothing to indicate that it was a hoax. The editor's perennial cry for more articles was also heard for the first time.

As to cricket, three players were awarded their colours and of six matches played, the school won four. However, three of the six opposing teams were played twice, implying that two games counted as one match.

Matches were played, as in later years, against local grammar schools such as Bishop Auckland, Coatham, Guisborough and Stockton. There were also games with the Durham Colleges, Seaton Carew Cricket Club, the North Eastern County School, Mr Beetham's XI and Mr Miller's XI.

The same magazine contained a report on the School Sports, with two photographs in the text. The weather was good, after heavy rain, but there was a low level of entries. As always, the sack race was popular in the Lower School. Incidental music was played by Hoggett's Military Band, and its performance was, as usual, followed by the 'Bandsmen's Race'. Some races were open to the entire school, whilst others were limited to the Preparatory Department or restricted by age. The swimming race took place at Kendrew Street Baths.

There was also a description of the 1912 Speech Day which mentioned that the report of an examiner from Balliol College, Oxford, read by the Head, was very satisfactory. The prizes were presented by Professor Hadow, who criticised the learning of Greek choruses by heart for examinations, regarding it as bad practice. He saw it as a custom of twenty years earlier, but the practice still continued at the Queen Elizabeth Grammar School. Indeed, fifty years later, candidates for A level Latin at the school were still learning by heart the English translations of those passages that they might be expected to translate in the exam.

The introduction of the magazine means that there is more information available about the sporting activities in the school than for the earlier period. At this time, there were only four school teams, namely First and Second XIs for association football and cricket respectively. Rugby was not played and there were no junior school teams. There was also an Old Boys' football team.

By this time there were eight forms plus the Preparatory Class. Those in the school proper were now Form I, Form II, Forms III A and B, Forms IV A and B, Form V and Form VI. A pupil arriving in the main school at the age of eight could be at the school for ten years and so would, at times, have to spend more than a year in the same form.

In 1912 Wood was 66 years old and had been Headmaster for thirty-five years. He was sharing the house with an unmarried daughter and his sister-in-law, Sarah Lawrence, and there were also three live-in staff: a cook and two housemaids. They were responsible for the seven remaining boarders as well as for the family. About 1,700 boys had entered the school since it opened in Vane Terrace.

During those thirty-five years the Headmaster had responded positively to the many challenges and obstacles that were presented to him, but he must surely have been battered by his continuing inability, through lack of funds, to provide the school with what was so badly needed. In October 1912 he faced the embarrassment of having the school threatened with legal proceedings for non-payment of Rates and £45 13s 5d had to be hastily paid. The Clerk to the Governors said that there had been no notification of any liability given until the final demand was received.

Then two months later, Philip Wood abruptly resigned. In the middle of the renewed crisis with Durham the Chairman of the Governors received a letter from James Wood, the Headmaster's nephew. It indicated that because of ill health, it was necessary for his uncle to resign as from the end of term, a couple of weeks away. The resignation was accepted with regret and a discussion followed about pension arrangements for the outgoing Headmaster. The Board agreed to pay an annual pension of £200 per year, a sum representing about 10 per cent of the school's salary bill, to Mr Wood, effective from 1 January next.

Back in 1900 a circular had been received from the Charity Commission proposing a new scheme for those secondary schools wanting to provide a pension fund for their Headmasters. The governors had assented to the proposal and a scheme had been prepared, encompassing a large number of grammar schools throughout the country. However, the scheme was permissive and the Darlington governors then did nothing to create a fund. As a result Wood's pension would have to be paid from the school's normal income, thus stretching the budget still further.

Then a potential problem about the appointment of a successor arose. Although the school was not yet a maintained one, its Division II status entitled the county council to control the appointment of the new Headmaster. The chairman of its Higher Education Committee had intimated that the annual salary of the replacement Head should not exceed £400, but the governors believed that this was inadequate, given the status of the school. They argued for a minimum of £500, plus the free use of the house. Even advertising for a successor would be delayed till the issue could be resolved, so the Chairman of the Governors was authorised to make any necessary temporary arrangements. At least nobody wanted to perpetuate the old system whereby the Headmaster was partly remunerated with a capitation fee and, on any basis, the new incumbent could expect a lower remuneration than his predecessor.

The Chairman used his powers to appoint David Carrick as Acting Head. As he would now have to live out of school, his salary was increased to £195, but he would also receive an additional £50 per term whilst Acting Head. During the interregnum, two staff members, Turner and Mutimer, requested salary increases, but it was decided to leave their requests in abeyance pending the appointment of a new Headmaster.

The Headmaster's retirement, coupled with the uncertain future of the school, had an unsettling effect upon Miss Ada Williams, who had succeeded Sarah Lawrence as the teacher in charge of the Preparatory Department. She obviously knew about Wood's resignation before his nephew's letter was placed before the governors, for the letter she felt obliged to write to the governors about her own position was considered at the same meeting. In it, she said that she had expected to be on the school staff by now rather than that Mr Wood would, as she put it, continue his responsibility towards her. As an employee, not of the governors, but of a Headmaster who was about to retire, her future was doubly dependent upon Wood's successor and the nature of any new regime.

The governors decided that, because of the uncertainty caused by the county's proposals, they would discuss the matter with Wood and urge Miss Williams to carry on for the time being. She did so, remaining at the school till 1918.

The gardener and 'odd-man' at the school, called Bowes, was also employed directly by the Headmaster. His retention was essential because he was needed for attending to the heating system during school holidays. At that eventful meeting, when the governors discussed the county's ultimatum, Wood's sudden resignation and Miss Williams' concerns, they also agreed to employ Bowes at 25/- (£1.25) per week.

The Local Studies Centre at Darlington has a letter from Philip Wood to A.J. Smith, the classics master. It is dated 9 September 1913 and the address is given as at 24 Cleveland Terrace. The letter is a printed one, even to 'Dear' at the beginning and Wood's name at the end. The word 'Smith' is handwritten; nothing else is. It refers to the sum in excess of £600 raised by colleagues, parents, friends of the school, and others for the Head's retirement. Wood says that most of the money has been invested in ordinary shares in Pease & Partners Ltd. He was also presented with a piece of inscribed plate and an enlarged photograph of him was to be placed in the school. The letter conveys Wood's thanks to everyone.

To put the amount in context it should be remembered that, for the year ending 31 March 1914, the endowment income was £488 16s 9d, fees were £1,088 5s 0d, and salaries, including that of the new Head, were £1,952 7s 2d. The outgoing Headmaster was clearly highly valued.

After a long illness, Philip Wood died at the house in Cleveland Terrace on Christmas Day 1917.

The Ultimatum

In early 1912, before Wood's retirement, Durham County Council renewed the offensive. There was an inspection of the school on 15 and 16 February and the first indication of trouble came from a Board of Education inspector during a discussion with the Chairman of the Governors following it. It was put to Edward Hutchinson that the Board might not be able to resist the establishment of another secondary school in Darlington unless the fees were reduced to the level of those in the other secondary schools in the county.

So the school could expect an ultimatum. Either comply with the terms presented in 1906 and become a maintained school charging lower fees at the county's rate, or lose all financial support from the council and face a rival county-maintained school in the town.

The situation was not helped by the school inspectors' requirements for the improvement of the school's facilities. Electric lighting needed to be installed, additional staff were required, and there should be additional classrooms utilising the unused dormitories. The governors recognised the validity of the suggestions, but, as usual, there was no money.

There was a complication and a source of hope. Because of the division of responsibility for education, there had been friction between Darlington Borough Council and the county for some years, relating principally to the funding of the Technical College in Northgate. Now there was the further issue of the county's desire to take over the Grammar School.

As a result, a movement had begun in Darlington to have the town apply for county borough status. A successful application would result in the town having a single authority exercising the powers of both the borough and county councils. A new county borough council could therefore have sole responsibility for secondary education in the town. Even though there was no certainty as to how such a council would treat the Grammar School the advantages of having Durham County Council off the scene seemed obvious.

At a meeting in May 1912, attended by Mr Wood and Mr J.A. Robson from the county council, the governors tried to decide what to do. They had before them a letter from one of their number, Arthur Pease, who could not attend. He accepted that improvements to the school were needed, but it was, in his view, pointless looking for public subscriptions, so they would have to rely upon the local authorities.

Pease proposed a middle course. He suggested the selling of endowments, with the money raised spent on school buildings, but he ignored both the need to obtain the Board of Education's consent and the loss of income arising from the disposal of the assets. As he accepted that both the Durham and Darlington councils would expect increased representation on the governing body he may have assumed that one of them would have been prepared to make up the deficit.

Pease's plan was to lease the school to the county. If this were to be possible, the governors would have to make sure that the necessary standards were maintained. Darlington had a large professional class and it would expect its sons to be educated to a proper standard. This was not the case in what he called 'the industrial districts' where boys were not likely to stay at school beyond sixteen. His thinking was that, if the school was leased, it could be more easily removed from Durham's control, should Darlington become a unitary authority.

There was also a letter to the Clerk from another governor who could not attend, J.B. Hodgkin. He referred to his experience of the 'subordination' of the Darlington Girls' High School to Durham, saying it was not a happy one. He was pessimistic about the Grammar School's future in view of its financial situation, but he had no suggestions to make.

Wood had prepared a report for the meeting. He was more pessimistic than Arthur Pease, but more realistic. He realised that the endowments were not large enough to bring results, assuming that permission to use them could be obtained. He also considered that any application to Darlington Council for help was likely to be futile, particularly as the borough paid a share of the county education rate. Wood thought that ultimately the County Higher Education Committee would have to be approached with regard to the school becoming a maintained one, but his hope was that conditions allowing the school to revert to the town, if and when Darlington became a county borough, could be negotiated. The governors agreed that a meeting with the Committee at Durham should be arranged.

The mood was sombre and Edward Hutchinson, Chairman of the Governors, expressed it openly at Speech Day on 23 July, saying that he ought to take the parents into the confidence of the governors regarding the future of the school. He then told his audience of the threat of the county council to set up a rival school with very low fees, adding that the new school would be in competition. He feared that the governors would not be able to resist the council's demands.

A deputation had gone to Durham to see a sub-committee of the Education Authority. They had been received courteously, but came away with the idea that it would be impossible to dissuade the county council from what it had already done in other towns, i.e. establishing a secondary school giving everybody in the town, rich or poor, the opportunity of a grammar school education.

Hutchinson did concede to his audience that if they went over to the county council, they would at least expect it to buy the playing fields and probably improve the buildings. He added that twenty-five years earlier, there would have been no difficulty in persuading the people of Darlington to pay to provide the facilities and modern equipment needed by the school, but that time had gone. They now said, 'The Government has taken over education, let them pay for it.' The Chairman ended by saying it was pitiful, but all they could do was to throw themselves into the hands of the county council, making the best terms they could.

Alderman Leach, for the county, attempted reassurance, telling his listeners that the provision of gymnasia to schools was a prominent feature of county council policy. He hoped that in its new state, the school would not disgrace, but would enhance its past.

Despite their concerns, it took the governors till October to discuss the memorandum prepared on their behalf. After their discussion, the governors set out the terms, seven in all, upon which Division I status would be acceptable to them. Some were not controversial, but others were. In particular, the governors wanted a lease of the premises to the county at a nominal rent of £5 and, in the event of Darlington becoming a county borough, they required the county council, after the necessary financial adjustments, to transfer the school to the Town Education Authority. They also expected that the option to purchase the cricket field would be exercised, that a gymnasium would be built and that such alterations as were suggested by the Board of Education would be carried out.

The governors seemed not to appreciate that, if the school became a maintained one, they would disappear, for they expected to retain responsibility for the scholarships and masters' salaries.

Durham's response was unsurprising. It dismissed the possibility of a lease of the premises. The transfer, including the field, would be by way of an Amending Scheme as had been used with other schools. Such alterations to the present building as were required would be undertaken by it, but there would be no commitment to buy the freehold of the field or to build a gymnasium. That the governors misunderstood their perceived continuing powers was also pointed out.

The governors felt that the response did not treat their proposals with the generosity they expected and they decided to submit a further statement urging more considerate treatment.

Yet, despite their intentions at the meeting, the governors did nothing about the county's proposals until October 1913, nearly a year later. By then the school had a new Headmaster, Leonard W. Taylor. He had been educated at Warwick School and New College Oxford and was engaged with a salary of £500, plus the use of the house. Given the situation at the time of his appointment, it has to be assumed that he was prepared, if necessary, to be Headmaster of a local-authority-controlled school.

The governors, banking upon the success of the application for county borough status, were undoubtedly trying to delay matters. Then a letter from Robson pressing for a response was received. It contained a clear threat. In the absence of an early acceptance of Durham's terms, the Committee would approach the Board of Education with a view to establishing a boys' secondary school in Darlington, on the lines of the Girls' High School, under the direct control of the county.

A special meeting of the governors to discuss the threat was convened, but still nothing happened. After two more months, the Secretary of the Higher Education Committee wrote again, saying he would be glad of a response from the governors after twelve months! He complained that the county council was continually receiving letters from residents asking about the situation. This time, there had to be a response. Edward Hutchinson, the Chairman, quickly went to see Robson at Durham and explained the difficulty over the resumption of negotiations in view of the expectation that Darlington would become a county borough.

In fact, A.C. Boyde, Darlington's own Education Officer, had written to the school at about the time of Robson's second letter, enquiring whether the borough could offer financial assistance. Nothing of substance then happened until July 1914 when a further letter from Boyde was received. He repeated the offer of assistance and wanted to know what was needed to conduct the school successfully. At last the governors responded and Boyde was sent a list showing the capital expenditure needed. The total amount was £5,560.

Every possible item appears to have been put on the list in an attempt to gain as great an advantage as possible. Considerable renewals to the existing building and a large amount of refitting including the provision of new desks were called for at a cost of £610. The fitting of new labs and the installation of an art room in the dining hall would add a further £450. Provision for a gym at £1,500 was also made, but all this was put in context by a massive figure of £3,000 for the cricket ground. Not only was provision made for buying the freehold for £1,500, but a similar sum was specified for buying and fencing an additional area.

There was more. The governors pointed out that the school had been in receipt, from the county council, of at least one junior exhibition of £60 per annum and merit grants of £100 per annum. Furthermore, the Head was meeting expenditure that should not fall on him. These included board, lodging and laundry for an assistant master in lieu of an additional salary, the salary of an extra maid of £50 and coke for school heating at, say, £5 per annum. There were also grants to the library, mural decorations and entertainments at an estimated £10 per annum. These items should also be taken into account, as should the level of the salaries of the assistant masters. They were below even those of the county council and would require further expenditure of £500–600 per annum.

Later in the month the governors met with a deputation from the town council. Also attending were Robson and an Alderman Johnson from the county council. After the list had been read, Edward Wooler responded on behalf of the town council, but he was cautious, saying he had no instructions to speak on its behalf pending the outcome of the county borough application. He did indicate, however, that the general feeling was for aided, rather than maintained, status. As a personal view, Wooler suggested that the gym be constructed in the Barnard Street area. It could then be used by local elementary schools too. Similarly an extended cricket field could have shared use with other schools. The governors, unsurprisingly, were not happy with these suggestions.

The Durham deputation of two was then seen. The county was having to make economies and the Alderman wanted to know whether the school would accept free a larger number of county scholars than was currently provided for. Given that the county was well aware of the school's financial problems, it cannot have been a surprise to Alderman Johnson that he received a negative response.

A further meeting with the borough council sub-committee, after it had had an opportunity to consider the matter further, was to be held at the conclusion of Speech Day on 8 July. It was clear that many issues would have to be resolved if a new county borough council were to take responsibility for the Grammar School. At that meeting the school produced a memorandum showing that a deficiency of £681 7s 6d was expected for 1914, saying it was explained by the lessening of fees and grants offset against higher salaries. It was calculated, taking an average over three years, that with an average number of boys of 163, there would be an average deficiency per boy of £1 4s 11d.

Overall, the county had paid the school £780 in 1912, £802 in 1913 and £740 in 1914. This income was essential, but it would be lost if the county council did not take over the school. On average forty-eight county scholars were educated at the school, close to a third of the pupils, but the future of these scholarships was unclear. The school needed to know whether the borough council would maintain them, or even add to their numbers, if it took over.

The school calculated that it would lose from the county a total of £956 per annum. Furthermore, the governors were contemplating, with Board of Education consent, the sale of endowments and a loss of income of £181 was expected as a result. The governors needed to know whether the borough would make up this sum, pointing out that a 1d rate would more than adequately meet the sum required. At the conclusion of the meeting, it was agreed that Boyde and the Clerk to the Governors would inspect the school, and after conferring with the new Head, would draw up proposals.

By now the borough council was anticipating a successful outcome to its application for county borough status, but its members had no intention of making a hasty commitment. The school was a valuable institution in the town and the council was sympathetic towards it, but it was mindful of the school's estimate of the expenditure required to put it in good order and of the long-term costs.

It had, as far back as 4 December 1913, passed the following resolution: 'In the opinion of this council it will be detrimental to the best interests of the town if the control of the Grammar School were transferred to the county council and it is therefore resolved that a Special Committee be appointed and requested to carefully consider the matter in all its bearings and, if thought desirable, they should be asked to seek an interview with the governors and to present a report as to the present condition of the School.' Nothing was now likely to happen before the committee, comprising Edward Wooler and Alderman Best, reported.

By then the country was at war, but the fate of the school was not to be postponed because of hostilities.

The Ending of an Era

The report, intended for members of the soon-to-be-constituted county borough council, was finally published in March 1915. It was a comprehensive piece of work and contained a large amount of information about the school in its current state. In its preliminaries, the report referred to an ongoing controversy about whether the school was a '<u>Free</u> Grammar School', as stipulated in its Charter. The report's compilers suggested that the various scholarships available satisfied any requirement, ignoring the lack of any scholarships for the centuries before 1878.

As the school was currently grant aided, the report also outlined the county council's rights of inspection and its powers of approving the curriculum and timetable. It also confirmed that if the school became fully maintained by either local authority, that authority would have the right to appoint all of the governors, but they need not be council members.

The report mentioned that the governors, apparently at Boyde's suggestion, had been in communication with the county council seeking further financial aid, but without success. The county stood by its existing position, requiring the complete transfer to it of the buildings and the endowments on its terms. It also required the reduction in fees to those in force in the county, namely £4 10s 0d (£4.50) per annum. To offset that fee reduction alone would require an additional income of £700 per annum.

Reference was made to the school inspections of 1906 and 1912 and their conclusions:

1. New desks, improved labs, a new workshop and a gymnasium were all needed.
2. Despite adverse criticism of certain members of staff, they were still at the school.
3. There was no more benefit from the prep classes than was likely from a well-managed kindergarten. The committee therefore concluded there was no justification for their continuance unless efficient staff could be provided and the fees raised to make the classes self-supporting.

The Board of Education's criticism in its 1912 report 'that the financial outlook was not bright' was warranted. An increase in the number of students might alleviate the situation slightly and the present level of debt might be sustained, but that would ignore the Board's requirements for improvements. Almost half of the income of the school now came from Board of Education and county council grants, including the county scholarship fees. The salary bill alone, of £1,952 7s 2d, comfortably exceeded the income that the school generated of its own accord.

The committee had concluded that an additional staircase at the playground end of the court, to ease accessibility to the classrooms made out of the dormitories, was needed. Additional accommodation for fifty boys would be provided, but further expenditure of £80 per annum would be needed. An asphalt playground and improvements to the heating system were also necessary.

The report recommended the taking over of control of the school by the new county borough, with conditions. The governors would have to agree in the interim to carry out no alterations or expenditure to buildings without the consent of the council and to refrain from increasing salaries in excess of the county council scale. They would also have to indicate their agreement to the transfer to the new council of the property and the control of the school.

There was one consideration in particular that influenced the committee. Durham County had overspent on secondary education and had been forced to apply to the Local Government Board to levy a rate higher than the 2d in the pound permitted by the Education Act. In response, the Board had suggested that the cost of higher education should fall upon the areas particularly served and the result was that Durham County Council was on the point of charging each constituent area for the cost of education in that area. The borough would therefore have to meet the outstanding costs of the Grammar School whether or not it took responsibility for it. Unless it did so, Darlington would have to bear the cost of the school without having any effective control of either its expenditure or management.

The rough estimate of the capital expenditure required remained at £5,560. This covered the conversion of two dormitories into physics and chemistry labs and into two classrooms, the provision of a gymnasium and the conversion of the present lab into a woodwork shop. It would also cover having an art room in the then dining hall and the purchase of the existing cricket ground, together with an extension.

The significance of the county council's proposal to charge each area for its educational costs had not escaped the local press. It asked why the fees charged at the Grammar School should be reduced when they caused no hardship. The Darlington ratepayers would have to meet the difference should they be reduced.

Although the borough council had inspected the school on 3 February, its proposals were still awaited by the governors on 26 March, six days before the new county borough was to come into existence. Still nothing had been heard when the governors met on 23 July 1915 and concern was expressed. It then transpired that, although the governors had counted on first hearing from the Education Committee, the Committee was expecting proposals from the governors! Communication between the school and the new council clearly left something to be desired.

Then Durham County suggested a conference at the school. The fees and other terms upon which the county scholars might be admitted to the school, in the event of Darlington controlling it, could then be discussed. The Girls' High School, as an existing maintained school, would automatically become the responsibility of the new authority, so a similar letter about its scholarships had also been sent to Boyde. The Grammar School governors agreed to have a discussion with

Boyde, but after the summer holidays. In the meantime, on 28 July they held a special meeting to prepare their proposals for submission to Darlington Education Committee.

The proposal listed the school's debts, stressing that the school could not carry on sustaining losses. Nevertheless, the governors persisted in their resistance to the school becoming a maintained one and requested that the county borough, whilst taking over the present indebtedness, treat the school as an aided one. The governors wanted to be given the discretion to reduce fees for individual boys, but they did not intend to reduce the fees en bloc to the levels proposed by Durham County Council. It was also proposed that endowments be used to buy the field. Initially the governors intended to ask for support at a suggested annual figure of £600, but, after further discussion, it was agreed to omit any reference a specific amount.

Communication between the parties involved was still unsatisfactory. At the governors' October meeting, the Chairman, having reported that nothing definite had yet been heard from the Education Committee, was told by the borough's representative governors who were present that the Education Committee had already resolved to take over the school, but as a maintained one! Ratification by the full council was merely awaited. The governors accepted their failure to obtain aided status, but attempted to make their acceptance subject to their desire that the standards of education be maintained.

After nearly ten years of uncertainty, the future status of the school was, at last, decided and the Darlington Grammar School would continue as a maintained school of Darlington County Borough Council for the rest of its existence.

There were many matters still to be resolved. A meeting between a committee of governors and representatives of Darlington Education Committee took place on 12 November 1915. The governors suggested that, as far as possible, the old rules and regulations of the school should be adhered to. It was also essential that the conditions attaching to the appointment of staff, including the Headmaster, and to the performance of their duties be adhered to. Everything should be taken over en bloc and the scholarships and exhibitions should not be interfered with.

Most of the proposals were accepted, but the governors were forced to accept that the Education Committee and not the Head would be responsible for the appointment of assistant masters. The transfer of the school to the county borough was therefore agreed.

The future arrangements for the county students had not been resolved. The county council had arranged a conference about the admission of such students to the Girls' High School, but the proposed similar conference with the Grammar School governors had not taken place. The governors, now mindful that their responsibilities were shortly to end, had their Clerk indicate to Durham that they could not commit themselves to future arrangements.

By February 1916 the formal proposals from the new county borough had been received. It would take the school over from 31 March, the end of the financial year, together with the assets and liabilities of the governors, and it was recorded that as at 31 March 1915 there was a debit balance of £1,591 10s 2d at the bank. The present staff would be taken over and the council would assure the governors that all steps would be taken to maintain the efficiency and the present status of the school.

The time scale for the transfer had been far too optimistic, for both the governors and Darlington Council seem to have overlooked the fact that the governors had no power to transfer the school and its endowments without the consent of the Board of Education. As soon as the existence of the requirement was realised, the governors agreed to make the request. Immediately they were advised that there would have to be a new scheme. It would have to provide for the trusts for the school's exhibitions and scholarships, for Wood's pension and for various other matters.

At this point, the governors had two other concerns. One related to the option to purchase the freehold of the cricket field. The pre-war residential development in the Abbey Road area had pushed up land values. This had led to a fear that if the county borough took over before the option was exercised, Lord Barnard might try to prevent its exercise by arguing that it was only available to the previous governing body.

Hutchinson, as Chairman, was therefore deputed to approach Fife, the Raby Estate's agent, to seek his views. If it appeared that the governors needed to exercise the option, they would require an indemnity from

Darlington Council to protect them from personal liability. It looks as if, before the delay in the transfer occurred, the governors had assumed that it was too late for them to be requested to exercise the option.

The second concern was that the county council had failed to pay the capitation and scholars' fees due in October 1915. Hutchinson communicated with Sir Frank Brown at Durham and he wrote back confirming that the sums due would be paid before the end of the month.

Then there was a further irritation; this one caused by the county borough. Doubtless assuming that the transfer was imminent, it brought the Easter holidays into line with the other schools, making them run from 20 April to 5 May instead of from 5 April to 1 May, thus creating a reduction of about ten days. The school was concerned about the inconvenience arising, particularly with the cleaning arrangements and with the boarders, for the matron who had responsibility for them had only been engaged as an employee up to 5 April. It fell to the governors to try to sort matters out, at least for the current year.

By 22 March the application for consent to the transfer had been approved by the Board of Education, but it had not drafted a scheme. With the proposed transfer only nine days away, the Clerk was forced to wire the Board stressing the urgency. The telegram produced no results and it was not till May that anything further was heard. Then, two letters came from the Board. One blamed the Local Education Authority for the delays, whilst the other warned the governors that their responsibilities continued until the new scheme was effective. The governors then asked the Board to expedite matters, but they also agreed that, for the rest of their term of office, they would avoid incurring any special expenditure for alterations or extensions.

There were still no clear arrangements for the fees for the Durham scholars attending the school and the governors decided that, until matters were clarified, they would have to be charged to the county. By July there was progress and it was agreed that Darlington would be responsible for the fees of scholarship boys living within the county borough.

Unfortunately, the county council declined to pay the fees of scholarship boys at the school who lived outside Darlington's boundaries, no doubt taking the view that pupils funded by it should be educated at a grammar school in the county's area. The Higher Education Committee therefore advised the school that the six boys concerned, who all lived in nearby villages outside the county borough boundaries, would be withdrawn at the end of term. The result of Darlington's new status was that scholarship boys living in villages close to Darlington would, in future years, normally have to travel to a county council grammar school.

The governors felt that the county's action was inconsistent with the agreement made and resolved to seek further information, but it looks as if Durham stood its ground for, by October, three sets of parents had indicated that they were prepared to pay the fees themselves. Another of the boys had died by then. At its December 1916 meeting Darlington Council agreed that the tuition fees for county scholars still at the school would be 6 guineas per annum, compared with the £4 10s 0d stipulated by Durham. Fee-paying pupils in the county area would be charged 10/- more than those living in Darlington.

Eventually the draft scheme regulating the proposed transfer arrived and was discussed at an Education Sub-committee meeting on 16 June 1916. After certain adjustments had been negotiated, it was approved and in October twenty copies of the draft scheme were received from the Board of Education. The proposals were then advertised in the *Northern Echo* and the *North Star*, with one month allowed for the receipt of objections. By this time the school's debit balance had been reduced to £730 11s 0d.

When it became operative, the Scheme provided that the governors were to submit an account of debts as soon as possible to the Board of Education. On receiving the Board's approval the governors were to discharge the debts from the endowments as provided. Those endowments, of course, included the ones that had come from Bellasses.

The last meeting of the governors of the independent Grammar School took place on 13 December 1916. The minutes refer to routine business only and make no reference to the significance of the meeting or to the changed future of the school. The new governing body would consist entirely of nominees of the county borough council, possessing significantly reduced powers.

On 31 March 1917, one year later than intended and with an absent Headmaster, the Queen Elizabeth Grammar School passed into local authority control. Under the Scheme the school was officially the 'Free Grammar School and Bellasses Foundation'. That the financial restraints dogging it for so long were now gone was evidenced by the increase in Darlington's higher-education rate from 0.45d in the pound in 1915–6 to 4.5d in 1916–7. Admittedly the increased rate also reflected the council's new responsibility for the High School. By 1920–1, thanks to inflation, the rate levied was 10d.

Once the new arrangements were in hand, the council was able to buy the freehold of the school field.

War

After his arrival in 1913, Leonard Taylor soon made an impact upon the school and in the year between his appointment and the coming of war, he introduced three innovations. The first was a prefectorial system, the introduction of which caused a degree of resentment to boys not accustomed to being told what to do by their fellow pupils. Initially there were four prefects, but by the autumn term of 1914 the number had increased to six, one of whom, designated Head Prefect, had served in the previous year. There was still no school captain.

Another development was the establishment of a library. The fiction section, with a borrowing facility, was housed in the dining hall. The Head was not ambitious in his expectations of his pupils. He recognised that the average boy was not likely to read Scott or Dickens in his own time, but he was concerned that the pupils did not read the cheap novelettes, described by Taylor as 'abominable trash', that were then common. Books by writers like the Brothers Grimm, Hans Christian Anderson and E. Nesbit were seen as suitable for the younger boys. So were books by Henty, Ballantyne and Marryat for the older ones. The non-fiction books had to be kept in classroom cupboards under the control of masters because of lack of space, making access difficult. By later standards the arrangements were basic and donations of books were frequently requested.

The third innovation was the introduction of a House system. There were three Houses and the idea was to provide sporting opportunities for boys who might not be in the school teams. Each House had XIs for cricket and football and each House team would play the other two during the season. Points would be awarded according to performance in matches and for successes in sports championship events, so a winning House would emerge each year. Reports of the first House matches were contained in the school magazine for early 1914.

The Houses were the Danes, the Normans and the Saxons and boys were allocated to them by reference to the initial letter of their surnames. Those with surnames in the A to G range became Danes and Blain was the first Housemaster. The Normans, with A.J. Smith as Housemaster, had H to P, whilst the Saxons took Q to Z. David Carrick was their Housemaster. Each of the three had a senior pupil as House Captain, but soon after the war started two volunteered for the army and were lost to the school. The system worked well, although, at the outset, the new loyalties led to mild hostilities amongst the leading lights of the Lower School in the court and in the playground. The new system led to a vast increase in the numbers competing in the annual sports, with the result that qualifying heats were needed on the Wednesday prior to the Sports Day.

Concerts were popular. A choir comprising masters' wives, together with ladies and gentlemen 'closely interested in the school', performed on 21 March 1914 and a second concert followed, this time with solo singers and a piano soloist. Then on 27 May, a concert, with a choir and soloists, was given by the school. Over 200 tickets were sold and the hall was packed to overflowing.

During the summer term of 1914, Carrick set himself the task of tracing as many post-1877 Old Boys as possible and a thousand circulars were sent out. The intention was to initially set up a register, followed by an attempt to form an Old Boys' Club. Carrick met with difficulty in tracing many of the former pupils, but the school magazine reported that 106 had been located and, of these, 47 gave Darlington addresses. There were ten abroad and eight were clergymen. Amongst those living locally was R.G. Brebner, who had participated in the 1912 Olympic Games. From 1907 to 1914 he was the England amateur football international goalkeeper. Sadly he died in 1914 having never recovered from an injury caused in a football match against Wolverhampton Wanderers. The onset of war brought Carrick's efforts to an end for some years.

Speech Day took place on 28 July 1914. The hall was seriously overcrowded, but at least the governors and staff had a platform to themselves. P.E. Matheson, a tutor at New College, Oxford gave the prizes. He said that it was not possible or desirable to give everyone a secondary education, but he stressed the importance of schools like the Grammar School taking boys from all sections of the community. The House Cup was awarded to the Saxons.

After the Chairman (Edward Hutchinson) had reported on the current situation with Darlington Borough Council and the county council the platform was vacated. A choir of boys from IVA Modern then sang two German students' songs. After the songs an excerpt from Moliere's *Le Bourgeois Gentilhomme* was performed in costume – apparently in French!

A week after the students' songs had received the audience's enthusiastic applause the country was at war.

The effect of the war was apparent from the start of term in September 1914. The mobilisation of the Territorial Army and the call for volunteers for the forces led to an urgent need for accommodation for men and equipment. Issue 7 of the school magazine, which covered the period up to September 1914, reported that the Grammar School, together with other schools, had been requisitioned and that Red Cross and other wagons had been seen in the school playground, with a sentry posted at the gate. The South Park had become a Royal Field Artillery camp and another camp had been set up in Hummersknott Hall's park. The initial requisitioning, by the Royal Army Medical Corps, was short-lived, perhaps during the school holidays only. Nevertheless a claim for damage and for cleaning after the billeting in the school was made to the War Office.

However, there was soon a more serious concern, for, very shortly afterwards, the school was inspected with a view to its being re-requisitioned for billeting. After correspondence with the Board of Education, the school was sufficiently concerned to write direct to the General Officer Commanding, Northern Division, but he did not reply. The governors tried to decide what to do if requisitioning took place and concluded that the best solution was to ask the county council to allow the school to take lessons at the Girls' High School. The Clerk wrote to Durham to this effect.

On 5 February 1915 the governors again met, but Robson from the County Education Committee also attended and he made it clear that the Darlington High School proposal was not acceptable to his council. He wanted to know whether enquiry had been made about using the Central Hall or somewhere similar. The governors passed the matter over to their Chairman, Edward Hutchinson.

There had still been no response from the army, but later in the month the uncertainty was ended. A letter came, not from the army but from the Board of Education, saying that no further commandeering need be feared. In this respect, the Grammar School was more fortunate than some elementary schools in the town. They had to organise teaching on a shift system, because parts of their buildings had been requisitioned.

Within a few weeks of the outbreak of war, fifty-one Old Boys had enlisted in the army. The first death in action occurred on 16 September. The victim, Lt. J.L. Huggan RAMC, was a regular soldier, and, at their meeting on 16 October, the governors had one minute's silence for him and sent a letter of condolence to his family. Unsurprisingly, given what was to happen, he was to be the only war casualty referred to in the governors' minutes.

The staffing of the school was also affected, for Ronald Mutimer, on the staff since 1908, joined up, as did E.S. Turner, who was President of the Games Club. Both were to die in the war. In the previous term Mutimer had received a payment of £10 to enable him to attend a geography course at Oxford, scheduled for the fateful month of August. The vacancies, together with the one left by Milner, were filled by C.J. Mitchell, J.A. Kirbyshire and C. Bride, all Oxford or Cambridge graduates. Kirbyshire was to receive £120 per year, the others £150. Because of the number of staffing changes, the Board of Education was asked to dispense with the examination of the Lower School.

Drill Sergeant Instructor Robson also joined the forces, but arrangements were made for drills to be continued by the existing staff. In particular, Ord was to be allowed the usual 4/6d (22½p) payment per lesson if they were given by him out of school hours. Also, at about this time, a pupil was appointed as a lab assistant at 2/6d (12½p) per week, the unusual circumstances justifying the decision. Then, in December, four Belgian refugee boys were taken into the school. Eventually Darlington Council agreed to meet half of their fees.

Mutimer and Turner were still employed by the school and the governors, who had to meet the salaries for their replacements out of the school funds, were aware that both had dependant mothers who could not be supported by their sons' army pay. It was therefore decided to grant the mothers £10 each for the current term, with the hope that some allowance might be continued thereafter, but it was recorded that the school's financial position might stand in the way of the governors doing as much as they would like.

Appeals for further assistance were soon made so, in December, the governors agreed to double the payments for the first term to both mothers. Turner remained unhappy about the provision made and by March 1915, the Association of Assistant Masters in Secondary Schools had intervened on his behalf. The governors asked their Clerk to reply, believing that the full circumstances had not been made known to the Association.

At least the staff still at the school gained a benefit. A decision made by the governors during the previous autumn to pay the assistant masters nine times a year, instead of once in each term, had led to A.J. Smith sending a letter of thanks on behalf of the staff in February 1915. The Assistant Masters' Association had encouraged the change.

Whether there was a connection or not is unclear, but the coming of war coincided with an increase in the number of pupils at the school and during the autumn of 1914 additional benches were provided for Miss Williams' Preparatory boys. The main school, however, needed a new classroom and tenders totalling £53 6s 0d were accepted on the basis that an unused dormitory would be converted. The conversion appears to have been insufficient, for in December 1915 the Borough Surveyor was asked to inspect the school. The governors believed that further classrooms were still needed, but, as always, there was no money. They were, no doubt, hoping that the new county borough would save the day.

The altered situation led to more changes of staff. Apart from departures of temporary staff, there were two retirements and one sudden death in 1915. The replacements were L. Ord (F. Ord's brother) at £150, R.E. Newton at £180 per annum rising by two increments to £200, and H.R. Hughes, who came to teach modern languages. He was to receive £150 initially, rising with three annual increments of £10 to £180. Hughes was born in a Welsh village and, according to his obituary published fifty years later, spoke scarcely any English until he was twelve. By now there were nine full-time assistants.

Amongst the temporary staff was a Miss Taylor, engaged for one term only at a mere £11 11s 0d. Around this time, Redpath, the manual instructor, applied for a salary increase but was put off, being told that consideration would have to be deferred because of the negotiations with Darlington Council.

During the spring of 1915 it was reported that the boys had proposed that the money allocated for school prizes be given to war charities. According to the governors' minutes one of their number, Alderman Wooler, objected, believing that the result would be unfair to the pupils. Despite the Chairman offering to meet the costs himself, the school magazine reported that there were no prizes and that the money saved went to war charities, mostly to the Red Cross.

In the midst of all this Taylor also had to organise urgent roof repairs, including the fixing of chimney pots. The payment of the pension to Wood was, at last, nearly three years after his retirement, approved by the Board of Education

On 3 November 1915 the governors attended a meeting, specially convened at Mr Taylor's suggestion, to consider a letter from him. In it, he referred to a great crisis at the school. All of the staff, including Taylor himself, had received Lord Derby's letter and none of them was 'starred'.

The subject of the masters' concern was the 'Derby Scheme', introduced in October 1915 because the flow of volunteers for the army had reduced to a trickle. The object was to make it compulsory for men aged from 15 to 65 to enter themselves on a national register, even though, at this stage, those aged over 40 were not expected to volunteer for service. The purpose was to reconcile the needs of industry with those of the army by categorising those registered by age, marital status and their importance to the national economy.

In effect, someone required to register had three choices. He could volunteer to join the forces immediately, he could indicate a willingness to serve under the scheme, or he could simply register, risking scorn for not being prepared 'to do his bit'. Because the object was to call up younger men and those who were unmarried first, an older married man might say he was willing to serve and be reasonably confident that he would not be called upon for some time.

There was a further complication in that essential employees, including those in reserved occupations, could be 'starred' and so would not be called up. They could safely volunteer knowing that they would not be called and would avoid public hostility by being entitled to wear an armband denoting both their exemption and their willingness to serve.

The staff were in a difficult position. Because they were not 'starred' they could not claim any justification for not volunteering and there was considerable hostility to those seen as shirking their duty. Furthermore it was well known that conscription was likely, so there was a strong temptation to anticipate the inevitable and gain some credit for being a volunteer. There was a perception, initially justified as it turned out, that the conscript force would be treated as being of inferior quality.

Because, in the words of Taylor's letter, 'the Authorities consider the staff's work unnecessary', no fewer than half of the full-time teachers, namely Messrs Taylor, Carrick, Smith, F.W. Ord and Todd, felt it incumbent to go by Christmas. In addition, Hughes, Newton and Hall were said to be uncertain about their position. L.C. Ord would stay, as his brother, although over age, would take his place in the army. Whilst the governors expressed their appreciation of the loyalty of the masters to their country, they were understandably concerned about the effect of their intentions upon the school. Taylor proposed a scheme for the temporary staffing of the school, but the matter was deferred to another special meeting to be held nine days later.

After the meeting steps were taken to dissuade him, but Taylor felt obliged to stand by his decision. His offer to resign as Headmaster was refused by the governors, but Taylor's offer to forgo his salary was accepted. However, the governors decided that certain expenses borne by him should be taken over by them on behalf of the school.

At the next special meeting it was agreed that Smith would stay. As a married man, he was somewhat down on Derby's list and it was decided that he would deputise for the Head for the time being, with a bonus of only £25 per term for doing so. Thomas Henderson had agreed to devote 13½ hours to teaching English, whilst junior Latin would be taught by two local clergymen. Nevertheless, as four members of staff were going, further teachers would be needed. The need for allowances for the departing assistant masters' dependants was also recognised, although Todd appeared to be already amply provided for.

By the end of term, the Chairman and the Headmaster agreed upon a new system for paying the staff. Ironically the upheavals improved the school's finances. The provisions for the salaries of Taylor and Todd at £500 and £150 respectively were removed and Carrick's salary of £195 was replaced by an allowance of £60. F.W. Ord was also to receive a reduced allowance, but he soon obtained a commission and declined to take anything from the school.

The staff who stayed, including those who worked part-time, all kept their existing salaries. Henderson was the exception, being awarded an additional £75 for his teaching of English. It was now possible to increase the annual allowances for Mrs Turner and Mrs Mutimer to £50 each. There were still sufficient savings on salaries to provide for the additional teachers needed, including provision of £120 for a replacement schoolmistress. Taylor made his own contribution by suggesting that, if the married masters provided the seeds, they might have the resultant yield from his garden.

Later, in March 1916, Mrs Taylor requested a wage increase for Bowes the gardener/furnaceman. An increase, in the form of a war bonus of 2/- (10p) was agreed, bringing his weekly income to 30/- (£1.50).

The staff needed had all been recruited. They were J. Williams (£180 salary), DC Craven (£150) and Miss Henson, who held a Certificate of Efficiency from the London Teachers Registration Council (£120). The numbers in the school grew to a record 187 by February 1916 and a new form was created, presumably using the converted dormitory referred to earlier. A further master was needed and John Henderson, not to be confused with the music master, was engaged at £50 per term to teach this class. At the same time, Dresser's salary was increased by £10 as his teaching time had been increased by 1½ hours per week.

The increasing number of pupils led to an improvement in the school's finances and there was a reduction in its debit balance at the bank. Of course, by now, it mattered less as the new arrangements for control of the school were well in hand.

There were still worries about the loss of further members of staff to the forces, particularly of Smith and Newton, and the governors decided to have the masters medically examined to ascertain who might be called up and whether steps to try to obtain exemption could be taken. They also considered attempting to have Smith and Newton 'starred', but they decided to take no action at that time. Concerns were eased by a letter dated 24 June 1916 from the Board of Education reporting that the Army Council had agreed to the school's retention of Smith and Newton 'except in the event of a grave crisis'.

By August 1916 both Mutimer and Turner had been killed in action. The Headmaster appears to have still been at the school in January 1916, for he presented two spoons as target shooting prizes, but the school magazine for the period up to April 1916 reported that he had been promoted to Captain. He served in the 5th Battalion, Durham Light Infantry, and also became a casualty, being wounded and captured by the Germans. He was not repatriated until 1919.

In the school itself, life went on, although the war increasingly intruded.

During that first term of war, the first proper school society was formed. Membership the Debating Society was initially confined to the Fifth and Sixth Forms and debates took place on Saturdays in the dining hall. The first debate, on Saturday 3 October 1914, was about the proposition that a modern education was better than a classical one and the motion was carried. At the next meeting a motion favouring compulsory military service was carried. There were six debates during the first term.

By early 1915 members of Form IVA were entitled to attend. Frequently masters were the principal speakers in debates, a practice that continued for many years. Perhaps surprisingly, the motion at one debate that 'the boys of the school have too little homework' was carried 11–10. Another debate supported the proposition that women should have the vote. The motion was lost, but the proceedings were enlivened by the intrusion of a woman described as a 'militant suffragette'. She was allowed to finish what the magazine called her 'amusing, but unreasoned, speech'.

One debate in early 1916 provides evidence that the long-standing tradition of forbidding pupils to use the front entrance to the school existed even then, for a motion was successfully proposed that the Sixth Form should be allowed to use it. The proposer claimed that boys were wasting twenty minutes per day through having to go down to the laboratory to gain access to the school. Presumably the result did not lead to change, for the magazine for the first half of 1921 contained a reference to the 'elect' who used the front steps, implying that their punctuality was not as it might be. During this period the Glee Club also resumed activities, with a fairly successful season, but it suffered from a paucity of trebles.

Paper chases seem to have been popular. On 9 December 1914 over 100 boys took part in one on a route through Cleasby and Low Coniscliffe. There was another on 16 February, with a six-mile route including Salutation Corner, Carmel Road and fields leading to Linden Avenue.

There were always reminders of the war, however. In the early days of the war the Belgian Refugees Fund was supported by the pupils, but later a weekly school collection was held for the YMCA Soldiers' Hut in North Lodge Park.

The members of the Fifth and Sixth Forms were urged to join the Old Boys' Drill Club, which was affiliated to the local Rifle Club, but it was hoped to form an Officer Training Corps at the school. Unfortunately, the Headmaster had to report at the 1915 Speech Day that the War Office had again refused its consent.

As an alternative, arrangements for the establishment of a platoon of Old Boys and older pupils, attached to the Darlington Volunteer Training Corps, were made. In addition, the three upper forms at the school were given military drill with dummy rifles. The drill became extremely popular. Charges, no doubt exhilarating for those taking part, were particularly so. In October 1916 it was reported that a number of the boys had joined the scouts and it was agreed that such boys should be known as 'the Darlington Grammar School Troop'. It was not made clear whether the boys had collectively joined one troop or whether they were scattered about existing ones.

The deaths of five Old Boys in the war were reported in Issue 9 of the magazine, including one in the army, killed in the Hartlepool bombardment. The magazine also contained a list of Old Boys who had joined up, seventy-five in total. Many ex-pupils had been wounded.

During 1915, George Spence, for twenty-eight years the school's cricket coach, retired, as he was suffering from problems with his sight. He had worked as a coach after putting in long hours in the Railway Wagon Works, and he appeared in most of the cricket team photos, then displayed in the dining hall but later to be found in the main corridor. Spence had played cricket both for the school and for Darlington and had also been a football player.

It will be remembered that the William Russell Scholarship had been established in 1911 in accordance with the terms of Russell's bequest. Unfortunately the £720 received had never been invested and in July 1915 the Board of Education wanted to know why. The governors felt that the query was uncalled for as the accounts for 1913, 1914 and 1915 all indicated that they had not invested the money. They chose to overlook the obvious point that the accounts provided no explanation for the omission. The reality was that the £720 had been retained in the bank to keep the school's overdraft at a reduced level. The governors' response was to ask the Board to provide them with (say) £1,700 out of the Consols invested for the Bellasses Trust. Such a sum would be sufficient to enable the £720 to be invested and the overdraft cleared off.

The proposal fell on stony ground, so the governors now used the argument that the Board of Education should have pursued the matter earlier, in time to allow some Consols to be transferred into a War Loan, for, with the passage of time, Consols had fallen in value. The governors also tried to extricate themselves by arguing that even though arrangements with the new county borough council had not been concluded, any new terms should be sorted between the Board and the council direct!

In February 1916 the Board relented to the extent that the governors would be permitted to take no action until the war was over, beyond giving an undertaking that they would ultimately invest the £720 and, in the meantime, would maintain the exhibition created. The governors were finally let off the hook under the terms of the Scheme of January 1917 which regulated the arrangements for the handing over to Darlington. The sum of £720 was to be taken by selling Consols vested in the Bellasses Foundation. It would then be held in trust for the Foundation of William Russell in satisfaction of the similar sum 'recently received by the school governors, as trustees of the Russell will, and temporarily appropriated by them for the purposes of the Grammar School'. The capital lost to the Bellasses Foundation as a result would not have to be replaced.

By late 1916 the war was having an increasing impact upon the school. The threat of airship raids imposed a need to further darken the hall and some classrooms and led to the payment of a £10 premium to provide £10,000 insurance cover for the buildings and contents under an aircraft insurance policy.

The continued effects of inflation were making the staff restive and in October the Acting Head requested a war bonus for the standing members of staff. The governors responded by pointing out that the county borough did not pay such a bonus to those in its employment receiving £150 or more. Although Smith did not press the matter, the staff did. They wrote directly to the governors repeating their request for a bonus and were supported by the Assistant Masters' Association.

Newton and Hughes attended the governors' meeting held on 13 December 1916 as a staff deputation. They gained an expression of sympathy, but it was pointed out that there were difficulties with the expected transfer of the school. However, the governors resolved that 'subject to information being obtained' a 10 per cent bonus for the year ending 31 March would be granted to married staff and those with other dependants. Bonuses would not be paid for visiting or temporary masters. The governors also decided to pay £100 per annum to the Headmaster after being advised of his altered financial circumstances. The matter had been before the October meeting when it had been left to the Chairman to 'favourably respond to any such approach on the subject as he rather expected to receive'. Whether the wording left him clear as to what was expected of him must be uncertain.

At this time Smith was keen to have a telephone installed in the school. The Clerk to the Governors was instructed to make enquiries, but there is nothing to indicate that anything happened and Ward's Directory of 1921 does not show a phone number for the school. One of the Fire Brigade's recommendations back in 1912 had been for such an installation.

Outside sporting fixtures continued with the school football team playing eleven matches during the 1914–5 season and, at this time, new cricket and football colours caps were introduced. The football one was divided into halves of dark and light blue whilst the cricket cap was in dark blue with a light blue button and a light blue ring. A new cap for prefects was also intended. The number of sporting fixtures had increased as a result of the House system being introduced. In early 1916 there were twenty-seven finishers in the House Run of 6 miles, with the Danes overall winners. In those days it was intended that all pupils took part.

Football matches against local schools such as Coatham and Bishop Auckland grammar schools still took place, whilst the Old Boys were still able to field a team to play against the school. There were also home games against what were presumably scratch teams such as Mr Henderson's XI or Mr Creek's XI. Eight members of the First Team gained football colours from 1913 on.

During the 1916 season the First XI had thirteen cricket fixtures, nine of them at home, and there were matches against the masters (Wednesday 14 June), Mr Henderson's XI and the Middlesbrough High School Old Boys, but there was no fixture with the school's own Old Boys. Seven players were awarded school colours.

Problems with fixtures increased as the war went on. The Local Studies Centre at Darlington has a postcard addressed to J.L. Sisman, who was Club Secretary for both football and cricket. It is dated 27 January 1917 and was sent on behalf of Middlesbrough High School Old Boys. The writer says that because of the increasing number of members being called to the colours it will be necessary to cancel their fixture for 10 March, but he hopes that playing can resume in better times.

A programme for the 37th Sports held on 7 July 1917, price 2d, survives. We can, therefore, form a picture of a typical Annual Sports Day during this period. According to the programme, J.L. Sisman was the Victor Ludorum for 1916. He was again in 1917.

Twenty-four events were listed, although one of these was a swimming race of two lengths in the Darlington Corporation Baths on an unspecified date. Amongst the events were the throwing of a cricket ball, a sack race, an Old Boys' race and a tug of war with a team from each house. Most events were open to anyone in the school, subject to age limits, but some seem to have been open to outsiders. The one-mile race had been run two days earlier and was won by Cox-Walker. The programme gives the record time as 5 minutes 17 seconds, yet states that the winner's time was 4 minutes 27 seconds! The Inter-House run had also taken place earlier.

Athletic events had their perils. Post-war, in 1921, the prospects of the Normans in the tug of war House final were reduced as two of their team managed to suffer broken wrists during training.

The ubiquitous Sisman has also left us his reports for his school career from Form IV onwards. For the academic year 1913–4 he was in Form IVA and the subjects studied by him included model drawing, scripture, arithmetic, algebra and geometry, but not trigonometry. He was also studying Latin and history, which were taught by the Headmaster. French was taught in sets, Sisman being in Set II, and only thirteen in the form were being taught Latin. Writing and spelling were reported . upon, but no placings were given. The July 1914 report shows Sisman as first out of twenty-eight in the form. He had shown considerable improvement during the year.

Other subjects listed on the report form, but not taught to Sisman, included reading, writing, spelling, higher maths, freehand and design drawing, Greek, German, woodwork and manual training. Biology was not taught. In December 1914, Sisman, despite his class placing, was still in IVA, though, by July 1915, he had reached Form VA. He was then studying higher maths, with nine in the class, and trigonometry, but not physics. He was now the first of eighteen.

By the beginning of 1916 Sisman was in the Sixth Form and the subsequent reports are all signed by Alfred Smith as Acting Head. He was now studying four mathematics subjects including higher (or applied) maths. His other subjects as a Sixth Former were scripture, history, geography, French, theoretical chemistry and Latin, ten subjects in all. This mixture of arts and science subjects would have seemed odd to a Sixth Former at the school forty or fifty years later. Sisman continued in the Sixth Form for a second year and in the summer of 1917 was placed second out of seventeen.

According to a report in the *North Star* in January 1917 the Education Committee was to consider whether the teaching of Latin and Greek at the school should continue. The nature and extent of the discussions is not known, but no change occurred.

At this time, the Cambridge Locals were being sat by Form IV as well as by those in V and VI, but an overdue change took place in 1917 when the School Certificate was introduced to replace the profusion of external examinations previously existing. As a result, by the end of the war the Grammar School had abandoned the Cambridge examination and replaced it with the Durham University School Certificate examination.

A note from the Education Office setting out the school's annual rental income as at 15 December 1917 also survives. The amounts were not high. Heighington provided £108, whilst the Darlington properties produced about £78. This figure included 2/- per week from a Mrs Fea 'payable if and when it can be got'.

By April 1917 the war was seen as never ending, the Tsar had been overthrown and the success of the German submarine blockade threatened Britain with starvation. The public mood was grim and public feeling was mounting against German nationals, suspected pacifists and anyone not participating in the war effort.

This mood was reflected in Darlington in connection with the proposed employment of a temporary master at the Grammar School. Williams, the chemistry master, had left to take up an important post in the munitions industry and his intended replacement was Rev. J.R. Missen, curate at Holy Trinity, Darlington, but also a certificated elementary school teacher with a degree. The salary was £150 and, as it had recently taken over control of the school, the responsibility for making the appointment fell upon the county borough council.

According to the *North Star* attempts were made in the council to prevent Missen's employment because of allegations that he had gone to Ireland to evade military service. It was argued on Missen's behalf that he had gone there in 1912, two years before war broke out, and furthermore that he also had an exemption from conscription. It was also alleged that there was a prejudice on the council against clergymen as teachers. The situation was discussed at various levels in committee and ended up before the full council. At that point, it decided to employ him. Rarely can a teacher have had his employment application subjected to such public scrutiny.

There had been, even at the beginning of 1916, fifteen fatalities amongst Old Boys serving in the forces but, as the intensity of Britain's involvement in the war increased, the numbers increased significantly. Deaths, if they were referred to at all, now warranted only a passing mention in the school magazine and pupils, particularly those in the Sixth Form, continued with their studies with the certainty that they would soon be in uniform.

One pupil faced with a dilemma was John Worstenholm. His father, the editor of the *Northern Echo* was a staunch Quaker and pacifist. Having gained a scholarship to Cambridge University, John left school in the summer of 1916 and in October, whilst the slaughter on the Somme continued, went to Cambridge. Most of those who should have been at the university were fighting and dying elsewhere, and Worstenholm must have found life there difficult. It is not known whether he was a conscientious objector or had obtained deferment, but John left Cambridge at the end of his first term and joined the army. He quickly transferred to the Royal Flying Corps and, in September 1917, as an inexperienced pilot, he was shot down and killed.

It is impossible to say much here about the lives of those who were killed, but two more can be mentioned as random examples. Joe Booth attended the Grammar School until July 1914, when he left to train as a teacher. Then he joined the Scottish Horse (later Duke of Atholl's Regiment) at Dunkeld in company with four others from the school.

They had all been in the Darlington Volunteer Training Corps together. At some point, he transferred to the Royal Field Artillery with the rank of second lieutenant and died of wounds on 8 October 1918, aged 21. He had been scorer for the school cricket team.

Thomas William Applegarth had been educated at elementary school and did not enter the Grammar School until 1907 when he was 14 years old and had gained a scholarship. Despite his late start, he passed the Cambridge Senior Local Examination in 1910 with first-class honours and with distinctions in Latin and geography. He was also the first winner of the Sir David Dale Memorial Exhibition worth £40 per annum. In 1912 a scholarship at Emmanuel College, Cambridge followed and he was awarded his BA in 1915.

After teaching in Derby, Applegarth enlisted, becoming a driver in the RASC. Subsequently he was awarded a commission and served as a second lieutenant in the Durham Light Infantry. Unfortunately, he was wounded and captured by the Germans, dying of his wounds on 8 April 1918.

The most celebrated of the Old Boys who fell in action were the Bradford brothers of Witton House, Milbank Road. There were four of them, collectively known as 'the fighting Bradfords', and three died in the war. The youngest, but highest ranking, was Brigadier-General Roland Boyes Bradford, who was born on 23 February 1892. He gained a Military Cross, whilst a lieutenant, in February 1915 and, after rapid promotion, was awarded a Victoria Cross as a temporary lieutenant-colonel in November 1916. When he was killed in action on 30 November 1917 Roland Bradford was, at 25, the youngest general in the British Army.

His brother James was a lieutenant in the DLI. In April 1917, he led his men into an enemy trench, capturing many men plus two machine guns. Having himself killed three Germans, he then repulsed a determined counter-attack. For this exploit James was awarded the Military Cross, but unfortunately he died of wounds in the following month.

A third brother, George Nicholson Bradford, was a permanent officer in the Royal Navy, reaching the rank of lieutenant commander, and was the second member of the family to be awarded a VC. He took part in the famous raid on Zeebrugge on St. George's Day 1918 and was in charge of the storming parties embarked in *Iris II*. There were problems in securing the vessel to the Mole and Bradford took charge of the securing, risking certain death in doing so. His body fell into the sea, riddled with bullets, but was recovered by the Germans and was buried 'with honour'. The award was, of course, posthumous, and was received by his mother in the following year.

The surviving brother was Captain Sir Thomas Andrew Bradford DSO, DL, JP, who died at the end of 1966. He too distinguished himself in the DLI, being awarded the Distinguished Service Order in 1916. In later years, he was knighted for political and public services and became Sheriff of County Durham.

The flagpole, which stood for many years by the entry to the school at the corner of Abbey Road and Vane Terrace, had its origins at this time. The pole and a flag were donated to the school and the presentation ceremony took place on Empire Day, 24 May 1918. Initially, the pole was on 'the Mound' referred to later.

The war ground to its end on 11 November 1918 and gradually the troops returned home. For those who were left it was necessary to determine the number of Old Boys who had lost their lives or who had served. Because many men had been posted missing, or had lost contact with the school, the task took time.

At the 1919 Speech Day it was asserted that 369 former pupils and masters had served and that sixty-four had fallen, but, over several years, additional names came to light. There are two Memorial Boards for the war in the hall at the Sixth Form College. One lists the dead, but the other, with many more names on it, lists those who served in the forces. In the past, this has led to an exaggeration of the numbers killed.

In 1934 the Headmaster wrote to the Chief Education Officer in response to an enquiry about the numbers, and he stated that 264 Old Boys served in war and that sixty-nine fell. He added that seven masters also served and two of these were killed. Actually three were killed, but John Milner's name appears as a former pupil, as he was no longer on the staff when he joined up. The 1934 figure for those who served is surely incorrect, given that over one hundred more had been listed fifteen years earlier. The relevant Memorial Board, which was updated when necessary, gives the names of 401 Old Boys and staff who served.

A further source of confusion arises because the names of former pupils who moved on to another school, such as the Bradford brothers, are not recorded on the board commemorating the fallen. It therefore understates the number from the school who died.

'Number One Council School, Darlington'

On 11 November 1918 the guns stopped firing and the school could anticipate a slow return to normality. But how would the normality of 1919 compare with that of 1914? At the Speech Day held a few days before the war began, when the governors were still fighting to maintain the school's independence, their Chairman, Edward Hutchinson, had complained that if they lost the struggle the school would merely become 'Number One Council School, Darlington'. Would he be right?

Decisions affecting the school were now in the hands of the local authority's Education Committee. In 1921 it contained fourteen council members, plus eight more who were co-opted. These comprised three lady members, one teacher, one trade unionist, and three clergymen – Anglican, Roman Catholic and Nonconformist respectively. The Committee appointed the school's entire governing body.

The immediate aftermath of war had produced ideas about the future shape of the school. In May 1919, Mr Boyde, the town's Director of Education, published a wide-ranging plan for education in Darlington. It was very advanced in concept and potentially very expensive. For secondary schools, including some proposed new intermediate ones, Boyde wanted an admission age of 12. Whilst he accepted the continuance of fee paying at the grammar and high schools, he proposed the closure of their Preparatory Departments. The Director expected a considerable growth in the size of both schools, possibly up to 500 pupils each.

At the same time there were changes in the awards for university and the authority now offered two scholarships of £60 and £40 respectively. There were also a number of school-leaving scholarships worth £45 per annum for three years and additionally, prospective teachers could obtain a four-year grant, covering a degree course plus 1 year in teacher training. Boyde considered that the awards were far too low, estimating that the annual cost at university was then £140, or £180 for Oxford or Cambridge.

In 1920 Boyde left for a post in Nottingham. Then, as the economic situation worsened, there were cutbacks and most of the memorandum was forgotten about.

The former independent school with around 160 pupils had now boosted its numbers to 267, none of whom were boarders. The last boarder had arrived in September 1917 and was the only one from sixty-eight admissions for the year. He came from as far away as Harrowgate Hill! Boarding had never enjoyed much success and its end had long been inevitable.

The new governing body showed no inclination to interfere with the normal running of the school and most of the changes in the next few years arose because of its growth and the provision of those facilities that had been needed for so long. Above all, the loss of independence resulted in funds at last being available to meet the school's needs. From its inception at Vane Terrace until 1914 the number of pupils had scarcely increased and the increasing demands of education had not been met. Yet within twenty years of the end of its independence the school would have a roll of 630, with facilities to match the pupils' needs. Hutchinson's fears were surely unfounded.

During 1919 those members of staff who had survived returned from active service, whilst new masters in the form of Richard H. Moar, G.R. Jenkins, S.W. Hughes and R.A. Burniston arrived. Mr Taylor also came back from his prisoner of war camp 'trailing clouds of glory' according to Charles Hinks, a prominent local solicitor and Old Boy who lauded his former Headmaster in extravagant terms in Norman Sunderland's history of the school. By 1921 the number of staff had expanded to sixteen full-time, plus five part-time.

Jenkins soon left, being replaced as a physics teacher by H.A. Ives, from Ossett Grammar School. A.R. Golland also came to be the General Form Master of the new Lower Shell. Both were to remain until after the Second World War. Two years later Messrs Todd and S.W. Hughes had left, being replaced by J.R. Canney and Mr Willmore.

The school hall was now no longer large enough to accommodate the increasing numbers, so the Speech Days from 1919 onwards were held in the Technical College lecture hall and even that was crowded. The practice also started of holding the event during the autumn term, rather than at the end of July.

The Upper School was now sitting the Durham School Certificate, in place of the Cambridge Locals, and in 1919 thirteen from the Upper V sat the exam and twelve passed. In the following year, the results eclipsed those of 1919, for all of the Upper V entered and all passed, with half placed in Division I.

However, the Durham Examination was short-lived. Most boys who went on to university did not go to Durham, so, as other universities did not accept the Durham Certificate in lieu of their own matriculation requirements, the school moved to the London General Schools Exam. Its qualification was more widely accepted and it was also thought to be of a higher standard. In 1922, five out of seven candidates passed the Durham Higher Certificate, but all twenty-three candidates passed the London General School Exams (one with Honours). The published results should be regarded with caution, however. Some boys passed in only one or two subjects and, for the London Exam, arithmetic, as distinct from maths, was a separate subject.

The school's adherence to the London Exam also proved to be brief and for reasons that are unclear, it reverted in 1925 to the Durham Certificate Exam. The number of former pupils graduating from university was still small. The magazine for autumn 1926, for instance, reported the graduation of five.

Space was at a premium. In 1920, when a record number of seventy-three boys entered the school, all of the former dormitories had been adapted, but the school was still at its limit and the hall and dining room had to be used as classrooms. Further alterations were made over the Easter vacation of 1921. Part of Room 14, the home of generations of English masters, became a cloakroom, whilst the rest of it was used for the erection of new stairs to serve the new classrooms made out of the old senior dormitories. Until then (apart from the one in the Headmaster's house) the only staircase to the first floor was the one below the tower.

Taylor stated at the 1920 Speech Day that the school had reached its limit of quantity, and that the aim was now for quality. He also appealed for parents to allow their sons to remain at the school for as long as they possibly could, saying that no boys could be admitted who at the age of sixteen desired a secondary education.

Until Taylor's arrival, the old system of numbering the classes consecutively in age order remained. This was now changed. Both the Fifth and Sixth Forms were separated into distinct Upper and Lower classes. Numbers continued to increase, leading in 1923 to the creation of two V Lower forms. In the subsequent year, there were also two V Upper forms.

The arrangements for the Lower School were far more complex. By 1920 the Preparatory Department had expanded considerably, having, in ascending age order, the Preparatory Form and Forms I, II and III. It appears, however, that the four classes had only three teachers. In the main school there was never a Form II and, until 1922, no Form III. Presumably, the object was to prevent confusion by not duplicating the numbers allocated to the Preparatory Department. Then, in 1922, Preparatory Form III became the Lower III, whilst, in the main school, an Upper III form was inserted between the Shell and IV forms.

The first-year class in the school proper was first designated as a Shell form in 1919; thereafter, with a brief interruption, the term was used until 1970. Initially there was one form only, but then for some years, apart from 1921–2, there were two, an Upper Shell and a Lower one. In this period, the Remove Form had its first of three incarnations at the school, but in about 1923 it disappeared for twenty years.

In essence we have a situation where, until 1922, the only form between the Shell forms and the IVs was the Remove, but then, for a year before its disappearance, the school had both the Remove and the newly introduced Upper III. To understand the relationship of these forms to each other, it is necessary to have some awareness of how boys progressed through the school.

It is not easy. There were no school lists at this time, so checking the progress of pupils through the school is more difficult than in later years. We are used to pupils within a given age range entering a school together and, in each successive year, moving up into the next age range. It was not so in the 1920s. Those entering the Grammar School proper were normally aged 11 to 13½, but some were outside that range. As an example, in one year, the youngest and eldest pupils admitted into the Shells were respectively aged 9½ and almost 14. Both were fees-exempt.

Whilst the minimum admission age of 5 continued for those entering the Preparatory Department, its four classes were taking new boys up to age 12½. It was possible therefore, in an extreme case, for an entrant to find himself going into the Preparatory Department, whilst another pupil, three years younger, was entering the main school!

What is obvious is that the pupil's level of attainment, not his age, determined the class he was put in. Equally his progress through the school year by year depended upon how he performed. At the beginning of a new school year, a pupil seen as not being ready for the next year's course would be held back in the same class for a second year. The records indicate that many boys in the Preparatory Department were kept back for years, possibly until they left school, because they were not ready for a grammar school education. The admissions register identifies one boy who had reached Form II in his fourth year in the department and, two years later, when he was probably fourteen, he had gone no further than the Lower III. However, even in the Grammar School proper, many pupils had gone by fourteen, so it is clear that expectations were low or opportunities few.

So what was the relationship between the forms in the Lower School, particularly between the two Shells and the Remove? In September 1920, when there were two Shell forms for the first time, twenty-six pupils went into the Upper Shell and twenty-three into the Lower, but it is not known how many had been in the school already. Interestingly, all but four of the Upper Shell entrants were prize winners or on local authority scholarships, whilst all of the Lower Shell entrants were fee payers. It seems clear, therefore, that the Upper form was intended for the more able pupils. The fees-exempt pupils, i.e. those on scholarships, also tended to be younger. No less than two-thirds of those entering the Lower Shell were aged 13 or over on admission.

The transition to an actual grammar school education was seen as starting in Form IV and, as the brighter Shell boys were seen as not needing further preparation, they went into Form IV direct, usually into Form IVA. It should be remembered that, despite the wide age range of those going into the Shells, the average age on entry was then twelve, so that many going directly into Form IV a year later would be of a similar age to IV Formers of later years. Boys were then normally aged 13+ on reaching this level.

The function of the Remove Form seems clear enough; it was to prepare the less academic boys, mainly in the Lower Shell for Form IV and beyond. That process could occupy more than one year. There are plenty of examples of boys spending two years in the Remove Form. One unfortunate was condemned to three years in it, but he seems to have benefited eventually, for he was in the Upper V three years later.

The relationship between the Remove and the Upper III is not entirely clear. The Upper III was presumably a replacement, but both existed together for a short time. For a few years there was only one Lower III class as against two Shell forms, suggesting that the old practice of having the more able pupils pass directly from Shell form to Form IV continued. By the end of the decade there were three Upper III forms, so there were then ample places for all former Shell pupils. There was one specific difference. Some pupils new to the school were also admitted into the Upper III. That was never the case with Taylor's Remove Form.

The continuing existence of fee payers perpetuated the school's unstructured admission arrangements. Preparatory pupils were liable to start at the school at any age from 5 to about 12 and might therefore enter any one of the four Preparatory forms. The stiffer entrance requirements imposed upon non-scholarship boys attempting to get into the main school and the resultant waiting list possibly increased the number entering the department at age 11 or 12. There was some alleviation in that, by 1927, the pressure on space in the school necessitated increasing the age of entry to eight. In consequence the lowest form in the Preparatory Department was abolished, permitting the creation of an additional form in the main school. The Preparatory forms were now I, II and Lower III.

The movement of pupils through the school at this period is complex and confusing and is deserving of further study by someone brave enough to attempt it!

What of the background of the pupils of this period? Although the great majority lived in Darlington itself, many came from the surrounding villages, but there was also a significant number of boys from nearby towns like Richmond and Shildon. Those living outside Darlington's boundaries with local authority scholarships would, of course, not normally be able to attend the Darlington Grammar School.

The occupations of the fathers were of all kinds and by no means all fee payers were middle class. In those early post-war years fee payers included the landlords of The Builders Arms and of The Greyhound, a railway signalman and a railway clerk. There was also a significant number of farmers. Reference has been made to the Preparatory pupils who had difficulty in getting in to the main school, but at the other extreme were boys who were earmarked for the public schools. Of the pupils entering the school in the year commencing September 1918, one later went to Whitgift, another to Oundle, another to Durham, whilst a fourth won a scholarship to Christ's Hospital.

On the other hand only four of that same entry reached the Upper VI, whilst two more attained the Lower VI. Only two of them went to university. Of the September 1920 entrants none is recorded as having gone into the Sixth Form or into higher education and that year's Bellasses Exhibition winner became a bank clerk. Many boys left in the middle of the year to take advantage of an available job. Some went into the family shop or followed their father into his business. Such examples presumably gave rise to Taylor's concerns about the poverty of expectations of pupils and their parents.

At the 1921 Speech Day, again held at the Technical College, an analysis of boys leaving the school over the previous three years was given: 15 per cent left whilst under fifteen and they usually went into the forces, into engineering works or became clerks; 38 per cent left when under sixteen with about one quarter becoming clerks; the rest going into various trades. Twenty-eight per cent left when between sixteen and seventeen, with 20 per cent becoming clerks or engineering apprentices. Only 19 per cent left when over seventeen with about half of them going to university. Most of the remainder went into teaching.

Taylor commented that in Durham, success in the Higher Certificate carried an £80 scholarship with it, but not in Darlington. This factor acted as a deterrent to parents who would like to keep their sons at school. Local firms, employing people were accused of preferring the semi-educated. Concern was again expressed about parents not keeping their boys at the school and about the low aims of many boys. Nevertheless, the Headmaster went on to express concerns about overcrowding.

At this time, the staff, apart from Taylor, were as follows:

Chemistry	D.R. Carrick
Classics	A.J. Smith
Maths	R.E. Newton, L.C. Ord and R.A. Burniston
Physics	H.A. Ives
English	R.A. Moar
History	J. Todd
Geography	S.J. Hughes
Modern Languages	H.R. Hughes and Miss Wilmott
General Subjects	A.R. Golland
Junior School (sic)	F.W. Ord, Miss Henson and Miss Ruecroft
Singing	T. Henderson
Drawing	A.B. Dresser
Woodwork	J.W.W. Redpath, W.E. Brown and Geo. Peacock

The last five listed were part-time.

By 1921 the school had a caretaker, William Kay, who was paid £4 2s 6d per week. He had a Chief Assistant who made do with £1 3s 4d, plus two helpers. They each worked 15 hours, sharing £1 2s 6d.

* * *

Since 1878 fee-paying pupils had been examined to demonstrate that they were able to profit from the education provided, though it is assumed, as more pupils were always needed, that the standard had not been unduly high. Any candidate who met that standard had been admitted, irrespective of numbers. Now, because of the pressure on numbers, a change had to be made. The number of places available would be fixed, so intending fee payers would have to compete against each other, not against a fixed standard, to gain one.

Nevertheless, growth still continued and by 1922 there were 353 on the roll, an increase of 12. It was awkward, for a high proportion of those who had taken the new competitive entrance examination had achieved a satisfactory standard and the school backtracked. Despite the intention to curtail increased numbers, the decision to admit extra boys was taken and no fewer than an extra sixty places for fee payers were allocated for the following September. There was also a long waiting list for the Preparatory classes.

Then, in 1923, another change was made. The Education Authority now required everyone seeking entrance to the school to sit the same exam, whether they wanted a free place or not. The top 25 per cent of candidates, later increased to the top 40 per cent, were offered free places and the remaining ones were filled by fee payers. There were two consequences. First, many boys whose parents would formerly have been prepared to pay would now have scholarships and second, those pupils who were fee payers were now defined as having failed to gain a scholarship place.

Because of the numbers in the school, it had become necessary to group the boys into two blocks so that the playing field could be used on different afternoons. For football a field on Carmel Road had to be rented. The field on Abbey Road, although now freehold, was still much smaller than in later years. An extra ground for cricket was wanted but there were difficulties in obtaining one.

Around now the school was painted. Presumably, this was a rare event for the editor of the magazine sarcastically claimed that he had asked Alderman Wooler, author of a history of Darlington, to delve deep into it to ascertain when the event had last occurred.

By 1923 there were 417 pupils in the school but, in contrast to the concerns expressed in 1921, the increase was seen as being due in part to boys returning to school after failing to find jobs. The low expectations of pupils and of their parents had become a recurrent theme and at the 1923 Speech Day, the Headmaster deplored the unwillingness of parents to allow their sons to stay on till age 18. He also spoke strongly of boys taking the London Matriculation and then sitting some exam of low standard such as the railway entrance exam. There were only thirteen boys doing definite advanced course work, the same as in 1921. The appeal to parents to let their boys stay on at school longer was repeated at the next Speech Day.

Until the conversion of the Headmaster's house took place, the former Housemaster's sitting room continued in use as a greatly overcrowded staff room, whilst the room above, once the Housemaster's bedroom, was now the Head's office. The shortage of space compelled Miss Willmott, who taught French and German, and the Head, when teaching History and Latin, to use whatever rooms were available. Dresser and Henderson continued to use the hall to teach drawing and music.

Until 1924 the huge increase in numbers had to be absorbed by the rooms created by the dormitory conversions, but in that year, after delays, the conversion work on the former Headmaster's house was finally completed. The rear half was now a flat for the occupation of Kay, the caretaker, whilst the remainder provided six new classrooms and a cloakroom, and what had formerly been Taylor's study now became a room for the prefects. An art room replaced the Form II classroom in the west wing whilst another room was converted into an additional chemistry lab. Whilst its conversion into a gymnasium was pending, the dining hall had part partitioned off to serve as a temporary Sixth Form classroom.

The respite was short-lived. At the 1925 Speech Day, postponed for a week because of Queen Alexandra's Memorial Service, Taylor reported that there were then 427 boys in the school, 26 more than in the previous year. He added that the recently completed conversion of the school house was not sufficient and there would have to be a slight reduction in admissions in the following year to avoid overcrowding.

The former dining hall became the gym, but the former cloakroom across the corridor had to be used as the changing room. Apparently, the atmosphere in it left much to be desired in hot weather. On 23 and 25 March 1925, it was possible for the school to give a small gym display for the first time. It was organised by Mr Golland and there were two teams of twenty boys. All seats were occupied, but the event was hampered through lack of space.

The increasing numbers in the school were now presenting problems at the Speech Days at the Technical College and at the 1924 event Alderman Leach, the Local Education Authority Chairman, presided and apologised for the cramped conditions. Despite the recent alterations, the school was again full, but the Head hoped that the alterations would make up for the deficiencies of recent years. In November 1926 a full inspection of the school was undertaken by the Board of Education, with satisfactory results.

Post-war, the school was able to expand its cultural activities. A concert was held in the hall on 17 December 1919 with the object of raising money for the Sports Fund. There was a choir of thirty boys, but as well as the singing, piano and cello solos were performed and £19 10s 6d was raised. There was another concert in the following June when an orchestra of twenty-three performers was brought in so that classical music could be heard. On this occasion over £7 was raised. In 1922 the first Inter-House Singing Competition took place, the test piece being 'Come Fairies, Trip O'er the Grass'. Each House sang in turn, but the points awarded did not count towards the House totals.

In 1921 a School Orchestra was formed under Mr Henderson. It was said to be an entirely new departure for the school, although there had been the short-lived 'string band' of 1886. The orchestra would, with the School Choir, take part in the School Concert. The school magazine reported that the string players were rehearsing each week, but that the flautist and 'piccolist' had yet to appear. The first public performance took place in a crowded hall on 21 December 1921.

In mid 1922 it was reported that the orchestra had at last won the respect of the school, so the work of Mr Henderson and Chris Bennett, then a pupil, but for many years the school's music master, had borne fruit. Undoubtedly, the pupils in the orchestra received their musical tuition elsewhere and there would be no systematic attempt by the school itself to teach pupils to play or to form permanent orchestras for some years. By the beginning of 1923 the orchestra, which already contained members of staff, was strengthened by admitting Old Boys to its number.

Perhaps oddly, there were also during this period a couple of concerts presented by the Debating Society. One took place in 1919 followed by a second in December 1920. On this occasion there were performances by staff members, including Messrs Hughes and Burniston, as well as by pupils. C. Bennett performed a violin solo and a farce, 'St Patrick's Day' by Sheridan, produced by R.H. Moar, was also performed. The evening's takings of £5 went to the school library.

The rationale for the Society's involvement seems to have been that it was the only school organisation for cultural events. Yet, despite the concerts, its existence came under threat in 1920, when attendances were seldom above twenty. There were appeals to allow it to continue and the result was that by 1921, the Society was attracting record numbers. Many of the speakers at debates were still staff members, including the Headmaster.

At the time of the 1922 General Election, the Society held its own mock election. There were election notices everywhere in the school and, according to the school magazine, the candidates made huge concessions and would have rendered the party leaders aghast with their policies. Heckling was allowed and 105 boys voted. The result was a Liberal win for Park with 42 votes, followed by Blakey (Labour) with 34. The Unionist, Campbell, had to be content with 29 votes. From time to time the Society had lectures, sometimes given by pupils, in place of debates. The normal practice at this time was to suspend the activities of both the Society and the orchestra during the summer term.

By 1923 the Debating Society was able to produce a printed syllabus. This was found to be particularly useful for Old Boys. Mock parliamentary elections were popular. Another was held on 1 December 1923, but this time the Conservative won. However, the magazine observed that the result could easily be understood as there were about thirty young members seated at the front of the hall wearing red rosettes (then the Conservative colour in Darlington) 'yelling at everybody and everything'.

A further mock election was held on 24 November 1924, at around the time of a real General Election, but this time the candidates were staff members and the result was an interesting one – a draw between H.R. Hughes (Conservative) and F.W. Ord (Bolshevik). A new departure, shortly afterwards, was the holding of a joint meeting (a lecture) with the Training College. There were no fewer than sixty lady visitors. A debate with students from the college took place in the autumn term of 1925 and was described as the annual joint debate, so it had obviously established itself. By this time the Society was holding its meetings on a Friday instead of on a Saturday.

The Debating Society Concert on 12 December had another first, in that it included a selection from the Newcastle wireless programme heard through the school wireless set. Mr Ives made the arrangements. He, with Messrs Burniston and Hughes, was amongst the singers at the concert.

The practice of holding a concert in December of every year continued for some time. Normally the object was to raise money for the Games Fund. In 1923, for instance, out of a total income of £216 for the fund, £22 was provided by the concert proceeds. A subscription 2/- (10p) per term was charged for each pupil for the fund.

Although there were still no other school societies, there were other events at the school. A production of *The Rivals* was staged by the Sixth Form. Incidental music was provided by Mr Henderson's orchestra and costumes were hired from London. Lectures and dramatic evenings were also held in the hall.

The school's first tuck shop was opened in what had been the boot room off the main corridor. Mr Willmore was the master in charge. After Willmore's departure in about 1925 L.C. Ord, who had been in charge of the library, took over and his brother, who was also the Danes' Housemaster, replaced him at the library. Sweets and fruit were sold at every morning break and the profits went to the Games Fund. In 1926 it was reported that the trade depression had not affected the shop.

Some of the Fund's sources of income, such as the concert proceeds and the magazine sales, were obvious, but there were others including the sale of postcards, producing £7 13s 3d in 1922, and grazing rent. The levels of expenditure seem minimal by modern standards; cricket cost £59 10s 4½d, football £30 10s 0½d and other sports £21 6s 7d, whilst magazine production accounted for £40 1s 11d.

In 1924 the school organised a visit to the Wembley Exhibition. Over sixty boys with three staff members went. After reaching Kings Cross at 1.30 p.m. the boys boarded huge buses labelled 'Darlington Grammar School'. They briefly visited the Tower, St. Paul's Cathedral and Westminster Abbey, also seeing Buckingham Palace. After staying overnight at the Park Royal Hostel the party spent the second day at the exhibition.

Two new members of staff, both of whom were to be at the school for many years, came in 1924. J.P. Leighton came as Form Master for V Lower B and P. Fothergill, a languages teacher, for Upper III. Fothergill had served in the Great War and had been awarded the Military Medal. He had lost an arm and an eye as a result of being hit by fourteen machine-gun bullets.

It should be noted in passing that, in 1925, St. Mary's Grammar School opened, so that, at last, a separate grammar school education was available for Catholic boys in Darlington.

In the early 1920s there were nine prefects, still headed by the Senior Prefect. One of them was Percy Moss, who was awarded school colours for both cricket and football. Later he served for thirty years as a master at the school. The growth in school numbers then led to an increase in the number of prefects. In 1924 the number had jumped to thirteen and in 1926 there were sixteen including the Seniors.

As always, there were complaints about a lack of contributions for the school magazine and the first issue of 1920 contained no articles by pupils. The revival of form magazines in the autumn term of 1922 did not help and the magazine editor expressed the hope, rather acidly, that would-be contributors to them would remember 'that little known periodical, the school magazine'. In 1923 the publication of one issue was delayed by a strike by members of the Typographical Association. At that time the magazine was printed at the *Northern Echo* Printing Works at Freeman's Place.

During the 1930s, there was an article in a school magazine by Charles Hinks. The article, written in facetious and oblique tones, referred to his term as editor in 1922 and to an incident involving his best friend when the nose on the bust of Queen Elizabeth was coloured red. Hinks implied that he had to relinquish the editorship as a result of the incident, drawing a comparison with the collective responsibility in the Cabinet. Unfortunately, the school magazines of the time are silent about any incident, but it is a pity that more is not known.

As to holidays the secondary schools, i.e. the grammar and high schools, were better provided for than the elementary schools. Their pupils were entitled to 3 weeks 2 days for Christmas, 3 weeks 3 days for Easter and 7 weeks 3 days for summer. In addition there were half-term holidays, producing a total of 15 weeks 2 days per year. In contrast, the elementary schools had to make do with 10 weeks and 1½ days. The Grammar School's finishing time was 4.15 p.m. The cost of staff per pupil at the school was £17 13s 0d, contrasting with £8 0s 7d for an elementary school child. By now, the school buildings were insured against fire for £10,250 and the contents cover was for £750.

In the 1920s the honours boards, now located in the old main corridor, adorned the walls of the hall, as did portraits of Philip Wood and Sir David Dale. Until its conversion into a gym, the old dining room had photographs of the school XIs around its walls. It is assumed that they were removed to their long-established place in the main corridor at the time of the conversion.

Once the war was over thought was given to how those who had died should be commemorated and the decision was made to install memorial windows in the end wall of the school hall. Before the middle of 1920, £420 had been donated towards the total estimated cost of £500 and on Wednesday 2 February 1921, the new windows were unveiled by Major-General Sir P.S. Wilkinson KCMG CB. The magazine referred to a sense of emotion during the ceremony, which included the reading of the names of all of the fallen, and of a feeling of tension during the sounding of the 'Last Post'. The eventual cost of the windows was £450, but offset against this was £7 raised from the sale of the old glass. A nameplate identifies the maker of the windows, which have narrowly escaped demolition more than once, as William Morris of Westminster. Luck and Sons donated the drapes used in the unveiling ceremony.

The programme for the dedication ceremony describes the windows. The Central one represents the Earl of Westmoreland and the Bishop of Durham receiving the Charter of the school from Queen Elizabeth. The seal is prominent, whilst the lesser panels indicate Religion and Learning. The East window represents Chivalry with a depiction of St. George, representing the Church. He is accompanied by Sir Galahad and Sir Perceval (sic), the finders of the Holy Grail. The West window represents sea power with an image of St. Nicholas, the patron saint of sailors. He, along with Drake and Frobisher, represents the Navy. At about the time of the unveiling, the Roll of Honour was again corrected and four more names were added.

On Friday 11 November 1994, twenty-four years after the school had ceased to exist, the windows were rededicated by Air Chief Marshall Sir David Parry-Evans GCB CBE. The service was based on the one that took place in 1921 and included the unveiling, by Capt. Richard Annand VC, of the plaque, now in the hall, dedicated to the Bradford brothers. The 102 dead of the Second World War were also remembered. Lt. Col. F. Phillips, familiar to generations of Old Boys as a games master at the school and a stalwart of the Territorial Army, was Chairman of the Rededication Committee.

A commemoration of the war of a different kind had taken place on 20 July 1920 when a trench mortar, presented to the school, was hauled onto the Mound by members of the Sixth Form. The Mound was a grassed area on the Abbey Road side of the school behind the hall and, according to Norman Sunderland's history, was 'sacred ground trodden only by Mr Allan's [sic] rabbits and the most foolhardy of boys'. The gun went in 1938 when a cloakroom was built on the site and one source says it was then sent to the South Park. It is believed that it then became a casualty of the World War II scrap drive. The gun still in the park is an older relic from the Crimean War. The flagpole, erected on Empire Day 1918, was on the same site, but in 1938 it was moved to the corner of Vane Terrace and Abbey Road.

* * *

In the immediate post-war period, sporting activities thrived and in 1920 it was reported that the football First XI had lost only two matches of ten played and that the cricket XI was unbeaten. What was described as the Football Club had fifty playing members and two school XIs. Not all opponents were grammar school teams and amongst those played by the football teams were St. Chad's College at Durham, the North Eastern County School, Central Commercial School, Greenbank Juniors, the Cleveland Bridge XI and the Old Boys. In 1920 Messrs Burniston and Ord were in the school team against the Old Boys, but they did not save the school from defeat. One magazine issue contained a critique of the football XI by A. Little. It examined and commented upon each player in turn.

Back in 1911 a boy called Riley had established a school cricket record by scoring 174 not out. Twelve years later, after the Old Boys' match, as Capt. C.L. Riley, he presented a cup to commemorate his record. It was to be held by the boy gaining the highest score of the season, but if a boy's score exceeded 174, he would keep the trophy permanently. The first winner was C.E. Creek, with 64 not out. His brother, F.N.S. Creek, an Old Boy, had the distinction of scoring two goals for Cambridge University against Arsenal at about this time.

The School Run still took place with mass entries, with all boys expected to participate. In 1920 there were 131 boys starting and two of the first three back were in their first year! Finishing within 35 minutes produced a point for the participant's House. In the following year there were over 200 competitors, of which 156 finished. In 1922 the House Run had to take place over the longer Teesside course because of an outbreak of foot and mouth disease in the Darlington area. No less than two-thirds to three-quarters of the members of each House took part in the House Run on 24 March 1926.

By 1924 the school had a harriers team. Unfortunately, there were few neighbouring schools with one, but fixtures were arranged with Bede College and with Darlington Harriers Youths. For practice, and for a change, the runners competed against cyclists, but the runners were given too great a time advantage. In autumn 1925 there were two running events against Barnard Castle County School and a triangular fixture against Darlington Harriers and Catterick Signallers, but in the following term there were separate fixtures against each of the three.

Contemporary photographs suggest that a change in the football team's shirts occurred around 1917 and 1918. By then, some players no longer had a badge on their shirts and some shirts had the colours reversed, with the lighter colour on the right side. By 1919 such shirts were in the majority, but, at the same time, the badge seemed to be coming back into fashion.

It now becomes complicated for by 1924 the majority of shirts are back to the pre-1917 pattern and whilst some have pockets, there are no badges! Then, in 1926, most shirts have reverted to the 1917 pattern and again have the lighter colour on the right-hand side. On about half of them, the badge has reappeared. At least the tradition of having the sleeve and collar in the same colour as the opposite side of the shirt continued. The 1926 pattern then seems to have survived without further change into the 1950s at least.

By 1925 shorts were becoming reduced in length and around 1929 there was a fashion for black ones. In 1930 striped socks made their appearance.

Jubilee

The coming of peace led to a revival of the attempt, thwarted in 1914, to establish an Old Boys' Association. On 26 June 1919 David Carrick sent out a circular letter, ostensibly about the Old Boys' cricket match on 19 July, but in it he mentioned that there would also be an evening meeting to form an Old Boys' Association. By 22 July a committee had been formed and the Rev. R. Drury, vicar of Darlington, had accepted the Presidency.

The first event, in February 1920, was a 'smoker' and sixty Old Boys, plus some masters, turned up. Mr and Mrs Taylor provided refreshments for them. Later in the year the first AGM was held and was presided over by Drury. A silver Challenge Cup, costing £14 including the engraving, was donated to the school to be awarded for the mile race at the School Sports. The recipient would hold it till the next sports day. The meeting also voted a Christmas box of £1 to George Spence, the former school cricket professional, who had become blind several years before. These donations, £2 in 1922, then of £5, continued annually until 1931. Larger payments were then made.

On 15 April 1921 the Association held its first Annual Dinner, with tickets at 7/6d (37½p). Although a threatened transport strike caused attendance problems, about fifty were present at the Fleece Hotel. After the toasts, a programme of songs followed including a school song, complete with rousing chorus, composed by Drury. Apparently the bill delivered for the printing of the song sheets charged for 'printing hymn'. The dinner gave rise to a deficit for the year of £3 0s 4d, against an income of £26 7s 6d. During the year a gift of £5 for an Old Boys' Football Cup had been made and £10 4s 0d had been incurred for providing school magazines for members. Receipt of the school magazine was a membership benefit.

At this time, well over half of the members lived in Darlington, but the remainder were widely scattered and there were addresses in places as diverse as Paris, Egypt, Ceylon, India and Java. In 1923 the Association dispensed with its entrance fee, thereafter relying upon the members' payment of the annual subscription. It also appointed a committee to organise its social activities and had the School Orchestra at the 1923 smoking concert.

By 1924 the Association had ninety-three members, paying 5/- (25p) each, but late payment of subscriptions appears to have been commonplace and the printed payment request for 1928 provided for payment of arrears back to 1925. It appears that, for many years, the officers were unwilling to withdraw membership benefits to those who were substantially behind with their payments. Even in 1919 it had been found that many Old Boys, when invited to join, readily agreed to do so and promised payment of their subscription. Then the initial enthusiasm of many of them waned and they never got around to opening their wallets.

It was reported at this time that the Association had started a fund to help a young Old Boy who was faced with difficulties and responsibilities. Soon it was proposed to extend the scheme to compile a register to enable the Association to aid unemployed Old Boys in finding jobs. In July 1926 there were said to be 5,000 Old Boys and a circular was sent to those whose addresses were known seeking details of their profession or trade in the hope that possession of this information would help in placing those needing help. In 1927, Charles Hinks, who was Solicitor to the Association, was instructed to write to the Labour Exchange about what the committee saw as unfair treatment of a member.

The Association would soon be preoccupied with the school's forthcoming Jubilee.

In 1928 the school would have been at Vane Terrace for fifty years and the anniversary was to be suitably commemorated, with both the school and the Old Boys' Association being actively involved in the organising.

The Association launched a financial appeal. It wanted funds for two purposes and was initially seeking £120. Part of the amount was to be used to place a metal tablet above the entrance to the school hall to mark the Jubilee and the rest was to provide for loans or gifts for the relief of 'necessitous cases arising amongst boys of the school'. The hope was that future benefactors would add to the fund over time. By October 1928 there was about £180 in the maintenance fund and a £3 loan was made to a boy starting employment in Manchester, whilst a grant of 10/6d (52$^{1/2}$p) was also made to provide a boy with football boots.

The actual commemoration took place on Wednesday 25 July 1928 and started with an early communion service at St. Cuthbert's Church at 7.30 a.m. The collection was for the benefit of George Spence. The main service took place at 10 a.m. on Wednesday 25 July and the pupils all marched from the school to the church. Each Old Boy was given a blue buttonhole at the church door. The offertory was on behalf of Darlington General (sic) Hospital and about £26 was raised.

In his sermon the vicar, Rev. R.F. Drury, himself an Old Boy, spoke of six and a half centuries of direct continuity for the school through the ancient Chantry School of 1291. He singled out for special reference Alfred Massingham, the classical and Fifth Form Master of thirty-three years, who had been a companion of Philip Wood on the golf links at Seaton Carew 'when golf links were few and far between'. He also referred to two pupils, Richard Luck, killed in the Boer War, and Jimmie Huggan, the first pupil to die in the Great War.

In the last two paragraphs of his sermon, copies of which were available for 1/- (5p) from local booksellers, Drury excelled himself with his extravagant language. 'So come along boys! "Finding, following, keeping, striving," – like the brave "Knights of the Round Table." Let us be diligent, let us be courageous. For Christ's sake and for the sake of our brethren we *must* be strong. For His sake and for *their* sakes, we must be pure. This then be our trumpet call of Jubilee – "Forward! Onward! Upward! – for the old School! For England! And for GOD!"'

At 11.30, after the taking of a panoramic photograph by Sydney Wood, a local photographer, the cricket match between past and present (Old Boys v. pupils) took place at Abbey Road. Tom Watson, the longest-surviving Old Boy at age 88 (he had attended the old Leadyard School), had the privilege of bowling the first ball of the match. The two teams were given luncheon by the Head, whilst 'the company' were entertained to tea by Mrs Taylor. The Old Boys won the match by the narrowest of margins.

Mr Watson's duties were not yet over. At 8 p.m. there was a smoking concert at the school and he had the task of unveiling the brass tablet over the school entrance commemorating the Jubilee. The hall was scarcely large enough to accommodate the Old Boys present and it was reported that 'The singing of the old choruses, the tumultuous cheering, the boisterous enthusiasm cannot be reproduced on paper'. The school magazine attributed the success of the concert to Chris Bennett and Mr Burniston. During the day, light refreshments had been served in the gym, whilst the committee of the Duke Street Club had thrown open the club for the day for Old Boys from out of town.

There was a commemorative book and 279 Old Boys signed it at either the cricket match or at the concert, T. Watson being the first. No fewer than four members of the Hinks family, who provided several generations of pupils, signed, as did three Drurys. A large photo of the participants was also taken. It was reckoned that no fewer than 450 Old Boys had attended the celebration.

The arrival of some of the boys and of guests at the church was filmed, as were the preliminaries at the school field before the cricket match. The film was shown in the school hall to interested parties on 9 November 1928, but was later presumed lost. Then, by chance, in 2005, the archivist at the Sixth Form College and the caretaker discovered a reel of film in the clock tower. Various members of staff are recognisable on the film including the Headmaster, David Carrick, Mr Fothergill, missing an arm and an eye, and Miss Henson, the Preparatory teacher. Tom Watson and Mr Drury also make their appearance, as does the AC car of 'Bug' Allen, seen being driven into the schoolyard.

Soon afterwards the school hall acquired an organ as the result of a donation of £500 by M.T. Anderson CBE. It was originally hand blown with the bellows handle extending on to the landing. As a result, if the person pumping, usually a pupil, became tired the organ would wail like a bagpipe. The instrument was seen as having certain inadequacies and eventually, in 1966, the decision was made to redesign it tonally using the existing pipework where possible. The work was done personally by the Head of the Music Department, assisted by six pupils, and on 3 November 1966, after completion of the work, there was an Organ Re-dedication Ceremony, preceded by an inaugural recital.

The tendency of grammar schools to emulate the public schools had not, in the north-east at least, extended to the playing of rugby football and its introduction at the school in March 1928 was received with mixed feelings. Indeed, it had to be stressed that there had been no definite decision to abandon soccer. The decision to adopt rugby arose because many of the schools against whom the Grammar School played were doing so, and it would have been left without fixtures had it not followed suit. Whether soccer could still be played against other schools was in the hands of those schools.

A further justification for playing rugby was put forward. It was said to provide an opportunity for what the magazine described as the more 'hefty' boys, who were not likely to be on a soccer team. The uncertainties about the introduction of rugby were reflected by the Debating Society, which carried, by a substantial majority, the motion that 'the introduction of Rugby Football into the School is undesirable'.

Soccer did survive. In the spring term of 1928, before the playing of rugby started, three association football matches were played, against Durham Colleges Union, Auckland Grammar School and Alderman Wraith's School, Spennymoor respectively. In the autumn term the First XI had six games including ones against Carrick's XI, Taylor's XI, Bede College and two against the Old Boys, but the lack of games against other grammar schools is noticeable. The Second XI had five games during that term.

The original arrangement was that no rugby would be played during the autumn term, for the intention was that it would only occupy the short period from March to the Easter holidays. In the first year the school XV won three of the four school matches and the new game proved so successful that for the following year the season was extended to the whole of the spring term. The playing of both types of football during the same period did not start until some years later.

Unfortunately, the adoption of rugby initially weakened the soccer XIs and, in the first season for both games, only four soccer matches out of sixteen were won. As an example of the frequency of games of rugby played after it had become established, the First XV played ten games in the season from 16 January 1932 including one against Darlington's Third XV. During the same season, the Second Team played seven games.

In 1929 cricket bats were awarded to five pupils for scores of over 50 and there was a new badge for boys winning colours at sport, but no description has been found. During the season, the cricket team played, amongst others, Darlington YMCA, the *Northern Echo* and Darlington Station Staff. For some reason that year, the School against the Old Boys football match was played at Hummersknott. The frequency of cricket matches was variable. During the 1927 season there were only eight played by the First XI and it appears that the first did not take place until 4 June. Yet, in the 1928 season, there were sixteen matches played from 5 May, although the Second XI played only seven.

In the autumn of 1927 a House Boxing Competition was held for the first time. The judging was undertaken by a Dr Kirk and the Saxons won. The competition then became an annual event, with Dr Kirk as the regular judge, lasting until about the late 1930s. By 1931 there was also an inter-school competition at the Royal Grammar School, Newcastle and the Darlington Grammar School competed regularly there. It had Junior and Senior sections. 'Gus' Golland was the member of staff responsible for both boxing and the gym display, by now an annual event.

Athletics featured strongly in the sporting programme at this time and there were many events against outside teams, not all of them from other schools. There were six runs in 1928 including the House Run. The others included competitions against 'F' Company, Royal Corps of Signals, Bede College, Darlington Harriers and Middlesbrough Harriers. The school then had a Running Captain but there was still no School Captain. In the same year a new annual event was introduced in the form of the Inter-Schools Athletic Competition. Initially there were only three competing teams, but by 1932, when the event was held at Coatham Grammar School before a large party of Darlington supporters, six schools were represented including Barnard Castle School and Stockton Secondary School.

The 1929 House Run took place in November on a considerably shortened route for both seniors and juniors and it was still expected that all boys in the school would take part. In 1932, there was, in addition to the School Run, a race with a school team of cyclists. The runners were given a start of seven minutes, but despite the muddy conditions the cyclists won. The size of the committees then supervising each kind of sporting activity is noteworthy.

The School Sports Day continued to be an annual event, but, in this period, it was customary to run the mile race on the following day. The 1932 Sports Day, held on 11 June and won by the Saxons, was distinguished by the breaking of nine school records.

On 20 February 1929 an ice hockey match against Barnard Castle School took place at Lartington Ponds. It was the first between them and it also appears to have also been the last. This is not surprising as the Darlington team was thrashed 13–0.

During 1930 new caps with green stripes were to be seen, for the decision had been made to have a fourth House. The new House, the Britons, was to take those pupils with surnames starting with the letters A, B or C, but boys outside this group could voluntarily transfer to it. Following upon the change, the Danes now took boys from D to J, the Normans K to R and the Saxons R to Z. The Housemasters were L.C. Ord (Britons), R.E. Newton (Danes), H.R. Hughes (Normans) and D.R. Carrick (Saxons).

The House results for 1931 indicate that there was then a Britons' First XI, a Second XI and First and Second XVs. To achieve this situation, pupils throughout the school with surnames beginning with A, B or C must have been reallocated to the new House and one wonders whether they were compensated for having to replace their caps.

There do not appear to have been any junior House teams at this time, so the only contribution those in the Lower School could normally make to House points would be by achieving the required time in the Junior House Run. Each House had first and second teams for association football, rugby and cricket and each team would play the corresponding House teams once in each season. The creation of an additional House enabled each team to pay three games per season as against the previous two.

The cap, with its colour denoting the wearer's House, was the only compulsory part of the uniform. However, school ties were available and could be bought from Masterman's shop on the corner of Post House Wynd and Skinnergate.

It was not until 1926 that a second school society was formed. It was the Natural History Society and would prove to be one of the best-supported and most consistently active of the many societies destined to be formed at the school. It soon had nearly a hundred members and was having many external visits. Initially it charged 1/- (10p) for annual membership. In 1928 a young Mr W.W. Allen, invariably known as 'Bug', arrived at the school from London, reputedly wearing spats. He was the first biology teacher and three years after his arrival he had the honour of being elected a Fellow of the Linnean Society. He was always known for his practical bias as well as for his eccentricities, and for the rest of the school's existence the society was indisputably his preserve.

Its mix of activities was impressive and wide ranging, including, in those early days, visits to the local engine sheds at Green Street, Haughton Road Brewery, the Cerebos Salt Works at Greatham, Rowntree's Chocolate Factory at York and the gas works. Other locations, perhaps more compatible with natural history, were visited, including Gainford Great Wood, Helvellyn, High Force and Crackpot. The attempts to view the eclipse of the sun were disappointing, but a good profit was made from the sale of 'Eclipse Viewers'. Many lectures were also given and in 1929 it acquired a photographic branch.

The Society then became more ambitious with a journey to the Dunlop Works at Birmingham, followed by a cinema visit. Thirty-five went, arriving back at 6.15 a.m. on the following day on a train that was two hours late. Pupils were a hardy lot then! One visit at this time provides a reminder of how attitudes change. A visit to the Tees Estuary, with the party travelling by train to Grangetown, was organised. The route from the station there passed a pond used by the locals for disposing of dead dogs and the school magazine reported that the group had counted two dozen in it.

Back at the school the Society not only provided lectures for its members, but it established a museum in the tower. By 1930 frogs were kept in captivity there and a large number of boys and well-wishers were reported as bringing specimens for the collection and the result was that additional cases had to be purchased to accommodate everything. At one time, to assist, Mr Ives was permitting society members to keep some specimens in the sinks in the physics lab. The growing collection necessitated the publication of a Museum Bulletin in which details of all exhibits were entered. The venture was not a total success, however, for the collection of stuffed birds was attacked by some kind of beetle.

The museum seems to have fallen into decline by the end of the decade and to generations of post-war schoolboys the tower remained a place of mystery where nobody ever set foot. Around 1960, but possibly earlier as well, the lower level found a use as a room for teaching Latin to the few who took it as an A level subject. Mr L. Readman, Senior Classics Master, would use a hippopotamus skull to provide a seat for himself. As will be seen later, sporadic attempts were made during the 1960s to find a use for this area of the school.

In about late 1927 two more societies were formed. One was announced as the Scientific Society under Mr Carrick, but it came into being known as the Philosophical Society and was open to Fifth and Sixth Formers. As well as organising lectures, it provided outside visits. Urlay Nook Chemical Works, Horden Colliery where the party went underground, Haughton Road Brewery, Darlington Gas Works, North of England Newspapers and Darlington Fire Brigade were amongst the many places visited. By 1932 its president was Bill Richardson, later Second Master. Amongst the lectures given by members were ones on Venus and on radioactivity. Parts for the Cunard liner under construction at the Darlington Forge were seen on a visit. By 1935 it had renamed itself the Scientific Society.

The other was the Stamp Club, the responsibility of Mr Ives. It too charged an annual subscription, but this had to be abolished in 1930 due to poor support. According to magazine reports, the club was still poorly supported through 1931 and 1932, but by then it was charging an entrance fee of 6d. The club obviously then died, because its revival was reported in 1933. A further society in the form of the Art Club appeared in 1931.

Over the years, many of the school's societies simply faded away without their demise being reported, though some, like the Stamp Club, were later resurrected. The committees of the early school societies seem to have contained a mixture of staff and boys.

The Debating Society continued to flourish and its dramatic ventures were now so successful that performances on two evenings were needed to cope with the audience sizes. The orchestra helped at some of the performances. A glance at some of the Society's debate motions is of interest. One deploring the Americanisation of England was supported by a large majority and, perhaps surprisingly for its time, a motion 'that hunting animals is un-British' was carried unanimously. The Society was also opposed to prohibition. As it always did, the Society had bouts of silliness with the result that a proposal that Darlington should be the capital of England (sic) was carried unanimously.

Masters still spoke at Debating Society meetings. For instance, on 18 November 1932 the Society had a mock trial with P.J. Osborn acting as solicitor for the defendants who were accused of theft. His clients were convicted. A year earlier, Mr Osborn had contributed an article on watching football matches to the school magazine. He displayed a touch of the common man, arguing that being in the crowd was definitely preferable to being in the directors' box.

The *Daily Express* journalist Chapman Pincher, nationally famous for his writings on espionage and his exposure of spies, had won a scholarship to the school and was involved with the Debating Society. He was the proposer of a motion that the advantages of colonies were outweighed by their disadvantages, but, unsurprisingly in an age of Empire, it was lost by a large majority. Earlier, in 1930, he had displayed his writing talents with an article in the school magazine about a school trip to White Scar Caverns. He lived to one hundred, surviving until August 2014.

Form dramatic performances had usually occupied two evenings and on the Saturday accommodation was in short supply, so that latecomers, mostly boys, had to stand on the floor at the back or on forms. From 1930 the performances were therefore extended over three nights.

Inevitably, the contributions of the youngest boys were of a limited nature. In 1933, for instance, Form I performed nursery rhymes – 'Hey Diddle', 'The Queen of Hearts' and 'Three Little Mice'.

School Concerts continued with an emphasis on singing and with the takings going to the Games Fund. The 1930 concert was the first without Mr Henderson, but Mr Martin provided solos on the organ and piano. From this time references to the School Orchestra cease, so it looks as if it disappeared following Henderson's retirement.

A new departure was the screening, on 5 March 1928, of the film *Rugger*. It showed, in slow motion, the important points of good rugby and was seen by a large crowd of boys and by Darlington Rugby Club members.

An early view of the school from Stanhope Park. The front door to the
Headmaster's house is visible near the right end of the building.
[Local Studies Centre, Darlington Public Library]

The Army Cadet Corps pose in the school yard. The toilet block, built a few
years earlier, and the adjacent Teachers' Training College are both visible.
Doctor Hare is flanked by the members of staff who held rank in the Corps.
[Queen Elizabeth Sixth Form College, Darlington; Local Studies Centre, Darlington Public Library]

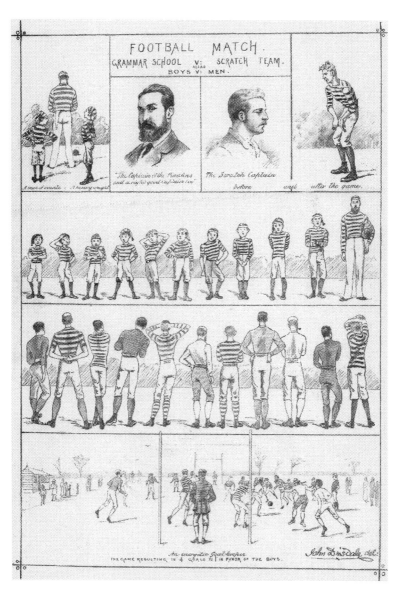

Darlington Grammar School Football Match from *Random Drawings of Darlingtonian Doings* by Jon Dinsdale. Photographs of the school's early football teams show that the dress of the players is accurately depicted.

[Local Studies Centre, Darlington Public Library]

The pupils and staff, autumn 1904. The unmistakable figure of Philip Wood is shown leaning against the vegetation on the left. The five other members of staff are all visible. The photograph emphasises both the small numbers in the school and the variety of dress then worn.

[Local Studies Centre, Darlington Public Library]

The interior of the school tower, with evidence of earlier visitors.

R. Gray
J. R. Sedgwick (Scorer)   J. A. Heddon   D. Russell   A. J. Muirhead   J. Longstaff   G. Spence (pro.)
         A. Matson   C. L. Riley   R. W. R. Miller (Capt.) H. J. Mein   W. Poynter
    J. R. Gibson   D. Drewery   S. Brown

The school cricket team 1910. George Spence, the cricket professional who went blind a few years later, is shown on the right.

[Local Studies Centre, Darlington Public Library]

The school cricket team 1957

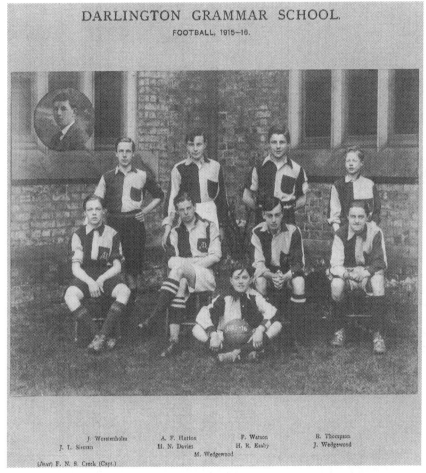

DARLINGTON GRAMMAR SCHOOL.

FOOTBALL, 1915–16.

J. Worstenholm   A. F. Hutton   F. Watson   R. Thompson
J. L. Sisman   H. N. Davies   H. R. Easby   J. Wedgewood
M. Wedgewood

(*Inset*) F. N. S. Creek (Capt.)

The school football team 1915–6. Three of those shown, F.N.S. Creek,
J.L. Sisman and J. Worstenholm, are referred to in the text. Only ten of the
team are present.

[Local Studies Centre, Darlington Public Library]

A 1944 photograph of Herbert Sutcliffe, Yorkshire and England cricketer, on the steps of the school cricket pavilion. Doctor Hare is seated in front of the window.
[Queen Elizabeth Sixth Form College, Darlington; Local Studies Centre, Darlington Public Library]

The surviving frontage of the former Headmaster's house in the final
days of the school. It was demolished shortly afterwards.

[Roger Butterworth and David Howlett]

The school staff in 1953. Bug Allen is seated sixth from the left in the front row, with W.S. Richardson between him and the Headmaster. Immediately on the other side of Dr Hare, from left to right, are R.A. Burniston, N. Sunderland, writer of the 1963 history, and P.J. Osborn. Third from the left on the same row is W. Hastie, who was prominent as a pupil at the school in the 1930s. Percy Moss is standing at the extreme right of the second row, whilst, further along, J.L. Bird, the art master, is distinguishable by his beard. Fred Phillips, who was drenched whilst on duty at the Coronation, is sixth from the left on the back row.

A presentation is made to the Queen Mother at the celebration of the school's 400th anniversary on 25 June 1963. The memorial windows in the school hall and the boards commemorating those who served and fell in the Great War are clearly visible.

[Picture courtesy of *Northern Echo*, Darlington; Local Studies Centre, Darlington Public Library]

The school's three Headmasters from 1913 onwards. Leonard Taylor (left), C.L. Hall and Dr Hare (right) are seen together at the Old Boys' Dinner held in late 1960.

[Picture courtesy of *Northern Echo*, Darlington; Local Studies Centre, Darlington Public Library;

David Carrick, on the right, Second Master for many years till 1946, with his successor, W.S. Richardson, who retired in 1965. His successor, Norman Sunderland, took the title of Deputy Headmaster.

[Picture courtesy of *Northern Echo*, Darlington; Local Studies Centre, Darlington Public Library]

OLD BOYS' DAY - JULY 9th. 1965.

President - Frank Goldsworthy.

The annual cricket match on Old Boys' Day 1965. Despite its size, the pavilion was incapable of accommodating more than a fraction of the pupils using the playing field on a normal afternoon.

[Queen Elizabeth Sixth Form College, Darlington; Local Studies Centre, Darlington Public Library]

The extension on the western side of the quad constructed in 1932. The first-floor veranda, with the art room behind, is visible, as is the archway behind the stacked desks. It gave direct access to the school yard, but was later filled in to provide another room. The entire quad is now roofed over.

[Roger Butterworth and David Howlett]

Mr Taylor's Later Years

During Leonard Taylor's later years at the school, a number of masters destined to serve the school for virtually the rest of its existence made their appearance. In 1930, two years after Bug Allen came, P.J. Osborn arrived to teach English, becoming in time Head of Department and a noteworthy producer of school plays. His lessons were always thought-provoking, although often not relevant to the subject, and his use of sarcasm made him feared without him having recourse to punishment. Bill Richardson, later Second Master, came at the same time.

In the following year, Norman Sunderland arrived, and was to remain for almost forty years. After becoming Senior History Master, he replaced Richardson as Deputy Head (formerly called Second Master) and, in the final months of the school, served as Acting Headmaster. He published a short history of Darlington, as well as his 1963 history of the school.

Two long-serving members of staff, both part-time and described by the school as visiting masters, retired during this period. Messrs Henderson and Dresser, who taught music and drawing respectively, both retired in 1929, having taught at the school since the 1890s.

Another loss was that of F.W. Ord, who died, aged 55, on 14 May 1928. He had come in January 1914 to take charge of the Junior School, taking under his wing all who entered through the Prep School. Shortly before his death, at the end of the Easter term, the masters had given the boys a concert and included in the production was a one-act farce, *Educated Ernest*, written by him. Miss Willmott, who came to the school during the war and was noteworthy as the first permanent female teacher outside the Preparatory Department, retired at Christmas 1932 and was succeeded by S.W. Hobson. Back in 1926 Miss Emerson had joined the Preparatory Department to replace Miss Ruecroft, who had left to marry.

Alterations in the structure of the classes were needed as the school expanded. In 1928 the separate Upper and Lower Shell Forms had fifty-eight pupils between them, but by 1932 there were three Shell Forms. They were now lettered A, B and C, and the designations 'Upper' and 'Lower' ended. In September of that year ninety-three boys were admitted to those forms, so there was no spare capacity. The Upper III, which now took all pupils leaving the Shell forms, was also expanded to three forms.

All of the years in the Upper School now had two classes, but whilst the forms in the IVs and V Lowers were lettered A and B, those in the V Upper were designated Modern and Languages. By contrast, the Lower and Upper VI each had separate Arts and Science Forms. It looks as if the setting up of two forms in each year in the Sixth Form was an innovation, for the prize list for the previous year shows only one form in each year. Then, in 1930, the two Arts Forms were re-designated Modern, in conformity with the Upper V, but, from 1935, the V Upper year had three forms, called A, B and C. That V Upper Language had been renamed V Upper Commercial a couple of years previously adds to the confusion.

Taylor seems to have had mixed feelings about the increased size of the Sixth Form. In his report at the 1927 Speech Day he stated that the large number of boys at the top of the school had tended to impair the efficiency of Higher Certificate work, because the individual tuition essential at that level had been practically impossible. Nevertheless, he conceded that a strong Sixth Form was a valuable asset to a school and that there was plenty of scope for the elder boys in the various activities of the school world.

He also reported that more boys than usual took the Higher Certificate exams, but difficulties in obtaining employment had caused many weaker candidates to stay on at school. Out of eight pupils, only four gained Higher Certificates, whilst in the School Certificate exam, twenty-six passed, with varying degrees of success.

It ought to be recorded that the steady growth in the size of the school was not constant. At the Speech Day in 1928, Taylor reported that there had been a decrease in the number of boys by 24 to 391. The reduction was felt most at the top of the school because of improved employment opportunities, but an increase in fees had also discouraged entry in the Lower School and a few boys had left as a result. Despite the easing in numbers, it was estimated that 200 pupils were being taught in the school hall each week. A year later, the situation had improved, with 399 in the school and with increased entry into the Preparatory Section. The prizes at the 1928 Speech Day were given by the Headmaster of Rugby School, making a change from the usual use of local dignitaries.

By 1929 the Upper School was very full and the number of Sixth Form courses available was placing pressure on masters. Some relief was obtained by dispensing with one form in the Lower Middle School. There were renewed accommodation problems, in particular for teaching biology and botany. The number of boys studying these subjects was increasing and a proper biology lab was desperately needed.

Despite the extensions to the school described in the next chapter, the pressure on space was relentless and was exacerbated by the decision to close the Central Secondary School (popularly known as the Commercial School).

The school had opened, in Gladstone Street behind the Technical College in 1911 and Mr W.G. Bainbridge was the Headmaster for its entire existence. At the beginning of the century, there had been a perception that something needed to be done to expand the availability of secondary education in the town and Darlington Council had promoted the school for the purpose of teaching pupils at a higher level than in the elementary schools. The quality of education in such schools was seen as inadequate for those leaving school to start engineering or similar courses. The new school became co-educational in 1916 and admission was by competitive examination. By 1921 it had 342 pupils, with seventeen staff, including nine women, and specialised in science and technical subjects,

Although it had enjoyed notable successes in the School Certificate exams, the school was expensive to run and its buildings were needed, so the decision was made to close it and to distribute its pupils and staff between the grammar and high schools. At the beginning of the 1930s, between thirty and forty-five boys gained scholarships to it each year.

In September 1932 the scholarship boys who would otherwise have started at the Central Secondary School went instead to the Grammar School and two masters, Messrs Graville and Crane, transferred there at the same time. A year later, the school closed and the rest of the male staff and sixty-two remaining boys also transferred, leading to a record number of 568 on the Grammar School roll. After the closure, the annual scholarship intake of the Grammar School was increased to compensate for the loss of places at the Central Secondary School.

The ingress of pupils following upon the closure resulted in an increase in the number of classes. In 1933 there were three V Lower Forms, and four each in the IVs and Upper IIIs. Despite recent extensions to the school, more were still needed.

In 1931 the school benefited from a new pavilion on the school field, replacing the one donated as recently as 1913. It was opened by Mr J.D. Hinks, who happened to be an Old Boy as well as being Mayor, and its facilities included showers, kitchen and tea room. Another Old Boy, Councillor J. Clayton, donated the pavilion clock. The new building was to be much longer lived than its predecessor, surviving well into the days of the Sixth Form College.

The field at Abbey Road was increasingly inadequate and the school had hired a field at Harrowgate Hill, situated at the junction of Thompson Street East and Whinfield Road, and known as Thompson's Field. It was certainly used by the Shell boys and it cost a halfpenny on the trolley bus to get there and the same back. Apparently it was common for boys to spend their return fare at a shop which they had to pass on the walk back to the bus stop. It is not known when the field was first used but, back in 1923, a House football match, between the Danes and the Normans, was played on it because of the condition of the school field.

The situation was relieved in the early 1930s when additional land at Abbey Road was acquired. The site then extended, as it still does, as far as Cleveland Terrace. The extension provided room for about three more games and the school now had the benefit of a motor mower.

The changing facilities in the new pavilion were totally inadequate for the numbers using the field, particularly on a Wednesday afternoon when visiting teams increased the numbers. The majority therefore had to make do with 'the Green Hut', built after the field had been extended. It was a long, narrow structure with a single door, located towards Cleveland Terrace, and it also lasted till near the end of the twentieth century, still painted in a weather-beaten light green. The road called 'Leconfield' is now built over the site. A bench seat ran along the walls and clothes hooks were provided, but there were no other facilities. The overcrowding, particularly when the entire Sixth Form was at the field, resulted in the hut's occupants standing shoulder to shoulder.

Not surprisingly, conditions were unpleasant, particularly in warm weather, and on one occasion in about 1960 a group of pupils, including the writer, decided that changing outside was to be preferred. Dr Hare, the then Headmaster, lived in Westbourne Grove on the far side of the field, and an observant neighbour must have reported the unwelcome sight, for, on the following morning at assembly, the Headmaster made it clear that there must never be a repetition.

The school might have gained a pavilion, but its library was in a desperate state. What had started life as Mr Wood's library – the small room at the side of the old dining hall – now served the entire school. Even with a mere 840 books, around one and a half per pupil, its shelves had reached their limits. During 1932 only thirteen books were purchased, so, unsurprisingly, there was a desire to revive the custom whereby boys, on leaving, presented a book to the library. Periodic appeals were therefore made. Usually the numbers donated were sufficiently small to enable the school magazine to print the title of each individual book presented. One donor was an Old Boy, Eric Miller, later Sir Eric, President of the Old Boys' Association in 1927–8. In later years he continued to assist the school, providing, via his firm, the rubber floor in the entrance vestibule and the main corridor. After his death a bequest provided the books for the new reference library in 1960.

By 1933 the library had to be open four afternoons per week because of the shortage of space, but matters improved to the extent that thirty-seven books were purchased during the year and an increased number were donated, several coming from Mr Taylor. A proper facility was desperately needed.

During the summer holidays of 1927 a party of boys from the Upper School visited Germany, joining boys from three other north-eastern schools. They spent most of their time 'in the haunts of the Youth Wander Movement' staying in what were described as Youth Homes. They had to carry all their possessions in their rucksacks. From Germany they had gone on by steamer to Vienna.

Subsequently, an attempt seems to have been made to hold a camp on an annual basis. In 1928 about thirty boys had a camp at Ruswarp which included a visit to Whitby Regatta, but fifteen pupils went, with Mr Hughes, on a fortnight's trip to Paris.

The Ruswarp Summer Camp was repeated in the following year, extending over fourteen days. Unfortunately the weather was so bad that the party eventually had to be housed in the village hall. Dinner one evening was unexpectedly augmented as a result of a salmon leaping into a boat crewed by three boys. It was quickly despatched with one of the oars. For 1930 the arrangements were more ambitious with a camp in Devon. Fifty-three boys left Bank Top station on 25 July in two reserved coaches travelling overnight to Goodrington Sands Halt near Torquay.

The form of school camp familiar to later pupils was established under Mr Fothergill and in 1931 was held in northern France. Unsurprisingly, given the short time since the Great War, places visited included Compiegne, Verdun and Vimy Ridge. For 1932 Mr Fothergill organised a camp in Denmark, at Elsinore, and forty-four boys went. Many snakes were encountered and one was killed and brought back to the school, doubtless being added to Mr Allen's collection. The visit occupied sixteen days including the travelling, which was lengthy.

The camp for the following year was not without its problems. A visit to Spain had been intended, but there were difficulties and emergency arrangements were made for going to Jersey as an alternative. Unfortunately, much had been left in the hands of an organiser on the island and, in Fothergill's opinion, he had much to answer for. On the outward crossing from Southampton, many boys had to sleep on the deck of the steamer and the return journey was also very trying. Furthermore, one pupil suffered head injuries on the ship when the bunk above collapsed on him! The camps for the following years, in Switzerland and near Koblenz respectively, were less eventful.

For 1936 the destination was Trier in Germany. On their arrival, after a tiring journey, the boys were obliged to attend a concert given in their honour by the Hitler Youth. As their hosts wanted to inspect the camp, they afterwards marched back to it with the visitors. Later, two football matches, one of them in a stadium, were played against the Hitler Youth and the Darlingtonians lost both. The travellers also had the benefit of a second concert and a social evening with their persistent hosts.

In 1937, a year before the Germans had absorbed the country, the school camp took place near Linz, in Austria, a twenty-two-hour journey. Many of the visitors to the camp wore national costume. In 1938 the camp was at Vaduz in Liechtenstein but, fortunately, Fothergill's choice for 1939 was Sweden, with the party crossing from Harwich to Esbjerg.

In 1959 Fothergill, who had left the school in 1943, published a book called *Camping Venture*. It recalled the series of camps made by the school between 1927 and 1940 and had a foreword written by Prince Emanuel of Liechtenstein.

The Old Boys' Association was still active and the school magazine published in February 1928 provided a list of members. Three, all still living in Darlington and including Tom Watson, had been at the old Leadyard School, whilst four more were from the first intake at Vane Terrace in 1878. Amongst the others were R.F. Drury, who gave the Jubilee sermon, David Carrick, the Second Master, and Percy Moss. They had entered the school in 1881, 1892 and 1917 respectively. Several names appeared in more than one generation.

In 1927 the Association's main income consisted of subscriptions of £32 5s 0d and its expenditure, as usual, included £5 to George Spence, the old school cricket professional who had served the school from the 1880s. In the following year, the subscription income was greater, at £43, but, alarmingly, the expenses were £77 8s 2d. In 1930 George Spence was paid no less than £30 and, in the same year, the large sum of £230 was raised in aid of the testimonial for Mr Henderson, the long-serving music master. In both 1930 and 1931 expenditure of £5 was approved for providing a gymnasium class for members, but the facility was short-lived and was dropped in 1933 because of insufficient enthusiasm

At this time, the Association revised its rules to introduce Life Membership and to provide for stronger enforcement of payment of arrears. A defaulter would now cease to be a member after notification was given to him that he was four years behind! He could rejoin after making payment in full. Life membership cost £2 as against 5 shillings for an annual subscription. Unsurprisingly, as life membership could be had for eight years' subscriptions, it became popular, but the corresponding reduction in annual payments in subsequent years seems to have created cash-flow problems.

The highlights of the 1928 Annual Dinner were the presentation to David Carrick of a grandfather clock and the showing of the film of the Jubilee celebrations. The 1929 dinner, held as usual at the Kings Head Hotel, had a record attendance of ninety. The music was led by the 'Senior Old Boy', Tom Watson, then aged 90, singing 'John Peel'. He seems to have become increasingly active in the association as he became older. His death, at the age of 95, was reported in the summer 1935 school magazine. He had, until a year or so earlier, continued to go salmon fishing in Scotland.

Three years after the singing of 'John Peel' there were about eighty present at the Dinner and the school song, specially composed and sung by Mr Drury, the vicar of Darlington, was supported in the choruses by the company present. The song seems to have disappeared into oblivion, but, given the content of Mr Drury's Jubilee sermon, it is perhaps as well. He was, by then, the oldest player in the Old Boys' cricket matches, having been a pupil fifty years earlier.

The usual attendance at the Old Boys' AGMs, which were held at the school, was in the region of forty to fifty. Often a smoking concert followed. The year 1932 was not a good one for Old Boys' mortality. Seven deaths were recorded; of these, one drowned and no fewer than three died in traffic accidents.

When Mr Taylor's departure to become Secretary to the Headmasters' Association was announced, a subscription list was opened, with a maximum contribution of 1/-. A silver tray and a photo album were purchased and no fewer than three hundred Old Boys were present in the school hall on 21 December 1933 when the gifts were presented to the Headmaster. Mr Taylor thanked the Old Boys for their support, saying he believed that he could name at least 60 per cent of those present. The audience sang 'For He's a Jolly Good Fellow' and they all then joined hands to sing 'Auld Lang Syne'. Community singing seemed to play a large part in Old Boys' events.

The assistance to Mr Spence continued. In 1932 there was a deficit in his pension fund, so an eight-guinea grant was agreed upon. Then in 1934, £5 was paid into the fund and a grant of £29 was paid to Spence. He died in March the following year, aged 76, and the payments finally ended.

At this time, the Association had no fewer than seventeen vice-presidents, together with two secretaries and one assistant secretary.

In November 1929 a branch of The School's National Savings Association was formed, managed by Mr Leighton. Under the scheme a boy would buy savings stamps which would be held for him at the school. When his holding of stamps was large enough it would be exchanged for a National Savings Certificate. By the end of 1930 there were ninety-five members. By 1933, when Crane, who came from the Central Secondary School, was managing the scheme, over £300 had been collected by the Association.

At the 1930 Speech Day, the Headmaster gave a breakdown of the known destinations of boys leaving the school, commenting that a higher proportion of boys was entering training colleges or universities because of the current employment difficulties. For the same reason, there was a larger number in the Sixth Form. This growth was, however, also partially accounted for by the increased number of pupils passing through the Lower School. This, in turn, arose from an increase in the number of free places available and from boys from outside the town being allowed in.

Of those leaving over the last twelve months, fifteen had gone to university or training colleges, nine to clerical jobs, fifteen to trade, nine to the professions, four to engineering, and four to the RAF or the merchant marine. Eight had no occupation and the rest (no number given) had left town or gone to other schools. Seven former pupils had graduated from university at the end of the previous academic year. This number indicates the comparatively low proportion of pupils then aiming for university and the number of places then available. At the end of 1931 there were six Old Boys at Oxford in total, but three had gone from the Grammar School to other schools, so they had possibly treated the school as a prep school.

By 1933 the Sixth Form had shrunk in size. This was taken to be a result of the fall in unemployment. During the inter-war period the size of the Upper School seemed to lead to two alternating complaints. Either boys were leaving school prematurely because their expectations were too low, or they were staying on beyond the stage when they were gaining any benefit for want of opportunity elsewhere.

In 1930 there were eight successful candidates in the Durham Higher Certificate exams and a creditable forty-two out of fifty-two were successful in the School Certificate, six pupils gaining Honours. Two years later, six boys gained their Higher Certificate, and forty-five out of fifty-five candidates were successful in the School Certificate.

The school magazine continued much as before and, as always, there were concerns about the quality of the articles submitted, with much being refused. Those published were a mix of intellectual outpourings and features on obscure topics unlikely to appeal to most readers. Issue number 33 of 1928, for instance, contained features on fire fighting and the salvaging of ships. Normally, at this time, the back cover contained adverts for Kodak cameras and for the North of England School Furnishing Company. A feature of the pre-war magazines was the various editors' enthusiasm for capital letters. There would be references to Masters, Summer Holidays, Cricket Season and School even when another institution was being referred to. When it was purchased for the school field, the Motor Mower was similarly dignified.

The School Concerts, now presented by Mr Martin, and the Form Dramatic Evenings continued as annual events. They performed the useful function of contributing towards what was now the Games, Magazine and Library Fund. The Concert of 15 December 1931, for instance, raised £18, whilst the 1932 Form Dramatic Evenings provided £32. Given that the overall income for 1932 was £341 16s ½d such contributions were significant. Small sums came from sources as diverse as advertising in the school magazine (15/-) and fines for mislaid library books.

Unfortunately, in that year, a deficit of £38 6s 8d arose, but a financial appeal raised no less than £183 13s 5d. The donations included £10 from the Headmaster and £16 19s 11d was raised by a concert organised by R.A. Burniston.

There was still no sign of a school captain, but the school continued to have a Senior Prefect. The number of prefects remained fairly constant, varying from fifteen in 1931 to seventeen in the following year.

For a time before 1928 the scholarship exam was in two parts and only those successful in the first went on to the second part, which included an intelligence test. Then it was decided to have the exam in only one part, but with the intelligence test incorporated. As the Education Authority considered that it would be useful to know the intelligence quotient of every pupil in the town, it also decided that all children, whether they wanted to go to a grammar school or not, would have to sit the exam. After that parental pressures on teachers began and the habit, in some schools, of practising for the exam began.

To save money, what was called the special places system came into effect on 1 April 1933. Parents of scholarship boys were liable to pay fees on a sliding scale based upon their income, but for pupils beyond the school-leaving age of fourteen, maintenance allowances for those on low incomes were available. Additionally, loans were available to supplement leaving scholarships for those going to college or university. However, many parents had to refuse scholarships because they could not undertake to keep the child at school until age 16 and during this period there were frequent early withdrawals of pupils for financial reasons. Many left early because the chance of a job came up, but, as has been seen, there were others who pointlessly stayed on into the Sixth Form, for want of employment. Many parents did not have an income sufficiently high to require a contribution from them towards the fees and, by 1937, the proportion of grammar school and high school pupils with a full or partial exemption from fees was 71 per cent.

More Buildings

In its final years of independence, the school had been unable to expand because it lacked the means to undertake any alterations or additional building, but then, from the end of the Great War until the 1930s, the school had an ongoing problem with overcrowding. Each measure taken to increase capacity at best only matched the school's continuing expansion in numbers.

By 1928 the school had gained additional classrooms, new labs including two for physics, the gym in the former dining room, a library of sorts and a small museum. There was now a reasonable-sized staff room on the first floor of the former Head's house. The old sitting room by the main entrance, now superseded as the staff room, later became the secretary's office.

It was not enough. There was an urgent need for further labs and one form did not have a classroom of its own. The school hall, in which about 200 boys each week were still having lessons, and the Abbey Road playing field were both too small for the number of pupils.

The next step was to enlarge the hall and plans were prepared in 1929 by Ernest Minors, the Borough Architect. The cost of the extension, which would add three side windows to the five of the existing hall, would be expensive because of the need to blend in with the existing structure and to relocate the Memorial Windows without damage. The building work started in the 1929–30 school year and was so skilfully carried out that the join is not normally visible. It is apparently possible, in wet weather, to see the difference in the roof slates if one looks carefully.

The first Speech Day held at the school since 1918 took placed in the extended hall on 15 December 1930 and, during the proceedings, Mrs Leach officially opened it. As usual, that event was followed on the next evening by the School Concert, but, this time, those attending were grateful for the reduction in crowding. It was expected that the larger stage would enhance the performances at the Form Dramatic Evenings, but there was no proscenium arch with curtains or an apron stage at this period.

The opportunity was also taken to provide the first biology lab. It was built under the new part of the hall and would remain the kingdom of Bug Allen for much of the school's remaining existence, housing all manner of flora and fauna, both dead and alive.

As more room was still needed, there was a further plan. The intention was to enlarge the so-called west wing to increase the capacity of the school to 500. It will be remembered that back in 1881 a short block had been built at right angles to the south wing. Now, an extension to it on the north side would provide three additional classrooms on the ground floor and an art room, plus a further biology lab at first-floor level. The new extension would effectively enclose the rear of the court and would follow the architectural style of the remainder of the building. Until this time the first-floor room at the Abbey Road end of the 1881 extension had been used as an art room. In the event, the proposal for the lab was abandoned and an art store was built in its place.

Until now the classrooms in the wing behind the main entrance had access from corridors. These were now to disappear. At first-floor level, both the existing wing and the new one at the rear of the court would have access via a veranda, open to the weather on one side but with a sloping glass roof above it. An open staircase along the outer side of the art room would give access from the first floor to the yard. The new veranda would provide some shelter from the weather to those going to and from the ground-floor rooms. An archway, nine feet wide, was to be provided in the new wing to give direct access to the schoolyard. After the work was completed in 1932 there were, in total, eleven ground-floor classrooms and nine first-floor ones, plus the labs and art room.

From 1932 the quadrangle, apart from having part of its area filled by a wartime kitchen, later replaced by a reference library, remained unchanged till 1970, but it is now roofed over and forms the Sixth Form College Library. The archway has since been walled in to create an additional room, but the different brickwork still identifies it.

The existing toilets were in the way of the new extension, so replacements were needed. The new toilet block was located closer to the Training College than the original and a covered way, with a flat roof, linked it to the end of the court. Originally, the roof was to be supported only by its connection to the buildings at each end, but, as an afterthought, it was decided to support it on pillars. The new toilets were provided with a pair of toplights in the roof for better illumination. It was also proposed to have two additional classrooms on the Abbey Road side of the 1881 extension, but, because of cost considerations, the project was postponed.

Despite all this work, still more rooms were needed. The closure of the Central Secondary School would result in the Grammar School having to accommodate those boys who were transferred, plus those who, in later years, would have attended it.

The caretaker's flat was seen as a source of additional space, so the next proposal was to replace it with a small house to be constructed at the front of the school site, adjacent to the boundary with the Training College. The removal of the flat would make space available for four additional classrooms, a cloakroom and a storeroom. The new house, with three bedrooms, was built in 1933 and was demolished shortly after the Sixth Form College took over in 1970. The view has been expressed that it provided a poor substitute for the accommodation available in the flat.

The expansion programme was not yet finished. The library facilities were inadequate and the gym left much to be desired, particularly as to its changing facilities, so the intention was to have new purpose-built gym, thus releasing the existing one for use as a library. By early 1937, when Dr Hare was Headmaster, building work was in hand on what, years earlier, had been the Headmaster's orchard at the rear of the yard. It appears to have been much neglected and there were sparse bushes and pear trees on it that had to be removed. It was also necessary to demolish part of the wall of the bike sheds.

The building work made slow progress and after a year, without waiting for the replacement gym to be available, the new library opened. Apparently the fiction section had been in use since the previous autumn and an average of fifty books was taken out each night.

The room was transformed. The 'unattractive walls, dingy ceiling and the wooden floor of the old gym' had all gone. There were now light yellow walls lined with new bookcases made of Austrian oak and there was linoleum on the floor. Assistance with the cataloguing had been given by the staff of Darlington Public Library, and the *Northern Echo* had donated an electric clock. There were spaces available for 7,000 books, but only about 2,000 were then possessed and a plea for gifts of books was made by the school.

Nearly every class was now provided with a library period and the library's facilities were available until 5.30 p.m. on four nights each week. Previously Sixth Formers with free periods had needed to find spare rooms as best they could, but they were now permitted to use the library. In addition, many pupils were staying after school to read the popular periodicals that were available and a new departure was the inclusion of a careers magazine. The small room next door, which had served as the library, now became its office.

Comments were made from time to time in the school magazine about the slowness of the construction of the gym and were coupled with observations about those working on the site. They were regarded almost as an alien species, with reference in one article to 'the mystical methods of the British Workman'. The writer implied that they did little work but count the windows of the school. At one point it was asserted that little had been done 'except for the addition of two doors to prevent the workmen inside from catching cold at their card games'.

At last, by the summer of 1938, after many weeks without gym lessons, the new building was ready. It offered a number of advantages over its predecessor. Four beams took the place of the two in the old gym and there was now a balcony for the benefit of spectators. It was claimed at the time that it enabled the nightly table tennis games of the prefects to be watched. The new building also had the benefit of a proper changing room with showers, a toilet and a small staff room. Its one drawback was the risk of rain faced by those going to and from it. Percy Moss, a dedicated Old Boy but not yet a master at the school, judged the first gym display at the new location.

Early in the war, there was a proposal to utilise the gym as a Gas Identification Office in case of a gas attack. A plan was prepared showing the alterations needed, but there is no evidence that anything happened. It is believed that there was no break in the wall along the Abbey Road side of the yard until the gym was built.

By now, funds were at last available for the building of the two additional rooms on the Abbey Road end of the wing. Like its counterparts at the back of the quad, the new first-floor room, which for many years was occupied by Norman Sunderland, had access by a veranda. Adjacent to it was the lecture room, with two physics stores next to it.

Because of the sloping site, the lower classroom was above ground level and steps from the playground gave access to it and the rest of the school. It too had a veranda. At the foot of the steps was the door to a small room below the classroom. No reference to its use has been found, but in the 1950s Mr Hastie had an elaborate diagram for timetable planning on the back of the door.

In 1936 efforts were made to improve the school's appearance. Repainting of the classrooms started, the lawn was re-turfed and the Mound, the area between the new extension and the side of the hall, was provided with shrubs and rockeries. Unfortunately, the winter of 1936–7 was a hard one and the appearance and cleanliness of the newly revamped school apparently suffered.

There was, however, one final stage in the building work and this necessitated the disappearance of the Mound – and the new shrubs and rockeries. Plans dated February 1938 show a proposed cloakroom and lavatories, with a flat roof containing four roof lights, on the site. On the hall side, there was to be a bookstore and a heater boiler area. The new development was below the level of the ground-floor classrooms in the south wing and, allowing for the sloping ground, was more or less on a level with the laboratories under the hall. With the completion of this work, there were, with the exception of the construction of the emergency kitchen and a dining hall, no changes of substance until the 1960 extension was built.

There was already ample provision for bicycles. Open sheds ran the length of the school yard along the rear boundary and there were similar sheds on the Training College side, between the gym and the toilet block.

Every extension and alteration to the school by the Education Authority seemed to justify a commemorative plaque. These were, for instance, provided for the new pavilion, the new gym and the library, as well as for the later 1960 extension.

Doctor Hare Arrives

Leonard Taylor's successor was Arthur Hare and, like his two predecessors, he was still in his thirties when appointed. A native of York, he had, after serving in the Great War, graduated from Leeds University with a First in physics and was, in 1924, awarded a PhD. Later, he was Senior Physics Master at King Edward VI High School, Birmingham.

The new Headmaster, invariably referred to as 'Doc' Hare, was physically big and remote in manner and these two characteristics encouraged the pupils to treat him carefully. On Dr Hare's retirement twenty-six years later, the Second Master, W.S. Richardson, paid tribute to him and having outlined his achievements, went on to say that Dr Hare was a martinet when he came, but over time his touch at the helm had lightened. It is perhaps unusual to find the word 'martinet' in a tribute, but its use probably emphasises the newcomer's intention to have his own way.

Arthur Hare took up his new position in January 1934 having very clear objectives. His previous teaching experience had been in large grammar schools with excellent facilities and it was Dr Hare's belief that a good grammar school could rival the public schools. He intended to put this belief to the test at his new school and his first few years in Darlington were characterised by a series of innovations.

The school now had 600 pupils, having boosted its numbers with the absorption of the boys from the Central Secondary School, and Dr Hare's first task was to ensure their integration. There was also an immediate change. In his first term Senior Prefects were introduced.

Initially there were three, plus the Head Prefect and twenty ordinary ones. It also seems that for the year 1934–5 a Captain of the School was appointed, for reference to him was made at the 1935 Speech Day.

Soon the Headmaster introduced the School Club. Its purpose was to provide – separately from the normal school budget – a source for funding the extra-curricular activities of the school and, hopefully, to expand them. The intention was that all pupils would pay 1/- (5p) per term for membership, although, in practice, the payments would come from the Education Committee. In addition, the profits of concerts and other events hosted by the school would be paid in. In many ways the new organisation echoed the Games Club introduced by Taylor twenty or so years earlier.

Associate membership of the School Club at 5/- (25p) per annum was also available and many of the teaching staff, including the Head, were early members. One of the benefits was the automatic receipt of copies of the school magazine. Members of the Old Boys' Association were automatically associate members, as their subscriptions were paid via the Association. At this time, programmes were provided, loose in the school magazine, setting out details of the activities of the School Club's components.

The accounts for the School Club for 1934–5 and 1936–7 provide an insight into the financing of school activities. The annual receipts for 1934–5, which included a balance in hand of £26 6s 3½d transferred from the library and a couple of school societies, amounted to £624 2s 3½d – roughly £1 per pupil. The largest items of income were £272 17s 9d from the Education Committee for the pupils' subscriptions and £53 8s 10d profits from the school entertainments. Tuck shop profits amounted to £18 5s 5d, and £13 11s 5d grazing rents from land comprising the school endowments were received. Pupils who cycled to school had to pay for cycle stalls, giving rise to a contribution of £11 4s 6d received via Miss Nicholson, the School Secretary. Surprisingly, library fines produced a mere £1 2s 1d (£1.10).

As to expenditure, the main item by far was for the Cricket Club at £130 17s 2½d. Football (apparently both varieties combined) managed with £20 13s 10½d, whilst the magazine and library section obtained £86 12s 4d. The costs for football for the following year were

£78, suggesting that the 1934–5 figure might be an error. The smallest individual item was an expenses claim of 10d for the Secretary of the Debating Society. Prefects' caps cost £20 10s 11d, but there is no corresponding item for their sale, implying that they were given to their wearers. A reserve Fund of £100 was maintained.

The sums involved increased as the school grew bigger and the accounts for 1938–9 show that £410 3s 6d had come from the Education Committee, whilst the total income was up to £759 11s 0d, less £58 12s 3½d in hand. After the outbreak of war income from the cycle stalls dwindled, possibly because many of them were displaced by air-raid shelters. Eventually, the receipts from the tuck shop all but disappeared, thanks to wartime shortages.

Dr Hare was both a trained singer and a cello player, and was keen to improve the musical facilities at the school. By 1935, occasional lunchtime organ recitals had been introduced, together with other performances, and the Headmaster often participated. One of his favourite songs was 'I must go down to the sea again'. According to his son, he once surprised the school assembly by singing from the organ loft.

However, Dr Hare had a greater ambition. The School Orchestra, having faded away after Mr Henderson's retirement, was revived after Dr Hare's arrival under Messrs Martin and Crane, but the plan was to have a new orchestra operating on both a different scale and a different footing. This one would differ from Henderson's in that the performers would be taught to play their instruments by the school.

Whilst music on the curriculum of local authority schools was virtually non-existent, orchestras had existed in public schools for many years. Private instrumental tuition, mainly piano, was often offered at such schools for an extra fee and orchestral instruments were taught by visiting professionals. As part of his plan to make the grammar school one of the finest in the country and the equal of the best independent schools, Dr Hare intended it to enjoy similar facilities.

The scheme had its beginnings in October 1938 when the first lessons, as an after-school activity, were given. It coincided with the return to the school of Chris Bennett as music master. Small classes of not more than four boys were formed with a fee of 15/- (75p) per pupil per term for ten lessons being charged. As an alternative, tuition in pairs at £1 per pupil, or individual teaching at £1 5s 0d (£1.25), could be provided, but Grade 4 or Grade 5 respectively was needed for these facilities to be used. There were a small number of instruments available on loan. Because of the low charges, it was not easy to find professional teachers of quality, but two personal friends offered to help, working part-time. Mrs Anna Gomez taught the violin and viola, whilst Miss Lily Gregory taught the cello.

Tuition was offered for orchestral instruments only, and piano teaching was left to the town's private teachers. The emphasis would be on learning to play to become part of an orchestra. There were to be two of these and pupils would start in the Second Orchestra, progressing to the First. It was recognised that, because of the need to teach pupils from scratch, it would take some time before an orchestra could be formed.

The initial take-up was poor with only thirteen pupils for the string instruments. However, by July 1940 there were twenty-five learning to play the violin and during the year an orchestra of twenty-five was formed. Thereafter recruits came in increasing numbers.

Teaching woodwind and brass presented greater problems for there was a lack of teachers in the town. The coming of war added to the difficulties as there was then a scarcity of instruments and a plea was made to parents and friends for the gift of any unwanted ones. For teaching, reliance had to be placed upon the bandsmen at Catterick Camp, but they obviously had other priorities. However, the school coped and the foundations for a post-war upsurge in the activities of the orchestras were laid.

Although it was said to be deficient in wind instruments and needed more viola and cello players, the School Orchestra, at its third concert, played on three successive nights in December 1941 and over a thousand parents and friends attended. Two hundred and fifty boys took part, although a large number of these were in the choir, conducted by H.O. Crane, known as 'Hoc'. The School Choir was now an established feature of the school, meeting at 4.30 p.m. every Monday.

On Monday 7 June 1937 the choir and the orchestra enjoyed an outing to Redcar under the charge of Messrs Crane and Martin. The boys deposited their 'encumbrances' at the Britannia Café and then had organised games on the beach until 2 p.m. This was followed by either the baths or the boating lake and then tea at the café. After that the boys were free till the 7.30 p.m. train but two of them are said to have missed it. The event was repeated in 1938.

During those final pre-war years the school also acquired an observatory. Back in 1904 the vicar of Eryholme had offered an astronomical telescope to Darlington Borough Council. His suggested price was £80 to £90, but, as the council was not prepared to pay for it, it was purchased by public subscription. After more than two years' delay, it was sited in the town's South Park, but then seems to have been largely forgotten about. This is perhaps unsurprising if the park was closed and locked at night. The telescope was housed in a revolving wooden observatory.

Then, in April 1936, Dr Hare wrote to the Parks and Cemeteries Committee about the observatory, requesting the removal of a number of trees surrounding it. The council seems to have found in Dr Hare's enquiry an opportunity to rid themselves of the telescope for an agreement to remove it to the Grammar School field was made with an estimated cost of removal and re-erection of £75. Despite the objections of the owners of some of the properties in nearby Westbourne Grove the observatory was moved to the field in 1937 and became available for the use of pupils.

Reference was made in the school magazine to 'the green structure forming the temple wherein is enshrined the Telescope'. Such was the high-flown and facetious language seemingly obligatory for magazine contributors in this period.

In early 1951 the observatory was broken into and equipment was stolen, but by June the police reported that the equipment had been recovered. The observatory continued to be used by the school's Astronomical Society for many years, but its use by other organisations seems to have been restricted because of the need to obtain night-time access. Ultimately, after the Grammar School had ceased to exist, the observatory suffered damage from vandals and its chequered existence came to an end.

The School List, published twice a year, was another innovation. With the exception of the Sixth Form, all of the pupils in the school were normally listed, form by form, in order of their overall examination placings. In addition, their position relative to their classmates in each individual subject was shown. For those sitting School Certificate or, later, GCE examinations, their grades were shown. The performance of each pupil was therefore public knowledge. By the 1960s, however, in response to changing attitudes, the pupils were listed, form by form, in alphabetical order.

In its early days, the list stated that the school was included in the list of institutions recognised by the Royal College of Physicians and Surgeons, and was approved by the General Medical Council as one where medical studies may be begun. The course of work provided in Lower VI science enabled boys to pass this 'Pre-Medical Examination' whilst still at school, enabling them then to be registered. It also set out details of the fees payable for those pupils not on scholarships. The normal amount was £14 per year, but for boys with parents living out of town it was £20.

The Sixth Form was costly for staff. At the beginning of Dr Hare's time, the Upper VI, whose form master was Ives, had nine arts pupils with a mere one each studying German, Greek and scripture. Latin, history and English did better with seven, five and six students respectively, whilst geography had to make do with three. However, there were only seven science pupils, with only one each studying pure and applied maths and, surprisingly, French. Although the Lower VI, under Hughes, contained only twelve pupils, the bias was reversed for there were nine science students with only three on the arts side.

From 1 September 1935 there was a third course intended to prepare pupils for the exams of the Civil Service or other bodies. This new group had their own form, the General VI, which spanned both years of the Sixth Form. In the December 1938 list, four pupils were shown as having been successful in the Civil Service Exams General Clerical Class, with positions ranging from 619th to 2,615th. A further ten in the form were merely shown as being candidates for the School Certificate Examination.

Although the numbers in the Sixth Form were nothing like those of later years, Dr Hare's enthusiasm for science teaching soon showed itself and, by the end of the decade, the proportion of Form VI pupils studying science subjects was much greater. By then the arts forms were designated Modern Forms. In early 1940 the entire Sixth Form only contained forty-seven members, eighteen fewer than in 1935. By the end of the decade the teaching of Greek seems to have ended, although it was certainly revived in later years.

Nobody seems to have opted for arts or science before entering the Sixth Form, but, once he did so, a pupil's specialisation for the Higher Certificate was complete. There is nothing to indicate that any science student chose a language, history or geography as a subject and those in the Modern (i.e. arts) classes had no science subjects. Three subjects only were normally listed for each pupil, but for the General class most pupils are listed for five subjects from English, French, history, geography, science, maths and arithmetic. All in the class studied maths and arithmetic.

Those in the Upper VI usually read for the Higher School Certificate or for open scholarships at the universities. State scholarships were awarded on the results of the Higher School Certificate examinations and some of those few hoping for a state scholarship would often stay on for an extra year in the hope of being able to improve their grades. By 1940 one or two Sixth Formers were sitting the Naval Cadet exams.

At the beginning of 1935 the new Headmaster proposed a scheme to enable boys of more than average ability to take the First School Certificate exams (effectively the equivalent of the later O levels) at the end of their fourth year, instead of the fifth. A trial was made for the academic year 1935–6 and the results were found to justify the scheme, with seventy-five out of the eighty-nine candidates passing, ten of them with Honours. Of the eighty-nine, thirty-five sat the exam after a shorter four-year course. Two obtained Honours and only five failed.

The express stream then became an established feature at the school. Participants took their First School Certificate exams in the year when they became fifteen (i.e. in what we would now regard as Year 10) and then entered the Sixth Form a year early. Two years' study would then enable them to sit the Higher Certificate exams whilst still aged 17, giving them a further year for improving results or for concentrating on university entrance exams. The normal pattern was that the boys in IV A formed the express stream when they moved up into V Lower A.

Later the system was revised. The normal practice at the school was for those pupils not in the express stream to sit five to seven O levels, but the changed system was based on the premise that express stream pupils should not need to sit more than four O levels. There was no point in their obtaining a pass at O level in a subject that was to be taken at A level.

As before, an express stream pupil would enter the Sixth Form a year earlier, missing out the Upper Fifth, but he would not now have sat any O level exams. Once in the Lower Sixth he would simultaneously study four O Levels and three A levels. The O levels would, of course, be in different subjects to the A levels. At the end of the year, he would sit (and hopefully pass) his O levels, and would then be free in the Upper Sixth to focus solely upon his A levels. As under the original system, the pupil would then have a third year in the Sixth Form available to him. There was some flexibility in the system. A pupil who was perceived as being weak in an A level subject might sit the subject at O level in the Upper VI on the basis that he could attempt it at A level a year later.

One consequence of the express stream was that as pupils were entering the Lower VI from both the Lower and Upper V, pupils of different ages were taught A level subjects together. Indeed, with subjects where numbers were few, such as English literature, pupils from the Lower Sixth to the Third Year Sixth, perhaps with an age range from 15 to 19, would be taught together.

For the academic year 1935–6 the school had a uniform curriculum up to the Sixth Form, except that there were limited alternatives as to language teaching. The four Shell forms now shared nearly 120 pupils and all of them studied seven subjects including French and art. Latin and German were not taught until pupils entered the III Forms, now no longer designated 'Upper', in the following year. Then they had to choose one or the other as a second language. The two subjects were taught by set, not by form, and there were three for Latin and two for German.

In the IV Forms, classes A and B studied eight subjects, including art, and with either Latin or German. For those in classes C and D, however, there were no options. For them, after one year's study, Latin and German ceased to be available. In the block, in 1935–6, there were sixty-three pupils studying Latin in three sets, as against only twenty-three taking German.

By 1940 those in the A form in the V Lowers were studying physics (which was compulsory), chemistry and biology in place of the single subject of science, whilst pupils in the A and B classes had to choose between history and geography. Classes C and D were taught the same subjects as in the IVs.

In the Fifth Form business knowledge was now available as an alternative subject. Perhaps significantly, the German option for those in Classes A and B had gone by 1940. The only language available, other than French, was Latin.

For those in Upper V, maths was taught in sets, so a boy in the A stream who was weak in the subject would expect to find himself in the B, or possibly C, set. All studied science, but it was still taught as a single subject, except that those in the A form were studying physics, chemistry and biology as separate subjects. By then pupils were also taking oral French, where appropriate, as well as geography and additional maths. The number of subjects studied by each pupil was also tending to increase.

In the summer of 1935 Upper V had thirty-seven School Certificate passes, plus seven more with Honours. Nine pupils failed and there were also three unclassified. The numbers fall well short of the total of pupils in the block, suggesting that there were many who, for one reason or another, did not sit for the School Certificate. By the end of the decade the number of candidates was greater. At the end of the 1939–40 year the V Lowers had seventy-eight pupils, in contrast to the V Uppers' fifty-seven. Presumably the difference arises because of the movement of express pupils directly from the V Lowers into the Sixth Form.

A familiar post-war pattern had already emerged in that the D stream in both the V Lowers and in the IVs was smaller than the other three. The December 1938 list, for example, shows that the IV forms had 28, 29, 25 and 17 pupils respectively. Most blocks had an age range extending well beyond one year, indicating that keeping pupils back remained common practice. In 1938–9 the range in the V Uppers extended over nearly 2½ years.

By now the timetable had assumed a complexity unthinkable even a few years earlier.

The School Lists also gave details of the recipients of form prizes, but it is difficult to discern any pattern in the number awarded to a particular form in a particular year. All that can be said is that the number per form varied from one to three, but there were odd instances when four were awarded. The value of the prizes apparently ranged from 3/- (15p) to 5/- (25p).

It is unclear whether his experience was typical, but Hector Parr found that, because he had his eleventh birthday in December 1938, he had to leave Dodmire School at the end of term. He was not permitted to stay until the end of the academic year. As a result he had to spend two terms at Eastbourne Secondary School, before entering the Grammar School in September.

The Preparatory Department had prospered since the local authority had taken control, but numbers could fluctuate. In July 1934 there were sixty-four boys in it, but two and a half years later the number had fallen to forty-three. Then it rose again. During the second half of the decade, the department underwent several structural changes, mainly short-lived and possibly involving little more than name changing.

When the new Headmaster arrived, there were three Shell forms and three Preparatory forms still designated I, II and Lower III, but in the year 1934–5 a fourth Shell form appeared and Lower III, which in the previous year had contained twenty pupils, disappeared. Then in 1935–6 the Shells reverted to three forms, whilst Lower III was restored to life! In the next academic year there were again four Shell forms, but, this time, all three Preparatory forms survived, retaining their customary designation. Mr G.H. Fisher's responsibilities as form master fluctuated between Shell D when it existed and Lower III.

Henceforth the number of Shell forms remained constant, but the arrangements for the Preparatory forms did not. In 1937 the Lower III continued, now under Miss Emerson, but Forms I and II were amalgamated into 'the Preparatory Form' with Miss Henson in charge. However, by the end of the academic year she was in charge of a separate Form I, whilst the Lower III had divided into Divisions A and B.

After the summer break in 1938 Miss Ellam replaced Miss Emerson, who had died, and the two Divisions now became Forms A and B. Then, by July 1939, Mrs Bowlby had replaced Miss Ellam. Her tenure was also short-lived, for by early 1940 Percy Moss was in charge of the Lower III, now in two Divisions again. Miss Henson continued, but now had a reborn Form II as well as Form I. Whether there were three or four classes, the department never had more than two teachers, each presumably using one classroom only.

The progression of boys through the Preparatory Department remained complex. As has been mentioned earlier, some newcomers, although well beyond the minimum age for entry, seem to have been put in Form I until they had been assessed. In addition, the practice of keeping boys back in the same form until their performance was seen as satisfactory extended the age range in a class. Normally boys would move up from Form I into II, but it seems that, increasingly, Forms I and II were intended to cater for a roughly similar age group, as were the two Lower III forms, so that a kind of streaming was being practised. It is perhaps borne out by the fact that two forms shared the same teacher.

In September 1934, after the Lower III had been replaced by the fourth Shell form, the boys from Form II who should have moved up into the Lower III were split. Some went directly into the augmented Shell block, but many were kept back in their old form. A year later, when Shell D was replaced by a reconstituted Lower III, the pupils from Form II were split three ways. Some went directly into a Shell form, others moved into Lower III and the rest stayed put. It is easy to see, with such movements, why so many forms catered for a wide age range.

As in the days of Taylor, it looks as if a significant number of boys in the Preparatory Department could not, even as fee payers, meet the Grammar School's entrance requirements. They were therefore kept back in the department until their parents either became tired of the situation or were discreetly requested to remove their child. A study of the School Lists reveals many names in the department's classes that are not traceable in the main school.

The subjects taught in the department were English, history, geography, maths and art, but by 1940 the final-year curriculum had expanded. Written English and oral English had become separate subjects and maths had been divided into arithmetic, geometry and, for Lower IIIA only, algebra. Grammar, science and general knowledge were also taught.

Old attitudes about grammar schools clearly persisted, for, in 1936, Dr Hare found it necessary to publish an open letter to boys and their parents in the school magazine. He proposed to answer criticisms heard on all sides about the value of exams, homework and the like and intended to point out the many opportunities available to pupils. The Head conceded that it was easy to denounce exams for their faults, but they remained and multiplied because it was impossible to do without them. They had saved the community from favouritism, corruption and influence reigning supreme and they served as a protection from incompetence.

Some said that, although a particular school had poor results, it built character in its pupils. Dr Hare's argument was that encouraging boys to stick in, to discipline themselves and to avoid laziness was, of itself, character building. The effort required to pass an exam had, irrespective of the result, a value in itself.

Homework was also necessary. Most attacks on it came from parents, and many boys said that they enjoyed it. Part of the trouble, in the Head's view, was that boys spent too much time on it. Sometimes, this happened because of the enjoyment, but it often arose because pupils did not understand what they were intended to do. He therefore urged every boy to make sure that he understood what he had to do and then make every effort to do it.

Dr Hare then went on to say that games and societies had been vastly extended in a short time, thanks to the School Club. It had been a very powerful force at his last school and he urged every boy to use its resources to the full. He would then find that the school was a really fine place.

In 1935 the school magazine changed its format and was now printed by James Dodds of Northgate in place of the *Northern Echo*. The long-standing adverts for Sydney Wood, the photographer, and North of England School Furnishing Co. disappeared. There were now more general articles that were usual in the earlier editions. A typical magazine of the time contained the customary letters from Old Boys at Oxford, Cambridge and London universities, with one added from Leeds, all written anonymously. There were articles about Life in India, Youth Hostels on the Continent, and Cuthbert Shaw, a local eighteenth-century poet and one-time master at the school. M. Emslie contributed poems for a number of issues. No one openly criticised the publication of articles unrelated to the school until the student radicalisation of the late 1960s.

The senior physics and chemistry labs were extended and, in addition, the lecture room was now revamped to make it more fit for purpose with new seating for 130 pupils. It was seen as being useful for school societies as well as for lectures, and, at some point, it began to be used for House prayers.

Notwithstanding the hall's extension a few years earlier, the continuing increase in pupil numbers led to its overcrowding. It was therefore essential to reduce the numbers attending assembly, and by holding separate Shell prayers in the lecture room on Mondays and House prayers on the remaining days, a proportion of the school population could be siphoned off. Even with the system of separate prayers, overcrowding in the hall remained a problem.

Until the conversion of the old gym, the problems of the library continued. In 1936, 165 extra books were bought, but there were problems accommodating them. The history, biology, general science and geography sections of the library had to be kept in classrooms, so accessibility for most pupils was considerably restricted.

In the previous year there had been a decrease in the number of books being borrowed from the library and the number of afternoon openings had been reduced. By the autumn, however, it was claimed that membership was increasing steadily, although most were in the junior school. In 1937 the library was closed for a term for stocktaking in readiness for the removal of the books into the new library. By 1939 the relocated library had started the practice of buying from the range of Penguin paperbacks then available. The books were popular and there was a saving on costs, but it was felt that seniors were not taking full advantage of the facilities offered by the library.

The traditional Form Dramatic Evenings continued. In 1936 they were held in the hall and nearly £50 was raised. Mr R.H. Moar, who was in charge, produced two of the plays, whilst other members of staff produced the others and were responsible for lighting and make-up. The stage was fitted up by Mr Busby, described as the 'school mechanic' and, presumably, the senior lab technician of the same name of the 1950s and '60s. The giving of entertainment benefited by the Education Committee's providing a grand piano in place of the old upright one.

Then, in 1937, the school's ability to provide dramatic productions moved forward. As a result of funds being made available by the local authority, a new stage, together with a proscenium arch designed by Mr McArthur, the art master, had been installed. There was now a four-foot apron stage, projecting beyond the arch, which significantly increased the acting space available. There were flats available for the scenery and lights of different colours. The switchboard and the wiring were designed by Mr Busby, now designated lab assistant.

A projecting wing masked the entrance onto the stage from the outside door. It was therefore now possible for a performer to use a dressing room elsewhere and, by using the exterior staircase, gain access to the sides of the stage without being seen by the audience. For appearances, there was a corresponding wing on the other side. Each wing had a door, so actors could enter onto the apron without going through the proscenium arch.

The new facilities made it possible to produce a proper school play for the first time. A full-length play with performers drawn from the entire school could now become a reality and on Thursday 18 March 1937 *The Shoemaker's Holiday*, an Elizabethan comedy by Thomas Dekker, was presented. The Morris dancers included in the cast received much applause and the School Orchestra (presumably a scratch one) provided incidental music, but they had to be squeezed into the organ loft.

For some reason old-style form plays were performed on the Friday night, so ticket sales for the school play were limited to the Thursday and Saturday night only. As a result conditions in the hall were cramped. The production was seen as a success artistically and financially, but the reviewer in the school magazine thought that the producers could have taken greater advantage of the new lighting.

The 1938 school play was *Henry V* and it had, including soldiers and monks, a cast of no less than fifty-one. The Shakespearean production was quickly followed by a puppet show presentation of *Faust*, but the reviewer had difficulty in knowing what to make of it. The 1939 production was *North Road*. Despite the production of a school play having become an annual event, Form Dramatic Evenings continued.

The House music competition, which was mainly for singing, but with classes for pianoforte and for other unspecified instruments, continued as an annual event, and music recitals were still held. There were, for instance, performances on 1 February and 1 March 1937 and Dr Hare sang at the second one. Because of demand, the School Concert was performed twice for the first time in 1937, realising over £17.

The stamina of pupils was put to the test on the trips that were occasionally organised. In June 1936 forty boys with two masters, enjoyed a day trip to Stratford-on-Avon, with a visit to Warwick Castle included. Then, on 20 May 1938, no fewer than 270 boys with 12 members of staff had an excursion to London. They had left Bank Top station at 11.35 p.m. on the previous Thursday evening, arriving at Marylebone station at 6 a.m. on the Friday. After touring various parts of London including the City, and the Buckingham Palace and Hyde Park areas, using motor coaches, the party went to the House of Commons. There they were met by C.U. Peat, the town's MP, and after a tour, the school party went on to the Zoo. The return journey started at 5.30 p.m., with an arrival in Darlington at 11.30 p.m. A 4.30 a.m. start was arranged in 1939 for an excursion to Edinburgh, with a trip on Loch Lomond included.

The King's Silver Jubilee of 1935 was celebrated with a knock-out cricket competition. The Mayor and Mayoress visited the school field and each boy was given a bag of cakes and tea in a presentation Jubilee Mug. Later there was a display of talking films in the school hall. On the King's death in the following January pupils were permitted to leave school to go to the Town Hall to hear the Proclamation of the Succession. The school also closed on the day of the royal funeral.

There was an innovation when King Edward VIII made his abdication speech, for it was broadcast in the school hall for the benefit of those pupils who could not get home to hear it. The Coronation of George

VI on 13 May 1937 was also celebrated by the playing of cricket, with a series of knock-out games. Afterwards there was the presentation of a Coronation Mug to every boy, followed by tea. For those who wanted it, there was then an evening cinema show in the school hall.

Dr Hare's first Speech Day was held in the school hall on 26 November 1934, and he reported that, at the end of the last academic year, ten boys had gone on to university or training college. It was the Headmaster's belief that far too many promising boys were leaving school at the School Certificate stage, instead of remaining to sit for Higher Certificate, University Scholarship or Civil Service exams. No institution could do so much for the boy aged between 16 and 18 as the school. On this occasion, his views contrasted with his predecessor's concern that many stayed on without purpose because of poor job opportunities.

The prizes were given by Alderman C.H. Leach, the Chairman of the Education Committee, who said that it was a national waste when promising boys left school early to take up some badly paid job with poor prospects. If they stayed on they could receive a maintenance grant from the council that could actually be more than the paltry wages they received. He doubted that there would ever be free education right up to university level for every boy – that would be a gross national waste – but he was glad that in Darlington there was free access from elementary school to university. If parents had not the means to send a clever boy to the university, the Education Committee might be prepared to give up to the full cost of the boy's education, even though it might run up to more than £200 per annum. The Alderman, however, was not specific about the extent of the assistance that might be available for funding a post-school education.

Almost forty years later, in 1963 after his retirement, it was Dr Hare's turn to present the prizes at Speech Day and in his speech he referred to the problems of obtaining a higher education during the 1930s. He presented a picture less glowing than Alderman Leach's. To qualify for a grant, it was necessary to obtain at least one distinction in the Higher School Certificate. The grant would be subject to a severe means test and, if awarded, would have a loan element of £40 in it, so a three-year course would lead to a debt of £120 to the local education authority (LEA). Dr Hare contrasted the restrictions with the wide availability of grants in 1963, adding that the uncertainties and the financial risks therefore kept Sixth Forms small during the 1930s.

Despite the views he expressed at his first Speech Day, Dr Hare also seems to have also been subject to the contradictory views expressed by Leonard Taylor about pupils staying on in the Sixth Form. In 1936 he wrote to the school magazine to outline the career directions pupils could take. In doing so, he made the point that those interested in entering business or certain professions should bear in mind that, as many employers placed no value on the Higher Certificate, the School Certificate might well be sufficient. He commented that boys should not stay on after sixteen merely to grow older. Unless they were to improve their qualifications, they should leave at sixteen. It was hardly an endorsement of his assertion that no institution could do so much for the boy aged between 16 and 18 as the school

From 1935 the Speech Day was held in the second week of the autumn term instead of in December. The change was made to enable boys proceeding to university to receive their prizes personally before the start of the university year. The post-war practice of inviting distinguished persons from outside Darlington was not yet established, for, in 1936, Alderman Leach again presented the prizes. In his speech, he said that the school had probably reached its maximum numbers and that after the scheduled alterations, there would probably be nothing else for a long time.

There were then 615 in the school, including sixty-five in the Sixth Forms. Sixty-seven out of eighty-four had passed the School Certificate, and at Higher Certificate level, six pupils obtained the Full Certificate. There were also excellent results in the Civil Service Examinations. The Speech Day concluded with a musical interlude and the labs were opened for inspection. By then there were four Senior Prefects and twenty-three ordinary ones.

The school suffered a flu epidemic in early 1938 and 220 pupils, together with 6 masters, were absent during one week. A magazine editorial also commented upon it. Apparently, the staff were surprised by the absence of two of their number believed to be immune to illness; one because of his strict adherence to a special diet and the other because he reputedly kept a secret cupboard full of medicines and tablets.

At the beginning of Dr Hare's tenure, the Old Boys' Association decided to adopt a blazer with the school badge for its members to wear. The new Head, although not an Old Boy, was a member of the committee and was always at the centre of the Association's decision-making process. He and David Carrick administered its Maintenance Fund to assist Old Boys facing difficulties, and in November 1934 were instructed that only one grant on loan should be made every year and that the amount should not exceed £25.

In 1936, when the Association's only real activities were the AGM, the school cricket match and the Maintenance Fund, it was acknowledged that it needed to enhance its activities. Dr Hare could well have been responsible for this initiative, for an article written by a prominent Old Boy appeared in the school magazine asserting that the Headmaster had accused the Association of not keeping up with the progress of the school. As a result, numerous committees had been formed and a special effort was to be made to interest boys leaving the school in membership. As numbers in the school were increasing, there was potentially a large group to recruit from. The Old Boys were also active as football players, but their football club was a separate entity and a proposal by the committee that it be amalgamated with the Association was not agreed upon, despite the willingness of the football club to merge.

The problem over life membership was resolved at the 1936 AGM. It was reported that out of 117 members there were 68 Life Members at £2 each, but the committee seems to have realised that the subscription was too low, for the meeting agreed that cost for future applicants be more than doubled to 4 guineas (£4.20). This was clearly a sensible change as Life Membership had been available for the cost of only eight annual subscriptions. The decision was also made that magazines would no longer be sent to those whose subscriptions were more than two years in arrears! A new development, shortly afterwards, was the holding of the Association's first Dance.

By 1937, when the Association had no fewer than twenty-three vice-presidents, there was a reduced 2/- subscription rate for junior members. Expenditure exceeded income for the last year by £10 11s 1d and both the Dance and the Dinner made losses. There had been a deficit in the previous year too. In 1938, with 115 full members and 7 junior members, the Association was considerably smaller than in post-war years. About half of its income went to the School Club to cover the cost of associate membership, but the payment included the supply of the school magazine to members.

The Association remained active until 1939. In that year a committee meeting took place on 4 April and usual routine business was discussed. There is nothing more in the minute book until 1946 when steps were taken to re-form the Association. There was no formal disbandment when war came.

By now the fee-paying pupils in the Grammar School proper were very much in a minority and in most years during the 1930s, about twenty-two to twenty-nine were admitted. Presumably this figure includes boys from the Preparatory Department who had failed to gain a scholarship place.

In each year to 1934 the register of fee-paying admissions contains references to agreements being cancelled or to damages being paid, so it seems that some fee-paying pupils were withdrawn by mutual agreement, whilst, in other cases, parents were penalised for withdrawing a son on short notice. It is assumed that 'paid damages' indicates a penalty for withdrawing a boy without giving the requisite notice, for it is difficult to see what else it could be. The register for the Darlington High School contains the same wording.

Often boys were admitted on trial, but it is impossible to tell how many of the withdrawn pupils had been in this category. Subsequent academic records of those taken on trial who stayed seem no worse than those who were withdrawn. In 1934, twenty-two fee-paying boys were admitted unconditionally, plus seven on trial, and damages are recorded as being paid for no fewer than fourteen of them, so obviously many admitted unconditionally were amongst those falling by the wayside. After 1934, with the exception of 1936, the register makes no reference to the cancellation of agreements or to the payment of damages.

A separate register for the recording of local authority scholarships indicates that in 1930 and 1931, forty and forty-five respectively were awarded for the Grammar School. However for 1932 there were no fewer than seventy-eight available. This jump in numbers resulted from the thirty or so scholarships available for boys to enter the Central Secondary School passing, on its closure, to the Grammar School. By contrast, in 1920, the Grammar School had possessed only twenty-one local authority scholarship places.

The book also gives details of pupils who missed the scholarship exam, through absence or illness. They were permitted to take the exam officially 'The Secondary School Qualifying Examination', in the following year. The first year recorded was 1930 when thirty-two absent pupils were permitted to take the exam for the various schools, including the Technical School, a year later. The number steadily reduced in subsequent years. The last entry was one for 1949, permitting the sitting of the exam in 1950. Some pupils with grammar school potential would therefore find themselves in a secondary modern school for the first year of their secondary education. It is not known whether a boy admitted to the Grammar School in these circumstances would start in a Shell Form a year late or go directly into a III Form.

There is little documentary evidence about changes to the school uniform and a lot of reliance has to be placed on monochrome photographs and personal reminiscences. It seems clear that when Dr Hare came to the school there were no blazers, but the cap was compulsory for all pupils. Prefects had their own distinctive one. It was similar to the normal one, except that it had panels of gold braid.

Photographic evidence suggests that by the late thirties some pupils were wearing plain blazers, as distinct from the striped-colour blazer with its silver wire badge, but that the practice was far from general. Some of these blazers had their edges braided with the colour of the wearer's house. The wearing of a navy blue blazer was encouraged, but it was not compulsory and it is understood that it was never so, even in later years, when the wearing of one was almost universal. It is ironic that in the 1950s, no pupils in the Lower V wore the school cap, even though it was supposedly compulsory, but they all sported the school blazer which was not!

Those with school colours wore the familiar striped blazer with the badge representing the seal of Queen Elizabeth instead of the interwoven 'DGS' and, at this time, the seal badge was made of silver wire. These blazers would normally have initials, e.g. C, on the breast pocket indicating the sport for which the colours had been awarded.

At the beginning of 1939 a new school cap was introduced. The new design had the coloured segments, denoting the House, replaced by concentric rings of a similar colour. The replacement design continued without further change until the end of the school. However, in post-war years, when the wearing of blazers became general and a coloured ribbon denoting the wearer's House was worn on the top of the breast pocket, all caps were coloured in two shades of blue irrespective of the pupil's House.

Opinion about the change appears to have been divided. A school magazine editorial, written in the facetious manner usual at the time, suggested that there had been a practice of school leavers burning their caps, but this was no longer possible, because the cap now had to be returned to the school when the pupil left.

The changing of the design of the prefects' cap was more controversial. The distinctive gold or yellow piping disappeared and the new caps were described as being 'very blue' and some prefects were said to be clinging on to their beloved yellow stripes. Initially, thirty prefects' caps were supplied to the school.

Dr Hare took a strict view about the wearing of the cap and pupils were expected to wear it even on weekends and there was always a fear of being caught by a prefect without one. Touching the cap to masters was expected. According to one source the Salvation Army bandmaster, who had a son at the school, was concerned about whether his son could wear the Salvation Army hat on a Sunday. He went to see Dr Hare for permission for his son not to wear the cap on Sundays and received a dressing down for even suggesting it!

Hard evidence is difficult to come by, but photographs and the recollections of former pupils suggest that during the war years few pupils wore school blazers. No doubt clothes rationing would have restricted their availability. A photograph of the prefects, taken at the end of the war, shows one wearing a striped blazer, whilst another is in a zip-up jerkin. The rest are wearing suits or sports jackets.

Milk had been supplied to other schools in the county borough for some years, but in 1939 the scheme was extended to the Grammar School. There was a charge of a halfpenny per day and the staff had the task of collecting payment, whilst the prefects were responsible for delivering the milk to the forms. At about the same time, Room 13 under the tower, formerly the staff room and, in earlier years, the resident Housemaster's sitting room, was allocated to the school secretary.

The Head's study was directly above on the first floor, opposite the museum stairs, and had been the Housemaster's bedroom. For many years there was a plate on the door taken from a pew in St. Cuthbert's Church. It had indicated that the pew was reserved for the Headmaster's use. It seems to have been removed after the Sixth Form College was established and its whereabouts are unknown.

In contrast to what was to come, there were few changes to the staff during this period. However, in 1938, no doubt in anticipation of the Head's plans for the teaching of music, Chris Bennett was engaged and went on to serve as music master until 1965. Another newcomer was Mr Snook, who came to the school to teach Latin and, in time, became Senior Classics Master. He had a Latin textbook to his credit which, inevitably, was called 'Snook's Book'.

Sadly Dr Hare's wife died on 8 May 1939 after a long illness.

Societies and Sport in the Late 1930s

The Headmaster seems to have been exaggerating when he referred to the extension of school societies, but the established ones continued to prosper during those final years before the war. At the meeting of the Debating Society held in February 1934 a mock municipal election took place. The candidates were an Independent, a Fascist and a Communist, the latter represented by F.W. Hastie, later a master at the school. The Independent candidate won, but the total number of votes cast exceeded the number present! At another meeting the motion that the BBC should lose its charter was carried unanimously. It was attacked for the quality of its programmes, the proportion of music to talks and for the excessive proportion of classical music. The final meeting of the term was a joint debate with the Girls' High School at the High School. Unsurprisingly, the attendance was unusually high. Shortly afterwards, a Junior Debating Society for the Lower School was formed.

The activities of the Natural History Society followed their customary pattern, with many field trips. A particularly interesting one consisted of a trip to a site at Norton-on-Tees, where human remains had been found on a previous occasion. A dig was undertaken and the Society recovered a hinge, several bones and a skull. The hinge was later dated at around AD 840, so it was assumed that there was a burial ground dating back to about that period.

The Society had a darkroom and members were encouraged to use it and to seek help from staff members if necessary. Animals were kept in the lab, but the death rate seems to have been high. In 1936 the museum was thoroughly overhauled and new rules, intended to keep it in good condition, were introduced. The ships of the German fleet scuttled at Scapa Flow were being raised for scrap at this time and the maker's nameplates from an anti-aircraft gun off the battleship *Konig Albert* were donated to the museum. A preserved shark's jaw from Aden and a piece of a propeller from a shot-down German plane had also been presented. It looks as if the museum soon reverted to a neglected state and some who were pupils at this time have no recollection of it.

The Science Club was flourishing. In January 1935 Dr Hare himself gave it a lecture about surface tension. During the first half of 1936 the club had visits to the Majestic Cinema in Bondgate, Darlington, Peases Mill, Swan Hunter and Armstrong-Saurer at Newcastle. During the following year there were trips to the gasworks, the Majestic Cinema again, Pumphrey's Sugar Mill at Thornaby and Warrenby Steel Works. A trip to Horden Colliery gave the members an opportunity to go underground.

In 1934 Mr Bowley, writing as 'EGB', contributed an article to the magazine on the benefits of chess playing. A Chess Club appeared shortly afterwards under his direction and was instantly successful. By the summer of 1935 it was estimated that between 150 and 200 boys were playing. It was necessary to use the art room and geography room simultaneously and, because of the numbers, leagues had been set up, with a Championship Contest for the stronger members. Matches with outside teams were soon being played and by the beginning of 1936 the club had begun to hold House matches

In 1937 the Belgian Champion gave a blindfold display against ten players from the school. W.R. Ireland, an Old Boy and a member of Darlington Chess Club, managed a draw against him. Matches against the masters and against the Darlington Club were also arranged.

Unfortunately, by about 1937 the Stamp and Cycling clubs appear to have become defunct. F.W. Hastie had been instrumental in forming both and they seem not to have survived his departure to Cambridge University. However, by 1939, the Stamp Club had been revived and an unofficial cycle club existed. There was also an Astronomical 'Section' intended to benefit from the recently acquired telescope, but, oddly, it seems to have been an offshoot of the recently formed Junior Debating

Society. Nevertheless, the number of school societies was still small in comparison with the post-1945 era. Most societies met after school on Fridays at this time.

Apart from the activities of the societies, lectures and film shows were regularly provided. Amongst them was a lecture about the 1933 Everest Expedition, given on 3 March 1939 by J.L. Longland, one of the participants.

Sporting activities carried on much as before under the new regime. Saturdays were occupied with sports fixtures including House matches and with three running events in the year. The practice of confining the playing of soccer to separate terms continued for a few more years, but the school magazine for spring 1939 indicated that the seasons were to be changed over. Rugby would now to be played in the autumn, followed by soccer in the winter term.

For players in the First Cricket Team an incentive was provided for the 1935 season as the decision was made to award a cricket bat to pupils scoring fifty or more runs. That a similar decision had been made six years earlier seems to have been overlooked. The practice continued until at least 1945.

In 1936 the Second XI played six matches, in contrast to the First XI's twelve. Amongst the teams played were the Moths, Barnard Castle School, Mr E. Brown's XI, the Staff and Cockerton Old Boys. For the House teams, the usual pattern continued, in that First and Second XIs played the corresponding team in each other House, thus providing each one with three matches in a season. By contrast, in 1937, the First XI played eight school matches plus four non-school ones, and most were won. Two were against Durham colleges.

The annual Inter-School Sports event continued. The ninth meeting was held at Stockton Cricket Field on 26 June 1936, followed by the 1937 event at Bishop Auckland, when the school finished sixth, i.e. last. The 1939 Inter-School Sports event was hosted by Darlington Grammar School and its team was placed third of six.

One change was made in early 1936 when it was announced that the School Run had been abolished. Although the event went back to the beginnings of the school at Vane Terrace, it was now thought absurd to make several hundred untrained boys run three and a half miles on one afternoon. It was also assumed that the change would be widely welcomed. Clearly the huge growth in the school population, plus the urbanisation of the route between the school and Carmel Road, encouraged the decision.

In 1936 the school's swimming activities were given a boost when the Second Class Swimming Baths, i.e. those in Kendrew Street, were made exclusively available every Tuesday and Thursday from 4.30 to 5.30 p.m. This arrangement went some way to make up for the lack of a swimming pool at the school. Fortunately several masters were keen on coaching and it was hoped to increase the number of entrants for swimming competitions.

The availability of the baths led to the formation of the Swimming Club, under the overall supervision of Mr Graville, and its first season was seen as successful. To celebrate, a gala was held in the First Class Bath in Gladstone Street. The first Swimming Sports, held on 9 June 1936, were won by the Danes with 78 points, in contrast to the unfortunate Saxons who managed 3! The 1938 Sports took place at the Public Baths with the 'Pearl Fishers' Race being held for the first time. Mrs H.R. Dent, wife of the famous publisher of the 'Everyman' series and founder of the nursery school in Elms Road, came from London to present the prizes.

By early 1938 the continuing out-of-school tuition had resulted in the award of seventy-five One Length Certificates and twenty-five Quarter Mile ones, and the standard of swimming was considered to have vastly improved.

By early 1939 there had been a complete change in the Housemasters. Fothergill now led the Britons, whilst Messrs Sunderland, Osborn and Richardson had responsibility for the Danes, Normans and Saxons respectively.

In Dr Hare's early days, the School Boxing Contest and the Inter-School Boxing Competition at Newcastle continued as annual events, as did the gym display. In 1936 both the Boxing Contest, which had the benefit of a new ring, and the gym display, organised by W.S. Richardson, had to be held in the hall, because of the inadequate seating in the school gym. It was, of course, still awaiting replacement. At the end of 1938 a display of vaulting was given at St. George's Hall,

Newcastle for the National Fitness Council. It appears from the limited evidence available that boxing, for which school colours or half colours could be awarded, had ceased to be a school activity by about the end of the decade.

A survival from earlier times was the practice of using the court for playing cricket and football. It is not known whether the practice dated back to the beginnings at Vane Terrace, but it was long established when it was described in the third issue of the school magazine in 1912. The article described in detail the full range of activities taking place at the end of the Wood regime. At that time, of course, there were buildings on three sides only, with the western side being open to the playground. The corridors on the classroom side were enclosed; the open corridors were to come later. Fortunately the windows facing on to the court all had grilles.

At that time there was always some activity in the court, whether at break time, at lunch, after school, during holidays and sometimes even during lesson periods. When there was no sport, boys would laze or gossip or, in icy weather, use it as a slide, but its popularity as a venue for fights was thought to be declining.

Football was played there at break, except for part of the third term. Most players were from the Sixth Form. There were five in each team and it was a recognised form of defence to jam an opposing player against the wall. The writer infers that minor injuries were common.

Games of cricket took two forms. One involved a system called 'Save Times'. Four or five bowlers were engaged at the same time and if a batsman was caught, the boy taking the catch then went to bat. However, for some strange reason, if the batsman was bowled out, the boy who had bowled the preceding ball went in to bat. The alternative was a 'Side Game', whereby runs were scored by hitting the ball against a wall, or better still, by hitting it over the roof. The rules were said to be complicated. Old bats cut down to about 2 to 2 ½ inches (5–6 centimetres) in width were used and wickets measuring 3 feet by 1 foot (90cm by 30cm) were chalked on the wall.

Fives was also played, but infrequently, using one wall only. For it and for the cricket a tennis ball was used.

The playing of football and cricket in the school courtyard survived at least until the end of the 1930s, but the rules seem to have changed. Court football was played after school, except on Wednesdays. Two captains would be chosen, and they would pick teams. Apparently older players were preferred, for younger pupils who tried to take part were usually pushed out into the main playground. The objective was to kick a tennis ball around at random amidst cries of 'sagging' and 'gooing'. Insofar as these words ever had any meanings, knowledge of them is long lost.

Two circumstances would bring a game to an end. Either the ball was lost on one of the surrounding roofs, or the janitor, accompanied by his reputedly fearsome mongrel, turned up. In either event the players then dispersed. The playing of the game was not universally popular and, back in 1921, Mrs Taylor, the Head's wife, had addressed the Debating Society on the topic. She had opposed the practice, giving a graphic account of the inconvenience caused to neighbours.

Court cricket, played during the season, was said to be a game that nobody lost or won. There were no sides and there was no scoring. The object was to knock as many balls as possible 'over the top', that is over the wing behind the tower onto the Mound. After the extension at the rear of the court was built, the bowlers used the archway giving access to the yard for running. Anyone was permitted to take part, including members of staff, but to qualify for an innings a player had to have caught or bowled a previous batsman out. There was no stumping, lbw or hit wickets. A catch was permitted even if the ball bounced off a wall or dropped off the roof.

Playing took place out of school hours, 4.15 p.m. being the most popular, and play during the morning break was confined to prefects only. The school's cast-off bats were used and they had short lives. Tom Pearson, who was at this time a pupil and was later a physics master, thinks the cricket master was responsible for providing a bat every year for the game. A dustbin was used as the wicket. By this time, of course, the galleries with their verandas were on two sides of the court. The buildings had netting running along at roof level and this often trapped the balls. The caretaker's son would eventually retrieve these and sell them back. It is as well, given the location, that soft balls were used.

As with the football, there were objectors and at the end of the decade there was an attempt by some unnamed person or persons to have the game restricted, but the attempt was unsuccessful. Recollections vary as to whether the games lasted beyond the end of the war or not. One belief is that cricket was played in the quad right up to about 1947/8, but there must be a high likelihood that the wartime building of the kitchen on part of the court curtailed these activities.

The Second War

Hector Parr, who came to the school as a Shell boy in September 1939, has expressed the view that the school was remarkably little affected by the Second World War. In a sense he was right for the business of the school, with its routines, largely went on as before. Yet that normality was intermixed with the radically different.

Some changes were immediate. It had been clear from the worsening international situation that war was likely and some preparations had been made. In particular, air-raid shelters were constructed around the edges of the yard and along the front boundary on Vane Terrace, with some cycle stalls being lost as a result. It is understood that the start of term in September 1939 was delayed until the building work was completed. The shelters remained for many years as an unsightly reminder of the war, with circles painted on their walls for use as targets. Complying with blackout requirements seems to have taken longer, with the autumn 1940 copy of the magazine reporting that the school was well on its way to becoming fully blacked-out. It also mentioned that the extension of Summer Time had allowed the old timetable to continue.

Boys in the Sixth Form were employed on fire-watching duties, using the school tower as a vantage point. Another early consequence of the war was that the scheduled December 1939 and March 1940 issues of the school magazine did not appear, but an issue for spring 1940 replaced them. The school holidays had been decreased, and in 1940, as a consequence, the first two weeks of the summer term were given over to football, with cricket then following.

The Speech Day of autumn 1939 set a pattern for the rest of the war. It was an informal event held in the school hall with no parents or friends present, and the prizes were presented by the Headmaster. Even so, there were still not enough seats for all of the 618 boys on the register.

In his address Dr Hare referred to the many staff and boys already involved in National Service in some form or another, going on to say that the school was settling down to the new conditions. He regretted that the government had cancelled the Civil Service exams, particularly as, in the recent ones, the school had been particularly successful. Twelve boys had received appointments in the clerical group, whilst in the executive ones two pupils had been respectively placed 168th and 267th out of 2,700 candidates. A plea for the loan or gift of instruments to enable the School Orchestra to be built up was made.

At the Speech Day next year, however, the Head was able to report that the school had suffered little because of the war and that the senior boys were managing well, despite their war work. He stressed the value of the National Savings Scheme.

The demands of the war led to the hall being used as a dining room for pupils. Morning assembly took place as normal, but it was then necessary to move the chairs to provide tables and seats for eating. Afterwards, everything had to be put back ready for assembly on the following morning. There was a rota system, whereby each form was delegated to do the job in turn.

It is believed that, initially food was brought in already cooked from a central kitchen, but, subsequently, in about 1943, a kitchen (and Emergency Feeding Centre) was built in the quad. The building, in the style of the rest of the school and with lantern ventilators, occupied about one quarter of the area. It lay against the main corridor but did not extend as far as the north wing, and had a chimney that was about the same height as the apex of the hall roof.

Most of the building comprised the kitchen itself, but the front portion at the north end was the tuck shop with a door onto the main corridor. The one it replaced had been a separate building projecting into the court with its entrance in the main corridor. The replacement shop suffered, throughout the war, from limited stocks and the 'sold out' notice sometimes appeared even as early as 1940.

Late in the war arrangements were made to build a proper dining hall. It was to be located in the area between the former Headmaster's house and the Training College with the entrance at the front, facing the school. By the end of 1944 most of the remaining trees in the school grounds had been cut down to make way for the new building, but their destruction was apparently not well received. At this time there were also plans for further additions to the school but they proved abortive.

David Carrick had been thwarted by the outbreak of the First World War in his attempt to compile a list of Old Boys. Now he attempted to produce a list of those from the school serving in the forces. It looks as if the task was passed on to Mr Maw for in the autumn 1940 magazine he published a list containing 149 names, including three already killed in action.

The magazine then went on to publish similar lists at periodic intervals and these included the numbers who were prisoners of war. It is not known how many served in the forces during the war, but in the spring of 1944, 520 were listed. There may have been omissions and, obviously, those who joined up subsequently would not be included.

At that time 53 were listed as having been killed in action, most serving with the RAF, but the War Memorial contains 102 names. British casualties in the Second World War were significantly less than in the First, but the Darlington Grammar School had more. There are two reasons for this. The school had vastly increased in size since the Great War and its pupils provided ideal material for Bomber Command aircrew, whose losses were disproportionately high.

The war ended any thoughts of school camps being held abroad and their replacement was to be a contribution towards the war effort in the form of forestry work. The 1940 camp was held near Selkirk and fifty-five boys participated, of whom thirty stayed for one month. The work involved cutting down trees and related tasks. There was a bonus in that the boys were paid 6d (2½p) per hour for their services. It was not all work and visits and other diversions were provided for them.

The 1941 camp was held on the Staffordshire–Shropshire border and the boys were again involved in forestry work, but, this time, they did little felling. In the following year, the participants found themselves in North Wales on a plain 1,500 feet high. They were involved in cleaning up forestry sites and burning unwanted timber and the work was said to more monotonous than in the two previous years. A sick bay was provided for the first time and it was needed. On 14 August a report on the camp, naming the school, was broadcast on the BBC one o'clock news bulletin. It was the first broadcast made about the schoolboy forestry camps.

The 1943 camp was held at Easter near the Forest of Bowland in Lancashire. Various forestry tasks were performed, but again there was no felling. Some pupils slept in converted buses, which were cold, but most were in the upper room of an old mill.

There was a change for 1944 with the forestry camp being replaced by an agricultural one, held in August and September near Chester-le-Street. Fifty-six boys participated, staying for varying periods up to a maximum of three weeks. Pig feeding, stooking and potato picking were amongst the activities undertaken. Some boys cycled there and back, although there was a suspicion that they benefited from lifts on lorries. The last camp, held under the auspices of Messrs Leighton, Hastie and Wrightson, was held in Somerset a few weeks after the war ended.

In 1941, 405 Squadron of the Air Training Corps was formed in Darlington. It had four flights and A Flight was composed of Darlington Grammar School boys, both past and present. They were drilled by a Home Guard officer, and for some weeks this drill was the sole training provided, with the result that the less enthusiastic left. Then a second town squadron (number 1435) was formed and twenty Old Boys were transferred to it from 405 ATC Squadron to form a nucleus, some going as NCOs. The two flight commanders attended officers' courses during the summer holidays. Lectures, the learning of Morse code and visits to RAF stations were arranged for the rest.

Until the following year, there was no corresponding provision for pupils who were keen on the army but, in March 1942, a decision was made to form a Darlington Battalion of the Army Cadet Force. The Grammar School was asked to form 'A' Company, 200 strong, and recruiting commenced with the result that at the beginning of the summer term 184 cadets paraded at the school. The other three companies were formed from Gladstone Street, Eastbourne and Albert Road schools.

The school staff provided three executive officers for the battalion, namely Lt. Col. Hare (Commanding Officer), Capt. Moss (Adjutant) and Capt. Leighton (Quartermaster). They also provided three company officers, Capt. Burniston, Lt. Golland and 2nd Lt. Allen. A squad of older cadets was formed to be trained by a Home Guard instructor with a view to promotion to non-commissioned rank. Most cadets had been issued with uniforms by early June, although greatcoats were not available until after the war had ended.

At 31 October 1942, the end of the official year, there were eight officers, plus 184 NCOs and cadets, and at a church parade at St. Cuthbert's Church on 15 November, 5 officers and 100 cadets appeared. Some cadets went on camp at Middleton-in-Teesdale. Next year the battalion had its second annual camp at the same location. It was much more ambitious than the first one and 7 officers and 124 cadets from the school attended. There was now a qualification called the War Certificate available and in 1943 there were ninety-three candidates for it.

By 1944 the Force was equipped with rifles and Sten guns, but Capt. Golland was keen to acquire Bren guns, plus equipment for W/T training. It looks as if he had, by this time, replaced Ray Burniston as Company Commander, presumably a result of the traffic accident that cost Burniston his leg. On 1 April 1945 the school's Company became a battalion in its own right as the 7 Darlington Cadet Battalion, DLI.

Former pupils disagree as to whether membership was compulsory. Dr Hare, as Colonel of the battalion, was understandably keen that as many boys as possible should join and no doubt a degree of pressure was applied, but the indications are that membership was voluntary. Compulsion could certainly never have applied to the entire school given the disparity between the population of the school and the numbers in the Force. In 1944 thirteen of the twenty-three prefects were NCOs, but others were not members at all. In the following year, when there were four Senior Prefects and eighteen ordinary ones, three and ten respectively were members of the Army Cadet Force and the majority were NCOs.

Photographs taken of events at the school at this time, such as the presentation of the House Cup at Speech Day in 1944, show a large number of pupils in Cadet Force uniform. In contrast, some boys appear to be wearing ties other than that of the school. There is no evidence to suggest any policy to encourage the wearing of uniforms during school hours and the explanation may be that pupils having parades or other functions after school were simply avoiding having to change at school. Parents, of course, may have considered that being in uniform avoided wear and tear to other clothes. They were, of course, subject to rationing.

Eventually a Naval Section of the Cadet Force was formed after a minimum requirement of twelve cadets had been met. On 1 March 1945 it came into being under the leadership of Lt. W.S. Richardson and Dr Wicksteed. There was no Air Force Section within the Cadet Force until later, but during the war the Grammar School held classes for RAF cadets in maths and aeronautics. Some pupils from the school went in the hope that when they were called up they would be considered for flying duties as a result.

The war led to staffing problems, with a large number of temporary teachers, many of them women, being engaged. Whilst only five masters from the school left for war service, the problem was compounded by the numbers leaving other schools and by those about to enter the profession going into the forces.

The first masters to go were Messrs Snook and Taylor in 1940. By 1941 Norman Sunderland had joined up, as had Mr Hobson. Jim Osborn, who had shortly before replaced Axford as Senior English Master, a post which he held until retirement in 1968, went into the navy and, from what he later told his pupils, had ample time for reading.

Miss Henson retired and died soon afterwards and, at about this time, the deaths of two former members of staff were reported: Ada Mary Williams, who had run the Preparatory Department from 1905 to 1918, was the lady who had expressed concerns about her future when Philip Wood resigned, whilst Alfred Dresser, an Old Boy, had been the part-time drawing master from 1896 to 1929.

Two long-term members of staff left in 1943. H.R. Hughes, who came to the school in 1915 to teach French and German and who had been the Normans' Housemaster for many years, retired. Fothergill, Senior

Classics Master and noted for his organisation of the school camps, also left. Eye strain and health considerations had resulted in him finding employment as a supervisor in the Forestry Camps under the Ministry of Supply. He had been the Britons' Housemaster and was replaced by Graville.

Then, in the following year, L.C. Ord, who had come in 1915 to teach maths, retired.

Appendix II, which lists in alphabetical order the known members of staff at the school, includes those temporary teachers during the war years who have been identified.

Inevitably, the school's sporting activities were affected by the war. Even at the beginning of 1940 it was reported that some sporting events had to be curtailed, but much activity remained.

Cricket seems to have thrived and inter-school matches still took place. The sporting highlight during these years was probably a visit by H.B. Sutcliffe, the Yorkshire and England cricketer. He gave a lecture and batting demonstration for all of the boys in the school. By 1940, possibly earlier, the school had a junior cricket XI as well as the two senior teams.

One difficulty faced by the teams was that Wilson, the long-serving groundsman, went into the RAF and, as no replacement could be found, his work had to be done by squads of boys, supervised by staff members. The Education Authority, however, agreed to lay concrete wickets and these would provide for three practice pitches, or batting ends and two complete pitches. In 1941 the First Cricket XI managed to play fifteen matches, many against scratch teams such as Mr Moss' XI and those of other staff members. There were the usual games against the staff and the Old Boys, but matches were also played against the Royal Ordnance Factory, Darlington Second XI and the Railway Athletic Second XI.

The following cricketing season was described in the school magazine as probably the most eventful in the history of the school. The laying of the concrete had resulted in an improved standard of play. Extended coaching had been introduced and a booklet containing suggestions was produced and distributed throughout the school. Yet despite the claimed improvement in standards, of the ten First XI matches played, only one was won, with two lost and seven drawn. The school had at least now acquired a temporary groundsman. By 1943 the First XI was more successful. It played twelve matches, winning five, drawing three and losing four.

At one point, the cricketers requested the Games Committee to consider extending the season to a full term, instead of devoting the first month of the summer term to athletics. It seems unlikely that the appeal had any success, for, in later years, pupils continued to be engaged in athletics during the early part of the summer term.

As to rugby, the autumn 1940 season was seen at the time as probably being the most successful in the school's history. Colours were re-awarded to five players, and awarded to another eleven, with five being given the right to wear the school blazer.

There is a brief, and tantalising, reference in the spring 1944 magazine to the school now having potatoes instead of football pitches. However, any contribution to the 'Dig for Victory' campaign does not seem to have adversely affected the playing of matches, for, during the 1944 season, eight soccer games were played by the First XI. Association football was still played in January and February, but whether the teams managed as best they could before the next crop was planted or played elsewhere is not known. Two of the 1942 matches were against University College, Durham, which must have had a depleted number of students.

At the beginning of 1941 the old requirement for House athletics that a competitor had to be in the first three to score points was altered. Henceforth each House member would acquire points for his House if he met one of two fixed standards. A competitor who now achieved a High Standard would be awarded two points for his House, and receive one if he gained a Low Standard.

The Athletic Sports Day continued to take place as an annual event, as did the Senior and Junior School Runs. The 1941 Senior House Run started at noon, but the entire school stopped work at 11.45 to watch. During the year, in addition to contests with other schools, the harriers had three competitions against army teams – a sign of the times. In 1942 the old idea of a contest against a cycle team from the school was revived. The runners won this time. Swimming activities continued, but it was stressed that the function of the Swimming Society was to teach as many boys as possible to swim, not to produce a few swimmers of individual brilliance.

As the war ground on, the situation deteriorated. The magazine of January 1945 reported that all Second XI and Junior XI cricket fixtures – presumably those in 1944 – had to be cancelled because of wartime restrictions and the lack of a full-time groundsman. There was also a restriction on the number of rugby games.

In the autumn 1941 magazine, the Britons' House report, not for the first time, complained of the House's disadvantage due to a shortage of numbers. It mentioned that the House contained only 10 per cent of the Sixth Form. By 1944, they were said to be doing a little better, as their numbers were now more nearly equal to those of the other Houses. Each House team continued to play each other House team once only.

There was, of course, much that was normal and there were also innovations unconnected with the war. One of these was the introduction of the Prefects' Dance. The first took place in 1939 at the Queen's Hall. Most of the Upper VI, some of the Lower VI and, by invitation, some of the Upper V were present, as were some Old Boys. Nothing was said about where their partners came from, so presumably those who attended brought their own. A rota of prefects was formed to keep out 'undesirables'. By December 1941 the Dance was being held at the Baths Hall. On that occasion 400 Old Boys, friends and pupils attended. There were still concerns about those without tickets attempting to gain admission and there were some problems at the door.

The 1943 Prefects' Dance was held on 2 November in the Technical College Hall, but in the following January there was a second function, described as the Annual Dance, at the Baths Hall. The event was a success, with music provided by the Dance Band of the Royal Hussars, no less, but again there were difficulties in keeping out undesirables. In later years tickets were sold at the Darlington High School, avoiding the need for boys to find their own partners beforehand, but it is unclear when this practice started. The recollection of those who were prefects at the time suggests that initially the girls who came were students from the Training College next door, not High School girls. At this time, Sixth Formers were invited by the Training College to provide men for their country dancing, so this is probably why, in the early days of Prefects' Dances, the involvement was with the college, not the High School.

That mysterious institution, the Prefects' Court, continued. Indeed, it survived for many more years. The prefects, or at last the seniors, had a room of their own on the first floor and the courts were held there. The number of prefects involved seems to have been small and Tom Pearson thought their powers were limited to dishing out lines to pupils, usually for failure to wear a cap. The spring 1940 magazine reported that the court had been put on a more businesslike footing. It was now held after school and was held in the presence of a 'public gallery', but spectators took no part in the proceedings. The courts were then regularly held on Friday evenings after school.

At the same time, several boys in the Lower VI became 'apprentices' to those prefects who had executive positions, but it is not known for how long this practice continued. At the beginning of the 1939–40 year, there were four Senior Prefects and twelve ordinary ones, but no fewer that eleven more were appointed during the early part of the year. The number of Senior Prefects seems to have remained constant at three but there was a tendency for the number of ordinary ones to increase. There were nineteen by early 1941, but twenty-three by 1944.

In October 1940, F. Weston, the School Captain, called a prefects' meeting to outline a scheme for a prefects' club. It was intended to govern the prefects' out-of-school activities and it would provide table tennis, chess, informal debates and the like. Hiking trips and an informal summer camp were also proposed. Although everyone present agreed with the proposal, it appears to have immediately sunk without trace.

More successful was the proposal to establish a youth club, called the Queen Elizabeth Club. It was formed in 1943 and was to cater for both pupils and Old Boys (presumably recent school leavers). It met on Wednesday and Saturday evenings and had a Drama Group, a Discussion Group and a Music Section. Sporting and Handicraft Sections were also intended. A canteen and a Smoke Room were provided, all for a subscription of 5/- (25p) per annum. It apparently had a shaky start, but according to the summer 1944 magazine was, by then, making an impact. Unfortunately, the club stalwarts were said to be all in the Lower School. By 1945 it was organised on a less formal basis; in other words there was less school control and, as a result, it was a bigger success. It still offered a canteen, films, an orchestra and drama. Then it seems to have disappeared.

As to music, by 1942 there were ninety boys in instrumental classes, with twenty-seven of them in the main orchestra. There were also thirty (including some 10-year-olds) in the second. However, shortages of players in certain sections and of instruments continued. A year later, there were 100 under musical tuition. The School Orchestra was also called upon to play during the intervals at the Form Dramatic Evenings.

After the war, in 1946, because of increased need, Dr Hare was able to persuade the LEA to appoint Miss Gregory and Mrs Gomez as full-time string teachers. Later, funds were also provided for instruments to enable the school to employ visiting teachers for woodwind, brass and percussion.

The House Music Competition continued throughout the war. On 17 July 1944 Sir Edward Bairstow, Director of Music at York Minster, adjudicated. The event was recorded with a photograph taken of performers with Sir Edward. Two out of the three are wearing open-necked shirts, whilst Dr Hare has discarded his gown, but is wearing his mortarboard.

During that summer there was excitement at the school in that there was a radio broadcast of the School Orchestra. It was even heard in Assam by an Old Boy, Capt. C.M. Bishop. The broadcast took place at the unsociable hour of 2.45 a.m. on the North America Service of the BBC and was described as 'Darlington England Calling Darlington America'. After the opening announcement the orchestra was heard to play about eight bars of 'Scarlet and Gold' before being faded out. There was a section in the programme about Pease's Mill, a sound track of the *Flying Scotsman* passing Darlington station, and the voices of various local personages were heard. The item had been recorded locally a few days earlier by the BBC's recording car.

Although the School Dramatic Evenings continued through the war, conditions precluded lavish productions and in 1943 the Preparatory boys' production did not go ahead due to illness. Later in the war each year of pupils, rather than individual forms, was responsible for productions. It looks as if the production of school plays was suspended.

In early 1941 the two Debating societies and the Natural History and Science societies were still functioning. It appears that the Astronomical Society had recently become defunct for a little while before members were being urged to take advantage of the blackout and to use the observatory. Despite the demise of the Society, Hector Parr was allowed to use the observatory and perhaps others were too.

Outside visits were still possible early in the war. In the period up to 1941, the Science Society was able to visit the Electricity Works, the Majestic Cinema in Bondgate and Darlington Gas Works, but, as conditions deteriorated, arranging trips became next to impossible.

The Debating societies had a patchy existence. The usual audience at a senior debate numbered about thirty, but, to increase attendances, the Head started to hold discussions in place of debates. It looks, however, as if the change was not successful, for in 1942 the Society reverted to holding debates. Then the Junior Debating Society folded but after a lapse of about twelve months was revived. During one term, at this stage, the Senior Society managed only two debates.

Yet not all was gloom. New societies, in the form of the Play Reading Society and the Aeronautical Society under the auspices of Mr Brydon, were formed and Mr Ives re-established the Stamp Club. In 1944 there was also a strictly unofficial society, known as the Roof Climbers. Its activities included going up on the school roof, but after several minor accidents it was, unsurprisingly, disbanded.

Another new activity, introduced in 1940, was a Sixth Form competition. Seven members of the Upper VI gave speeches not exceeding five minutes in length to the entire school and the winner was H. Bowe, who argued that prefects were necessary. It is not known whether the competition continued into a second year.

After the production delays during the earlier part of the war, the school magazine continued to appear on a fairly regular basis, but in 1942 and 1943 there were intervals of a year between issues. In addition, the restrictions on paper supplies reduced the magazine's size and from the spring 1944 issue it no longer had an outer cover. Nevertheless, there were still photographs in it.

There were other factors affecting production. For instance the library report for summer 1944 had to be held over because the navy had whisked away the Head Librarian before he had had time to write it! At the same time, despite the ongoing difficulties, it was intended to have a magazine every term and there were, apparently, plenty of enthusiastic contributors, except in the Sixth Form. Nevertheless, a year later, the editor was complaining about the lack of magazine contributions, saying that the Prep boys were the best in this respect. The intention was fulfilled, except for a lapse back to two issues in 1947 and 1948.

In 1944 the editor's complaint about a lack of general support for sporting and other school activities from the Shells to the Fifths provoked a letter from a Lt. Col. Wood, an Old Boy and possibly Philip Wood's son. He was unhappy about the then current fashion, encouraged by such people as Professor Joad, the broadcaster, to denigrate the Victorians. He went on to urge all pupils, past and present, to honour the school tie. By autumn, the editor had discerned an improving spirit in the school both in societies and on the games field.

If anything, the library prospered during the war. In the spring of 1941 School Certificate forms were permitted to use the library at break times and, later in the year, an increase in the reading of 'serious' books was reported. A year later it was said to be still growing in popularity, particularly as to the reading of periodicals about the war and aviation. The wartime shortages, however, prompted a request for donations of books. The intention was obviously to benefit the younger pupils, for amongst the authors mentioned were Enid Blyton, W.E. Johns, Henty, 'Sapper', Arthur Ransome and Conan Doyle.

The many outside activities that had sprung up during the war worried the Head and he mentioned the subject at the 1943 Speech Day, which, like all of the wartime ones, was an internal event. He was concerned that academic training might suffer as a result of boys 'spending an uncontrolled amount of leisure' in these activities. He wanted them to join school organisations where better control could be exercised compared with outside groups.

Changes to the structure of the forms continued. In the academic year 1939–40 Lower VI General disappeared. This form had been introduced largely for the benefit of those intending to take the Civil Service exams, cancelled on the outbreak of war. Zoology was introduced for the first time as a subject for Upper VI science in this period. The numbers in forms seem to have held up during the war. In July 1943 the Upper VI, for instance, numbered nineteen pupils, with forty-three in the Lower VI. These figures stand comparison with the late 1930s.

It appears that inkwells were still in use at this time, as Hector Parr remembers boys putting calcium carbide in them to produce horrible classroom smells. The familiar sight of boys going about with ink patches on their blazer pockets as a result of their having to carry with them a bottle, often insecurely closed, belonged to a later era. It is as well that the school blazers were navy blue. The idea of anyone using a ball pen in the post-war era was, of course, unthinkable.

Despite the upheavals and uncertainties of war, many looked ahead to the years of peace to follow, and the implementation of far-reaching changes to the school even before the war had ended was the result.

The structure of education, particularly for older pupils, had been regarded as unsatisfactory by many for some years. In broad terms, secondary education was the preserve of those attending grammar or technical schools. There were exceptions – the recently opened Eastbourne School in Darlington seems to have been one – but most children were leaving school at age 14 with nothing more than an elementary education.

The Education Act, passed in 1944 with all-party support, represented an attempt to remedy the situation. All children would receive a secondary education from the age of eleven, with a post-war minimum school-leaving age of fifteen. Those not educated in a grammar or technical school would attend a new category of school, a secondary modern. Given that most secondary modern schools were housed in old school buildings, with the same teachers and with no significant improvements in funding, there is scope for argument as to how successful they were.

More to the point, however, is the impact of the legislation upon the existing local authority grammar schools. Most of them, including Darlington, were still admitting a proportion of fee-paying pupils. Whilst Darlington Education Authority's provision was considerably greater, nationally only 14 per cent of places were free. The principle adopted by the new legislation, which did not extend to independent schools, was that grammar school places should be made available only to those who passed an entrance examination designed to measure intelligence.

The 11-plus exam was therefore born and fee paying was to disappear. Furthermore, it was no longer appropriate for a grammar school to provide for under-11s, so the Preparatory Department was doomed.

At the same time the Education Authority decided to give those who failed to enter the school after sitting the 11-plus a second opportunity. Upwards of thirty boys, successful in a 13-plus examination, would now be admitted to the Fourth Form and, for the second time, the school would have a Remove form. The summer 1944 issue of the school magazine recorded that the changes were viewed with mixed feelings. The Education Committee also decided to convert maintenance allowances into scholarships and to lower the qualifying standards. Financial assistance for staying on beyond the school-leaving age would therefore become easier to obtain.

The changes were quickly implemented. In July 1944 there were still three Prep forms, containing eighty-seven boys, occupying Rooms 23 and 24 on the first floor above the library. At the end of term, Form I ceased to exist and there were no new entrants to the department. The disappearance of Form I coincided with the arrival of the first Remove pupils ready for the 1944–5 year.

It should be mentioned that most of those who were successful in the 13-plus exam went to the Technical School in preference to the grammar and high schools, but there were also a few pupils at the Grammar School who, after a couple of years, transferred to the Technical School.

Austerity

The war ended but rationing did not, and the nation, beset by shortages and heavily in debt, struggled to adjust to a changed world. For the Darlington Grammar School the immediate concerns were the ongoing effects of the Education Act of 1944 and the need to find permanent staff. The need to contend with wartime bureaucracy also continued. A memo to the Headmaster, dated 25 January 1946, still exists. It requests him to provide information about school leavers, apparently to enable a check to be made as to the whereabouts and condition of their gas masks.

There were ongoing anxieties about the effect of the recent Education Act upon the future of grammar schools and the editor of the school magazine addressed the subject in the first post-war issue, number 67 dated September 1945. Having started by regretting the growing number of intellectual snobs deprecating loyalty and respect towards any 'alma mater', the editor went on to express concerns about what he saw as a levelling-down tendency afoot in the academic world. Issue number 69 returned to the subject. The editorial repeated the concerns about the effects of the new legislation. The issues were a little more specific this time and included a reference to the reduction in schools' holidays to bring them more in line with the secondary modern schools. In was claimed that account was not being taken of the special circumstances – perhaps a reference to homework – of grammar schools. Only eighteen days off were now allowed for Christmas.

The Headmaster was also worried. At the 1946 Speech Day, held at the Baths Hall instead of in the school hall and the first one attended by friends and parents since 1939, he stressed the dangers of the new Education Act to schools like his own. He warned of the tendencies to level down, arguing that a widening of the gap between public and grammar schools would be the result. Dr Hare was not deterred from expressing his views by the presence of Mr Hardman, Darlington's MP and Parliamentary Secretary to the Ministry of Education, who presented the prizes.

The topic was also raised at the next Speech Day, but this time, the Headmaster had an ally on the platform in the form of his predecessor, L.W. Taylor, who was to present the prizes. Dr Hare repeated his concerns about the lowering of standards in the name of equality and was disturbed by the proposed abolition of the School Certificate, arguing for having a modified Higher Certificate as an exam for university entrance. He also considered that the threatened abolition of external exams altogether would discourage the necessary belief in hard work.

Taylor expressed doubts as to whether the country at large realised what grammar schools stood for and pointed out that a very great percentage of commissioned officers in the war were from such schools. The 1944 Act was permeated with a desire for equality and attempted to bring all secondary schools to the same level. Parents would not be persuaded when the leaving age was 15 and schools had inferior facilities to grammar schools. He stressed the need to avoid lowering the position of grammar schools to level the gap between them and the secondary moderns. The leadership must come from grammar schools.

Taylor ended by requesting two extra days' holiday for the pupils. The request was greeted with 'a fervent demonstration of approval'.

There were perhaps two strands to these concerns about the future. One fear was that the perceived need to provide a better education for secondary pupils elsewhere would lead to a diversion of expenditure from grammar schools to secondary modern schools. The result would be that any improvement in the secondary moderns would be at the expense of the grammar schools. Furthermore, because the same constraints would not be imposed upon public schools, any gap between their standards and those of the grammar schools would widen.

In a sense, the argument was a rehearsal of the one that would, a few years later, dominate the debate about comprehensive schools.

The second issue was about exams. The Norwood Report of 1943 had recommended that there should be no external exams in any schools before university entrance and that a detailed school report should take the place of the School Certificate at sixteen. Undoubtedly Dr Hare was referring to this proposal when he expressed his fears about the abolition of external exams.

In the event, the proposal was not implemented. Instead the General Certificate of Education (GCE) was to be introduced in 1950–1 as a replacement for the School Certificate. It was seen as offering greater flexibility in that the old requirement that passes in a block of subjects were required was ended. Initially no pupils under sixteen were to be presented as candidates, so secondary modern pupils, with a leaving age of 15, were automatically excluded. No doubt the grammar schools were relieved by this stipulation, although it proved to be short-lived. Perhaps it was the imposition of the age limit that led to Dr Hare adjusting the express stream arrangements to his later system.

By the end of the decade the introduction of the GCE had been effected and at the Speech Day in November 1951, the Head was able to report that, despite misgivings, the new GCE had proved itself a success. He had, at the 1948 Speech Day, expressed the hope that the universities would clarify their attitude to the changes and make known the standards expected of entrants and it appears that he was satisfied that they had done so. At the 1952 Speech Day he suggested that a pass in the School Certificate had been possible for an intelligent boy without real effort, but the GCE had raised standards. The new system was more flexible.

The situation in secondary modern schools continued to be unsatisfactory. For many years, until exams like the Northern Counties Certificate were introduced, large numbers of secondary modern pupils were leaving school without any paper qualifications. The situation in Darlington was slightly ameliorated because of the possibility of moving from a secondary modern as a result of passing the 13-plus exam.

During this period of uncertainty, the school faced the possibility of another change; perhaps a more welcome one. The Education Authority prepared a plan for future education in Darlington and it provided for the moving of both the High School and the Grammar School to a new site at Hummersknott. There was, however, an option of extending the Grammar School on its existing site. It was seen as not complying with the standards required by the Ministry of Education for school and playing field sites. As early as the first post-war Dinner, the President of the Old Boys' Association referred to the school being located at its new site, with building work starting in 1951.

The girls obtained their new school; the boys did not and the Grammar School had to make do with what it had. The Ministry's standards were modified, with the result that the Grammar School then complied with them without the need to move elsewhere. Additional buildings were promised, but the school had to wait till 1960 for them. The Authority's plan also provided for new secondary modern schools at Branksome and Haughton and, when building work eventually started, the new school at Branksome would provide another threat to the Darlington Grammar School.

During the post-war period of adjustment, steps were taken to re-establish the school uniform. According to the magazine, the school cap had been practically extinct since the war, but it now became compulsory wear for the first four years, but, as mentioned earlier, by the 1950s no one in the fourth year (Lower Vs) was ever seen with a cap.

In addition, all pupils were required to wear the school tie, which, at this time, had colours similar to the Normans. A magazine editorial implied that till this time some fairly striking neckwear was being worn. The wearing of blazers, although not compulsory, was encouraged, but they were difficult to obtain, doubtless due to continued rationing. Contemporary photographs indicate that, apart from the occasional striped-colours example, blazers remained a rarity.

The staffing of the school also returned to normality. At the beginning of the summer term 1949 Mr F.W. Hastie, Old Boy and former Cambridge Senior Wrangler, joined the school staff. By then Messrs Brydon, who came in 1933 as a science master and was latterly the Normans' Housemaster, Bowley and Maw had gone. The masters who had been in the forces came back and, amongst the other new members of staff were Messrs Thompson and Hancock, who were to serve for many years. Miss Fearon the temporary secretary also left, being replaced by Miss Fail. Others returning were Busby the laboratory technician and Wilson the groundsman.

In 1946 W. Kay was still caretaker and the school now had a Welfare Officer, Miss K. Banks. She left in the summer of 1948 and her duties were then reorganised, making a replacement unnecessary. School dinners were now an established feature of school life and by the end of 1945, double sittings, with 150 boys each, were the norm, with nearly half of the boys at the school staying for them. By 1950 there was a third sitting in the dining hall.

The high turnover of staff continued into the later part of the decade. Amongst the long-standing members of staff who left were Ives, who came in 1920 to teach physics, and Gus Golland, who had arrived in the same year. He was succeeded as Senior Geography Master by G.T.L. Chapman. In 1950 J.P. Leighton, who had come to the school to teach science in 1924 and been Quartermaster for the Cadet Force, died suddenly.

The last of the masters, including Crane and Graville, who had transferred to the school when the Central Secondary School closed, also retired. Crane's eventual replacement as scripture teacher was Maurice Lumsden. Amongst the other new masters who came at this time were 'Cosh' Graham and J.H. 'Jasper' Green, both Old Boys and former House Captains of the Danes. Of six new members of staff who came in early 1950, four served the school for many years. They were Len Griffiths, Eric Pratt, John ('Jet') Turner and Harry Welding.

Outside the school Eric Pratt was notable for his leadership of Greenbank Operatic Society which specialised in productions of Gilbert and Sullivan. He was able to recruit as lead singers both 'Jet' Turner and Maurice Lumsden. Interestingly, the lead comedy singer from 1959 with the Doyly Carte Operatic Company, John Reed, was an Old Boy of the school.

At about the end of 1949 Ray Burniston and Percy Moss exchanged their rooms, so Shell A moved from Room 1 on the Quad to Room 24 above the library. Burniston's artificial leg appeared to have no knee joint, so using stairs presented him with a problem. After 1950, as the then longest-serving assistant master, he would take morning assembly when both Dr Hare and W.S. Richardson were absent and he would manfully swing his leg through a wide arc on each tread of the stairs to gain access to the hall platform.

In 1944 thirty-three boys entered the newly established IV Remove, but after two years the number entering the form had fallen to twenty, reducing to fourteen in 1949. At this time the IV and V Lower years still had a 'D' form, but the two forms were later renamed 'General' and for teaching purposes were integrated with the Remove forms. One result was that, to bring them into conformity with the Remove boys who had never been taught a foreign language, the pupils in the General forms ceased to have any language tuition. A significant number of the pupils entering the school at thirteen were found to have the potential for a university education and by the time they reached the VI forms they therefore needed to undertake a high-intensity course of study to acquire a language GCE to satisfy matriculation requirements.

Until 1947 there were three V Upper forms, each identified by the name of the Form Master, but a fourth – V Upper Remove – then appeared. Clearly, there was a perception that even after two years in the school, the 13-plus entrants still needed to be kept in a separate category. By 1950 the V Upper had swollen to five forms, including the Remove, but the separate form for the 13-plus entrants disappeared shortly afterwards.

The VI Form was still divided between Science and Modern forms and there was, as yet, no separate Third Year VI. The subjects taught increased in number and by 1949 they included economics, Greek and geology. The Head estimated that if a multilateral school were to offer the same facilities, it would need to have over 2,000 pupils on the roll. The school was entering pupils for state scholarships and in 1948 three were awarded, with two more boys on the reserve list. Two years later two pupils were successful, with a third on the reserve list.

The coming of peacetime did nothing to diminish the Cadet Force. If anything, it thrived, broadening its appeal by extending its range of activities. The expected ones continued with various parades and visits to army camps. The Force's Annual Camp was held at Amble on 2 July 1945, with the 149 cadets attending being housed in wooden huts. Training was limited to the mornings. The magazine report stated that the location could be mentioned because of the relaxation of reporting restrictions following upon the end of the war. Greatcoats were at last available and there was also a scheme for the supply of good army-type boots at reasonable cost.

Cadet Force dances became popular. The first was held at the Baths Hall on 8 December 1945, followed by two in the following November at the Queen's Hall. The dances then continued as an annual entry in the social calendar, supplemented in 1947 by an officers' dinner, held in the school library. The Force also had the distinction of providing a Guard of Honour when Field Marshall Montgomery visited Darlington on 22 April 1947. Many athletics events were also organised by it.

Perhaps more surprising was the organising, at the invitation of the Cadet Battalion, of a concert given by the Halle Orchestra under Sir John Barbirolli at the Baths Hall on 12 October 1945. The school had a block booking of 320 seats for it. Then, in 1947, the Cadet Force organised a return visit of the orchestra.

Candidates continued to present themselves for the War Certificate exam. In January 1947 it was reported that ninety-seven had passed Part I, whilst four had failed. For Part II there were forty passes with five failures. In the following year, however, the exam results were described as disappointing. By then Gus Golland was Battalion Major, whilst Dickie Fairbairn was OC of 'C' Company, assisted by Lt. Magoon. Moss and Leighton were still captains and there was a Lt. Mellor who was not on the school staff. During 1947 seven members, presumably from the Signals Platoon, were able to obtain their certificates as Cadet Assistant Instructors in Signalling after attendance at a course at Sedgefield.

The Cadet Force, including the Naval Branch, went for training at Whitburn Camp from Thursday 2 October 1947 to the following Sunday. Training was given for both parts of the War Certificate and there was also map reading, fieldcraft and squad drill. As a test the cadets were left several miles away from the camp and had to make their own way back. They were, however, in wireless communication most of the time. In addition, shooting on the ranges was provided and there was free time, either in Sunderland or on the cliffs.

The Naval Section also remained active. In the summer of 1948 twenty-six cadets went on a naval camp to HMS *Adamant*, a Submarine

Depot ship at Portsmouth. They experienced sleeping in hammocks, took a sea trip in a destroyer and had flights with the Fleet Air Arm. In June 1949 fifteen cadets had a training week in MS *Hunter*, a tank landing craft. One of the less agreeable tasks was the scrubbing of the mess. A Naval Camp was held in HMS *Diadem* at Chatham, from 13 to 20 August 1949. The cadets scrubbed the deck and learned about gunnery and rope making. They were fed a large amount of soup and bully beef.

On 26 September 1948 a contingent under Maj. Golland attended a service at Durham Cathedral. Four days later, the camp, under the Headmaster's command, was held at Whitburn and eight buses took 200 cadets with 13 officers there. The Part II candidates engaged in a mock battle. The Battalion also competed at Roundhay Park, Leeds in athletics championships. During 1949 the Force ceased to be the 7th Battalion, becoming 'the Queen Elizabeth Grammar School Combined Cadet Force'.

An Air Force Section, commanded by Mr Magoon, was finally formed and it visited an unnamed RAF station on 1 March. The cadets later went to camp at Manby, where they had some flights. The bystanders at the railway station and the RAF personnel were apparently intrigued by the cadets' uniform, for, apart from RAF blue forage caps, they were dressed in khaki.

The existence of the Force ended on 31 March 1950. In the previous September a survey had shown that an overwhelming majority of parents did not wish their sons to join the Cadet Force and, after several meetings, the decision to disband was taken. The attitude of the army seems to have played a part. In 1949, despite 12 months' notice being given to the army asking for a camp, it failed to materialise at the last moment. The impression was given that the situation would never improve. Of the thirty-one Sixth Form leavers recorded in 1949, only eleven had been CCF members.

During the Force's existence, 369 cadets in the Army Section had obtained a War Certificate 'A' Pt. I, with 133 gaining Pt. II. In the smaller Naval Section thirty-one cadets passed the Leading Seaman's exam with fourteen passing the one for Petty Officers.

* * *

252

There were post-war revivals too, including the Old Boys' Association and the school camp. Steps to restore the Association to life began with a meeting chaired by Dr Hare on 29 January 1946. Those present appointed themselves as a sub-committee to get it running again. The Association was soon resurrected and, by September, secretaries for the badminton and rugby sections had been appointed. It had also been agreed to pay 3 guineas per term to the school groundsman for his services and to have 300 of each issue of the school magazine, at 1/- (5p) per copy, provided to the Association.

About 100 attended the first AGM of the restored Association, held on 8 October 1946. The organisation was to be called 'The Darlington Queen Elizabeth Grammar School Old Boys' Association', with a subscription of 10/6d (521/2p) per annum.

The tolerance shown pre-war towards defaulting members was not in evidence, for membership benefits would be now lost when a sub was four months in arrears. There would be an additional subscription for each section and the section committees would decide the amounts. Initially there were sections for association football, rugby, badminton, cricket, gymnastics, the magazine and the orchestra, but when desired, others could be formed. There was a requirement, later to cause some problems, that all members of sections, except for ladies playing badminton, had to be full members of the Association. The initial annual subscriptions for membership of the soccer, rugby and badminton sections were 5/- (25p) each. There were also PT sessions held by W.S. Richardson, who became Second Master in 1946 on Carrick's retirement.

The holding of Annual Dinners (dress optional), with tickets priced at 10/6d, and Dinner Dances was resumed and during 1948 there were also recorded music meetings and a film show. The first Annual Dinner, held at the Imperial Hotel on 6 December 1946 and presided over by Lord Henderson, attracted 120 members. The guests extended from J.W. Malkin, the last survivor from the Leadyard School, aged 87, to A.G. Nokes, who left the school in 1945. A year or so later, Lord Henderson, the first Old Boy to receive a peerage, was appointed Parliamentary Undersecretary at the Foreign

Office. Later, he was elected to the Association's committee, but seems not to have attended any meetings.

At the 1949 AGM, following upon a suggestion by Percy Moss, it was resolved that all members of staff who were not Old Boys would be made Honorary Members. An amendment to include all staff members was withdrawn, with the result that Old Boys on the staff still had to pay a subscription to enjoy membership benefits. It was also decided that female staff members would be excluded from membership. The rules of the re-established Association originally made no provision for life membership, but the omission was made good in 1951 when such membership again became available. Initially, the once and for all subscription was £10 10s 0d.

Unsurprisingly, the provision of a war memorial for the Old Boys who had died in the recent war had to be considered. The topic was first discussed in 1946, when Dr Hare, who normally attended committee meetings, suggested that an electric blower for the organ could be provided. At an AGM of the Association, held in the school library on 7 October, Dr Hare outlined the plan for a war memorial and it was agreed that an appeal letter was to be sent to members.

By 1949, a proposed design for a memorial tablet was produced and Almonds, the local engravers in Duke Street, undertook the work at a cost of £110. Arrangements were also made for repainting the names on the 1914–8 memorials for an additional £54. At an Open Day in 1951, a service of dedication of the Memorial took place. Parents and next-of-kin of those named were invited.

By now the Association was thriving, although few members had enthusiasm for attending AGMs, and on 2 February 1950, Mr Snook was able to report that 168 new members had joined, increasing the total to 463. The buoyancy of the Association must have been helped by a 1947 survey that indicated that most parents were keen to have their sons join it on leaving school. The Association agreed to provide a new flag for the school, but instead, it became a gift from the Hinks family. On Old Boys' Day, 8 June 1950, after a service at the school, a flag-raising ceremony took place in heavy rain at the school field.

There was a proposal to establish an Old Boys' Club, presumably with bar facilities, but many members were hostile, fearing that the

Association would have to assume financial responsibility for it. In the event, a resolution against the Association itself founding a club was successful. There was also a successful motion in favour of acquiring a sports field, but the idea seems to have been denied the light of day.

In December 1949 one of the days allocated for the School Concert became an Old Boys' night, but a new arrangement was agreed for future years. A whole day was to be devoted to the annual cricket match, with an open day at the school and a reunion in the evening. The intention was that after a service at the school, there would also be matches with the school at cricket, badminton, chess, table tennis and basketball. In addition, science and art exhibitions were to be held with music provided by the School Orchestra. At the first such Old Boys' Day L.W. Taylor, Dr Hare's predecessor, who in 1947 had been awarded the OBE for his services to education, read the church lesson.

The Old Boys' rugby and soccer clubs were very active, with many fixtures, and both had flourishing second teams. In 1951 the introduction of a colours tie for Old Boys, costing 12/6d (62½p), was announced, but it was limited to those who had received school colours. By 1951 there was also a tennis team and the badminton section had to increase its membership capacity to forty, including provision for seventeen females. A couple of years earlier there had been interest in forming a philatelic section, but nothing seems to have come of it. An attempt to form an athletics section was also stillborn.

Despite the growth in both membership and number of activities, concerns over the financial position of the Association were expressed early in 1951 and default in paying subscriptions was blamed. As a consequence, people who were strictly no longer members were receiving magazines that had to be paid for by the Association. Letters were sent out, apparently producing some response. Unfortunately, by the spring of 1952 there were 250 subscriptions still outstanding and more letters had to be sent. At this time the majority of Association members lived in the Darlington area.

The forestry camps ended with the war, but it was not until August 1947 that it was possible to provide a school camp abroad, with Holland chosen as the venue. The Head led the camp, assisted by five staff members. At the following Speech Day, Dr Hare reported that there was a new policy and that the intention was to take the boys to five different countries. The numbers going would, if possible, be increased to 300. Presumably he meant 300 in total, not 300 per camp. The first camp produced a profit of £20 5s 1d. Insurance had cost £3 0s 6d.

Because of unspecified difficulties, the 1948 camp was again held in Holland, with no fewer than 150 boys attending. The next camp was in France, with the party staying in a *lycée* at Versailles. The food, particularly when compared with what was then available in Britain, was said to be superb. In 1950, 105 boys went to the Copenhagen camp. For three of them it was their fourth school camp.

It is not clear whether the Queen Elizabeth Club survived the end of the War. Its Senior and Junior Drama Groups had both given performances earlier in 1945, although the acting was said not to have been subtle. Then the decision was made to close the club during the summer term, but with the intention that it would re-open later. The first job afterwards would be to 'raise the tone' of the club, so pupils in the higher forms, in particular those in the Sixth, would think it worthwhile to attend. There is nothing to indicate, however, that the club ever re-opened. The School Savings Group continued into the post-war years and in early 1948, 491 boys out of 730 were members. Then it seems to have faded away.

Peacetime conditions enabled the school magazine to return to its former size and frequency of publication. Then, for issue 71 of September 1947, the cover reappeared. There was also artwork of the kind familiar to readers of the magazine during the 1950s and '60s, including the images of the 'Briton' and other warriors to accompany the House reports. Adverts for local businesses, now largely forgotten, also reappeared, including ones for Stuart's Shoe Shop on Stone Bridge, Luck's for scout and cub uniforms, William's Music Shop and Minories Garage for Rootes cars. A possible first for this issue was the inclusion of a crossword puzzle.

An innovation in the January 1946 issue was the provision of form reports, but not all forms were covered. Most coverage was given to IV Remove. The same magazine also contained what was then believed to be a full Roll of Honour, listing seventy-four names – mostly RAF, but as had happened after 1918, the names of other Old Boys who had died came to light over time. The May 1948 issue had a redesigned cover in blue and was entitled *Darlington Grammar School of Queen Elizabeth, Darlington*. However, by the following September, the cover was green with the image of a wicket keeper on it and by 1950 red artwork on the inside pages had appeared. Possibly, the magazine was benefiting from the influence of J.L. ('Dicky') Bird, who had come to the school to teach art.

In January 1948, the magazine announced that it had a new policy. The January issue each year would be for individual contributions, whilst the other two issues would cater for the society and games reports. Nothing was said about the undesirability of readers having to wait for many months for reports or about the perennial problem of individual contributions not being forthcoming. At the time it was said that much material was coming in from the Lower School – too much in fact for everything to be published – so the then editor might have had a short-lived optimism. In the event, the proposed change was short-lived. One of the more amusing contributions came from J.A. Henderson, Lower VI Arts, and appeared in January 1950. It was entitled 'Kay's Elegy' or 'The Caretaker's Lament' and was a parody of the work by Grey about the toils of Mr Kay after the end of the school day.

By now, advertising had increased. Other familiar business in Darlington, such as Thornley's Toy Shop, Lear's Ironmongers and department store Bainbridge Barker were now represented, as were Valet French Cleaners of Bondgate, who offered repairs to silk stockings at 2/6d per stocking. Larger organisations, such as the Darlington Co-operative Society and the Newcastle Savings Bank now also placed adverts.

By January 1946 a new rung had been added to the prefects' hierarchy in the form of an unspecified number of sub-prefects. At that time, there were, apart from the School Captain, four Senior Prefects and twenty-three ordinary ones. The new appointees were excluded from the Prefects' Room, but after some delay, managed to acquire a rectangular space, with lockers, adjoining the chemistry lab.

It was claimed that there had been a reduction in the number of ordinary prefects resulting from more rigorous selection, yet, two years earlier, there had also been twenty-three. In the year 1948–9 there were three Senior Prefects, twenty-five ordinary ones and seventeen sub-prefects. Then, there was a return to growth, for in 1950 the numbers were, respectively, five, twenty-four and thirty. The new system also led to the appointment of prefects at a younger age. In early 1946 there were four full prefects and nine sub-prefects in the Lower VI.

Prefects' Dances had continued during the war, despite difficulties with venues because of wartime requisitioning. The last one took place at the Baths Hall on 11 January 1945 and a large part of the proceeds went to the school's musical instrument fund. The post-war venues kept changing. The Queen's Hall was used in 1947 and 1949, whilst the venue for the 1948 event was the Palais de Danse. Tickets were reportedly much cheaper than in previous years. An innovation around this time was the introduction of an annual Prefects' Dinner.

In late 1945, there were over a hundred instrumentalists in the school, with forty of them in the First Orchestra, but some Old Boys had helped out at the 1945 concert. By 1947, however, the school was able to set up a third orchestra. The annual concert remained an important feature of school life and those of 1945 and 1946 were each held on three evenings in the school hall.

In 1947 it was only possible to hold the concert on two nights at the school, so a repeat performance was arranged in early 1948 at the Baths Hall. Here, the three orchestras were able to play together for the first time, using a specially erected platform. There were ninety-five performers in the combined orchestras with an audience of twelve hundred. The arrangement was repeated two years later, when the concert at the school in December 1949 was oversubscribed. A repeat concert in February 1950 at the Baths Hall was therefore arranged. Prices for reserved seats were 3/6d (17½p), for unreserved 2/6d (12½p).

The school's first competitive venture in music resulted in the First Orchestra winning the School Orchestra Class at the North of England Music Tournament at Newcastle. Furthermore, five pupils were selected to play in the National Youth Orchestra. At one Old Boys' Dinner, Dr Hare felt sufficiently confident to assert that the school had the finest music scheme in any school in England.

The House Music Competition continued as an annual event and in both 1945 and 1947 some pupils attended the Schools' Music Course at Sherborne. Fifty out of fifty-five candidates passed the music exams in April 1949.

The school library suffered during the immediate post-war years from a continuing difficulty in obtaining books, but the situation gradually improved. In early 1949, however, there were concerns that it was not being used as much as it should be. On average, each pupil borrowed only four or five books in a term. It was conceded that the popular magazines were well read, the serious journals not so. Discipline in the library had improved at break and dinner times and there was now a more studious atmosphere. A reference cupboard had been established for more valuable books and for those unspecified ones whose use it was desirable to control. Presumably application had to be made to some responsible person with a key.

Till 1949 there had been a long period without any bookbinding because of the unavailability of materials, but at the end of the summer term a large consignment arrived and those pupils who volunteered as bookbinders worked through the holidays to reduce the backlog of books requiring repair. In the following April it was reported that there were now nearly five thousand books available in the library and that 7,454 had been borrowed during the previous year. It was clear, however, that many boys, particularly in Forms IV and V, never borrowed at all.

An innovation was an art exhibition with over 100 works on display, held in the library on 27–29 June 1949. Blackout material was used to cover the bookshelves. Some of J.L. Bird's own work was shown, including a still life recently accepted by the Royal Academy. Two examples of tapestry work by Dr Hare, plus two of his watercolours, were also exhibited. A second exhibition was held in the following year, but the hope that the exhibition would become an annual function seems not to have materialised. Another claimed innovation, following upon Dicky Bird's arrival, was the sale of school Christmas cards designed by him. Cards had been sold at one time before the war, but it is not known whether they had been specially designed for the school.

On 11 April 1949 a science exhibition was held at the school. Its size was such that it used the hall, chemistry labs, physics labs, the new geography and science rooms and the biology lab.

The old Form Dramatic Evenings continued, usually with the performance of several one-act plays, although by 1948 each school year – rather than individual forms – was responsible for a play. However, the production of a full play was not resumed until April 1949 when Capek's play *And So Ad Infinitum*, otherwise *The Insect Play*, was staged. It was noteworthy for its huge cast, with many boys playing insects. The 1950 play, *The Zeal of Thy House* by Dorothy L. Sayers, was regarded as having been the most successful yet and, for the first time, prizes were awarded for performances. There were eight of them.

From 1945 onwards many new societies sprang up. By the end of the war there was a Film Society, followed shortly by a Junior Science Society. The school magazine of January 1946 contained their first reports, but there were also reports from the Student Christian Movement, the Classical Society and the Play Reading Society, apparently re-formed in October. The long-established Chess Club had now opened its membership to the entire school. By 1949 there was also an Art Society. A year later it acquired a Marionette Section with a theatre.

Nineteen fifty was a good year for new societies, with the appearance of the Recorded Music Society and the Literary and Philosophical Society. Two defunct societies were also revived; the Stamp Club, re-formed under George Chapman, the new Senior Geography Master, and the Film Society which had died at some point after 1945. Unfortunately, the Literary and Philosophical Society was not destined to continue for long.

The Chess Club prospered. Competitive events regularly took place and school colours were awarded. By 1948 the club was meeting weekly and it was now holding a junior trophy competition. Two years later, it reportedly experienced a sudden surge in popularity, largely because of its beginners' classes. One consideration undoubtedly encouraged the playing of chess in the school. By the early 1950s, if not earlier, after school exams had finished and the staff were using class time for marking, pupils were permitted either to read or to play chess. The result was that nearly everyone soon learned how to play.

The Senior Debating Society, the longest-established society, was active initially. In the first term of the 1945–6 academic year there were two debates, plus a mock trial enlivened by the appearance of the famous detective Lord Peter Wimsey on a bicycle, but as far as can be seen, no verdict was ever reached. Soon the Society went into decline and, even in 1950, after a reported revival, it was managing only two debates per term.

The impression is given that the number of meetings provided by societies fluctuated considerably depending upon their changing fortunes, and that the quiet or dormant times were often unreported. The Junior Debating Society, for instance, had eight meetings, including a mock parliament, after the war, then was moribund, but in the two terms up to April 1950, managed to have three meetings. In the summer term 1949, the Classical Society had only one meeting, when a pupil gave a talk on Julius Caesar.

The Science and Natural History societies both called upon the services of outside speakers and, particularly during the summer term, provided field trips and other visits. In 1949 a three-day geographical and geological expedition, starting on 30 March and based at Langdon Beck Youth Hostel, was organised. It was reported that cooking consisted of rendering nearly all of Mr Heinz's fifty-seven varieties to being almost unfit for human consumption, although nobody apparently suffered any ill effects. There was a similar outing in 1950, so presumably nobody had been put off.

In November 1948 a group of thirty boys visited Bank Top Engine Sheds, but the identity of the organiser is unclear. Another outing had been arranged to enable 140 boys to see Michael Redgrave in the title role of *Macbeth* at Newcastle on 9 January 1947. Sixth Form Talks had been established by this time, most of them given by masters, not by outside speakers.

In 1949 a collection of animal heads, including those of a rhino and two buffaloes, was presented by Mr H.E. Whitwell. The heads were placed in the biology lab or in the room of Mr Lovell, the assistant biology master. In addition, an Old Boy, Ronald Snowden, presented a case of stuffed birds to the school. According to Tom Pearson, there was a school inspection at about this time. It led to a good report, except that it was critical of the biology department. The lab contained too many dead specimens.

There is insufficient space to say much about the achievements of former pupils, but four can be mentioned randomly. One, Edward Graham, achieved distinction whilst still at the school. After winning a talent show at the Darlington Hippodrome, he was the successful applicant out of a thousand boys who auditioned to play William Brown in the film *Just William's Luck*. He then starred in a second film, *William Comes to Town*. He also appeared on stage at the Astoria Theatre in High Northgate, now the site of a filling station. After National Service as a private in the RAMC, he worked at London's Windmill Theatre until its closure.

Jimmy Blumer, started a successful motor racing career by entering the 1950 Monte Carlo Rally driving a 1938 Morris 10. The car was the oldest in the event, and at eighteen, he was the youngest entrant. The start was from Glasgow and, because of the appalling roads, the crew had to replace a front spring in Paris. Later they had to withdraw after running a big end.

Someone older who had become prominent was F.N.S. Creek, who had been awarded the Military Cross whilst serving in the Royal Flying Corps in the Great War. He was later a cricket writer with the *Daily Telegraph* and was manager of the British Olympic football team from 1952 to 1968.

Geoffrey Cass, later Sir Geoffrey, who was School Captain in 1950, became an Oxford Tennis Blue and in 1954 played W. Seixas, the reigning champion, at Wimbledon. Later Sir Geoffrey was President of the Lawn Tennis Association, Chief Executive of Cambridge University Press and Chairman of the Royal Shakespeare Company.

In 1947, the First Rugby XV had the distinction of not losing a single match all season, although, of the twelve games played, seven were drawn. During the 1947–8 season four of the First XV were selected for county trials, and three were selected for the Durham County Public Schools XV. In 1949 no fewer than ten members of the First XV were selected to play at the Durham Public Schools trials match on 17 December. Those who were in the First XV in early 1948 had their individual playing strengths and weaknesses analysed in a report in the school magazine.

It looks as if, in about 1947, there was a move to end soccer playing, for at the Old Boys' Annual Dinner, held at the Imperial Hotel in December 1947, Dr Hare said that association football would be included in the 1948 timetable. He stressed that his task was to provide physical recreation for pupils, not specialised training in one sport or another.

The decision was then made to stop having rugby and association football played in different terms and in 1948–9 there were both rugby and soccer fixtures from September to March. Then in 1949, for the first time since the war, the staff, with Norman Sunderland in goal, played the school at soccer. Although the referee had the usual black shorts, he also sported a salmon pink rowing blazer. Conditions were very muddy and the school won.

The number of cricket matches played in a season was variable. In 1945 the First Cricket XI played fourteen, compared with ten in 1948. As usual, most matches were played against local grammar schools, but the annual games against the masters and the Old Boys were always in the fixtures list. In 1949 the first team played fifteen matches, eleven at the home ground. That year, for the first time, two Meritorious Performance Awards were given as well as the usual colours and permissions to wear the striped blazer.

An interesting innovation, reported in January 1947, was that promising school cricketers were given a year's free membership of Darlington Cricket Club, but it is not known whether the practice was continued into future seasons. There was at this time an established Masters Cricket XI. It played about five or six games, including the usual one against the school, in a season.

The School Sports were still an annual event, but bad weather was common. There were various other athletics meetings, including the regular Inter-School Sports at York. For the first time, in 1948 the school competed in the Darlington School Sports at Feethams, whilst in 1949 the Shells and IIIs had their own Sports Day on a separate date from the rest of the school. The arrangement was repeated in the following year.

The Harriers remained active with meetings with other teams and, in 1948, the Inter-School Event (Darlington Grammar School, Acklam, Coatham, Stockton and Middlesbrough) was revived. The entire school also had the opportunity to see a film of the London Olympics.

The Swimming Gala remained a regular event, except in 1949 when, for some reason, the Baths Hall could not be reserved. Swimming classes were still regularly held on Tuesdays and Thursdays after school, with the life-saving classes being provided by Lovell. In 1949 he took responsibility for all of the swimming activities from Graville. One year later eight pupils were awarded the Bronze Medallion of the Royal Life Saving Society.

In about 1948 a table tennis club was formed for the Upper School, with tables for both singles and doubles. There was a hope that a school team could be formed. By then there were annual matches between Sixth Formers and the High School tennis and hockey teams. By 1950 the Housemasters were Graville (Britons), Fisher (Danes), Allen (Normans) and Richardson (Saxons), and school rugby was under the charge of Norman Sunderland.

There was always a lighter side to school life. At the time of his leaving the school in 1946, Hector Parr and some others played a prank at the end-of-term service. They suspended various items, including toilet rolls, in a box above the stage. A string ran the length of the hall into the organ loft and when it was pulled, the contents of the box spilled out around the Headmaster. He was not amused.

The Fifties: the Quiet Years

It is the author's belief, hopefully not coloured by his time at the school, that the 1950s were the least interesting period during the school's time at Vane Terrace. Although building work started towards the end of the decade there were no significant alterations to the school buildings and no events of great note affecting the school. Dr Hare was now long established as Headmaster, but the reforming years had gone. Pupil numbers continued to rise, adding to the problems of overcrowding, but the school prospered, untroubled by external threats, and enjoyed an excellent reputation.

Perhaps, by now, some complacency had set in. There was stuffiness in some of the attitudes found in the school, with Bug Allen complaining of boys in uniform being seen in Woolworths on a Saturday morning, or in Percy Moss' attempts to make Shell boys into 'young gentlemen'. However, such attitudes have to be seen in the context of the time. Hierarchies were still important and the challenges to authority experienced in the late 1960s were a long way off.

A supply teacher called Watson demonstrated attitudes that would never have been expressed in a school in later years. On one occasion when he was having difficulty in maintaining control he appealed to his pupils' better natures, asking them 'to play the game', adding that they were British, 'not Wogs or Dagoes'. In doing so, he lost all credibility. His experience was untypical, however. Classroom discipline was not normally a problem, although Jim Osborn recounted how, when he was a young teacher at the school, he had once gone into a classroom to find the master on the floor with a pupil on top of him.

The school had a skeleton, used in science lessons. It was reputedly of a German soldier of the First World War and was invariably referred to as 'Fritz' without anyone feeling self-conscious about it.

Elitism was still acceptable and for the grammar and high schools it appeared in more than one form. Their pupils wore uniforms, whilst those in the secondary modern schools did not. Their summer holidays extended over seven weeks compared with five for other schools, although this may have been a compensation for grammar and high school pupils having to face homework. When the Mulheim Exchange started in the 1950s, the participants from Darlington were limited to the two schools.

A new pupil had to familiarise himself with various aspects of school life. Because of the unfamiliarity of primary school pupils with rugby football, the games staff used to organise a couple of days at the school field during the holidays before boys started at the school. The purpose was to introduce them to the game. At their first English lesson, new boys were required to abandon the fancy capital lettering they may have learned at primary school and were taught to write in a plain script instead.

They also had to provide a small padlock with key for their desk in the form room. Each desk was fitted with a hasp and staple to enable it to be locked, but, as there was no certainty that he would be in the room other than at roll call, each pupil had to carry everything he needed for the day from classroom to classroom. Traditional satchels were most definitely out, other than for new boys. Most boys used haversacks, often army surplus.

New Shell boys arrived at the school on their first day having heard that new boys were put in the dustbins by older pupils, but, in practice, nothing seemed to happen beyond the odd cap being snatched off a boy's head and being hurled a distance. A dispute between two boys in the yard would immediately provoke a cry of 'fight' and an immediate stampede towards the area of conflict always resulted.

Physical contact, both by way of formal punishment and in other forms, was seen as normal and the risk of prosecutions or disciplinary proceedings was not contemplated. Corporal punishment, applied by the Headmaster using a leather strap on the offender's backside, continued and the summons given by Dr Hare at assembly to see him in his study afterwards carried grave implications. Percy Moss would threaten the use of a slipper, but it is not known whether he ever used it. One modern languages master had a propensity for hitting pupils on the head with a book.

The writer witnessed one incident when a small boy was incautious enough to run along the main corridor when Jim Osborn was approaching from the opposite direction. As they were about to pass, Osborn seized the offender by his collar and, without a word being spoken but still holding him, marched him back to his starting point.

The wearing of gowns by the graduate staff when teaching was usual, with one or two exceptions including Osborn. Perhaps an edict about the practice was occasionally delivered, for, on rare occasions and for a short time only, Osborn would appear wearing what could only be described as the remnants of a gown, consisting largely of shredded strips of cloth! At Speech Day and for the Founders' Day service the full robes with hoods were worn. Only the Head wore a mortar board, but more often he carried it. Pupils, as always, were invariably addressed by their surnames only.

Inevitably, the school placed much emphasis upon tradition, but some of it was recently born. The school celebrated Founders' Day, with a service at St. Cuthbert's Church, to which the pupils walked in procession, followed by a cricket match between the staff and the school team. The match was long established; the service was not. The author, having assumed that the practice went back over the centuries, was surprised to find that the first Founders' Day service took place on 13 June 1952.

As 1953 saw the 75th Anniversary of the school at Vane Terrace, Founders Day and Old Boys' Day were commemorated together on 12 June. On the previous day there had been a procession of pupils to the Odeon Cinema in Bondgate to see the film of the Queen's Coronation. One person from the school had been directly involved. Fred Phillips, a long-serving games master, commanded a section of the 6th/8th Battalion Durham Light Infantry on the Coronation processional route and was rewarded with a good soaking.

As part of its tradition, the school also had a school hymn and a school prayer. The age of the hymn, sung to the tune of 'Eternal Father', is not known, but it certainly existed during the Second World War. Its frequency of use is uncertain, and, during the 1950s, might have been confined to the Founders' Day service. Whether it fell into total disuse is unclear, but it was certainly revived in the late 1960s when Hector Parr, who replaced Chris Bennett as music master, composed a new tune for it.

Former pupils who were at the school in the 1930s or during the Second World War have no recollection of a school prayer, so it was almost certainly a post-war creation, possibly written by Maurice Lumsdon. Every boy new to the school was required to furnish himself with a copy of the *Songs of Praise* hymnbook, but he was also required, by Mr Lumsdon, to learn the school prayer within a stipulated time. The penalty for failure was to face being strapped. The prayer was recited every day at morning assembly.

It appears to have be rewritten at some point, possibly in conjunction with the Queen Mother's' 1963 visit, for it is the belief of the writer and of other contemporaries that the wording used in the sixties, whilst following the thread of the original prayer, is not the same. No other written version of the prayer has been found and the passage of sixty years has effaced the detailed memory of the words from those compelled to learn it by heart!

For those who wish to recall them or are simply interested, the words of hymn and of the later version of the prayer are set out in Appendix I.

By now the school uniform was established. The wearing of the navy blue blazer was almost universal, but the striped blazer for those with full colours permitted to wear it remained in use. Except as mentioned below, boys in the Lower School had a badge with a cipher of 'DGS' on the breast pocket, but in 1953 it was decided that Fifth Formers without colours could wear the oval badge depicting Queen Elizabeth I. The wording implies that Sixth Formers already could. A coloured strip denoting the wearer's house was worn above the badge.

Boys in the Lower School wore the ties showing the House colours. They were made of a woollen fabric with the bottoms cut square. During heat wave conditions, pupils were permitted to dispense with their ties, but they were then required to wear their shirt collar outside their jacket collar.

At the beginning of 1953 the practice of having a formal presentation of badges to those awarded colours was reintroduced. One of the purposes was to encourage the wearing of blazers. The school magazine contained drawings describing the colours awarded. There were four groups:

1. Junior House colours. The recipient had the school badge on his breast pocket with the coloured House ribbon above. Initial letters in blue indicating the sport would appear in a bottom corner of the pocket.

2. Junior school colours. The oval Queen Elizabeth badge would be worn, surmounted by the school ribbon. Blue letters would indicate the sport.

3. Senior House colours. As for junior school colours.

4. Senior school colours. The Queen Elizabeth badge would be in silver with silver letters and would be worn on a striped blazer. The holder was also entitled to wear a dark blue tie with the Queen Elizabeth motif.

There was a rumour current at one period in the decade that those members of staff who were Old Boys and who had been required to wear the cap in the Sixth Form were attempting to have the requirement reimposed. Attempts to find out more have been unsuccessful.

There seem to have been few changes to the uniform after this period, although the seal badge rather than the DGS cipher seems to have been adopted for the entire school during the 1960s. Photographs of that time also suggest that all pupils were by then wearing the diagonally striped tie and that there was no longer a House ribbon on breast pockets. Although they were never part of the uniform requirements, short trousers for Lower School pupils seem to have survived till then.

Prefects' lapel badges were now in use. They were rectangular in shape and depicted the keys of St. Cuthbert's. Senior Prefects had red ones, ordinary prefects white ones, whilst the sub-prefects' were coloured blue.

The number of prefects continued to fluctuate. For 1951–2 there were thirty prefects and forty sub-prefects, plus the School Captain. The rank of Senior Prefect had recently been abolished. By January 1953 the tendency for the numbers to increase was again showing itself. Apart from the School Captain and Vice-Captain, there were then thirty-nine prefects and forty-five sub-prefects, but by the end of 1955, when there were 742 pupils in the school including 166 in the Sixth Form, there were no fewer than eighty-five in total. Of these, seven including the School Captain and Vice-Captain were Senior Prefects – now reintroduced. There twenty-four were ordinary ones and the rest, including two in Upper V, were sub-prefects.

Within a year the inevitable purge took place. Senior Prefects numbered ten, the ordinary ones twenty-seven, whilst the lowly sub-prefects disappeared. Then, over time, the total number more than doubled. By the autumn of 1960 there were twenty-nine Senior Prefects and sixty-two ordinary ones, but such was then the size of the Sixth Form, that by no means all of the Upper VI were prefects. By then there were two School Vice-Captains.

Concerns about Health and Safety appear to have been non-existent. Overcrowding in the hall was always a problem, hence the need for separate Shell or House prayers. The hall was always more crowded for Monday assembly because each House took away a quarter of the school, the Shells less. At assembly it was the norm for pupils to sit on the heating pipes at the sides of the hall whilst the seats always accommodated more boys than they were designed for.

An incident at the Remembrance Day service in about 1960 is recalled. A trestle table had been set up beside the hall entrance for the purpose of selling poppies, but the crush became so great that the table was knocked over, and one hall door came off at least one of its hinges. Someone was heard to shout that his feet were not touching the floor, but fortunately nobody seems to have been harmed.

In 1957 there were twelve governors, including three aldermen and four councillors. Amongst the remaining five were Miss Stanton, Principal of the Training College next door, Canon Wansey, vicar of Darlington, and Lady Starmer. The governing body was, of course, subordinated to the Education Committee.

It is impossible to record in full the arrival and departure of every member of staff, but many who left had been at the school for a short period of time only and, overall and in contrast to the late 1960s, the staff turnover was low. Amongst the most notable amongst the staff leaving was Dr Izzard, who left in July 1954, and Mr Snook left at the end of the same year, having come straight from Cambridge sixteen years earlier. His stated aim was to convince schoolboys that Latin was actually spoken by the Romans and was not a kind of linguistic crossword puzzle devised for their confusion.

G.T.L. Chapman, the popular teacher of geography, left for a post in Stoke-on-Trent in 1958 and was followed, within a few months, by two Old Boys, 'Cosh' Graham and Tom Pearson. Probably the most significant departure was that of R.A. Burniston, who retired in 1958 after thirty-nine years at the school. He had been a keen soccer and cricket player even in the 1930s, being a regular in the masters' teams. He had also played golf and badminton, but had unfortunately lost a leg in 1944.

Amongst the newcomers were Fred Phillips, Keith (otherwise 'Captain') Blood who replaced Mrs Gomez, Jack Waltham who taught geography, and L.G. Reedman, Senior Classics Master in succession to Snook. Three new members of staff who came in September 1954 were all Old Boys, but only Jack Dodds, assistant biology master, remained for any length of time. The school always employed a large number of its former pupils, but there is no evidence of a policy in favour of doing so. New members of staff at the end of the decade were John Stanley and another Old Boy, David Mackenzie. They taught French and maths respectively.

Another change in 1952 was the replacement of Kay the caretaker by Mr Jennings, who lasted into Sixth Form College days. By 1953 the school also had a careers master.

The school magazine, now established at three issues per year, thrived and the range of adverts carried is, perhaps, a testimony to its influence. In issue 82 of May 1951, for example, the advertisers included Luck & Sons, Northern Radio (located on the corner of Skinnergate and Bell's Place), Trustee Savings Bank, Haward & Robertson the removal firm,

The Admiralty (for a career in flying), the Co-operative Society and the department store Bainbridge Barker. Various local garages, estate agents and other business, now largely forgotten, also featured.

There was, by school magazine standards, controversy in January 1953 arising from the publication of a letter from the Second Master, W.S. Richardson. He started by praising the magazine for its improvement over twenty years, but then attacked it for the poor quality of the articles and the artwork in the previous issue. He referred to 'half-baked, woolly headed effusions' and wanted more sports reports, as they were more likely to appeal to the Old Boys – the most interested group of readers. A joint letter from the editor and art editor rebutted Mr Richardson's 'witty trivialities' whilst J.L. Bird, the art master, wrote to defend the quality of the artwork, criticising those 'dismal jimmies' who did not like it. Finally there was a letter from Snook, the Chairman of the Magazine Committee, written in more measured tones, explaining the various considerations that had to be taken into account.

The correspondence was heated by the usual standards of the magazine, but one has to wonder whether the strong feelings were intended for effect, bearing in mind that all of the correspondents were members of the Magazine Committee and presumably had some influence over the magazine's policy and its content. In his letter, Snook had said that the magazine had assumed its current form in 1947 when the Committee was reconstituted. It comprised a member of staff as chairman and included the Senior Art Master, the editor and the art editor, both pupils, together with a dozen or so interested Sixth Formers. The Head, the Second Master, the School Captain and the Treasurer of the School Club were also members ex-officio.

The next issue, by way of commemoration of the new reign and the impending Coronation, carried the name *Elizabethan*. The name continued in use until October 1969, almost at the end of the school's existence, when it was changed to *New Elizabethan*.

Three years later, the cover had a depiction of the heads of a Briton, a Dane, a Norman and a Saxon, two on each side of the oval seal. Pen-and-ink drawings in the text were normally found. One issue of the time contained some lively correspondence about the quality of the poetry published in it, with a strong response to a contributor in the previous magazine who had deplored the lack of originality. There was at least one letter complaining about contributors borrowing material from published poets or from text books.

The old problem of having sufficient material of the right kind continued and, at times, one is left wondering whether the articles published, although often of a high standard, attracted many readers. As an example, the issue of September 1953 had no less than eight pages occupied by an article on lead mining in Teesdale and Swaledale. There were also features on the trade unions and the water supply, plus correspondence, written in strong terms about the conflict between the autonomy of the artist and the autonomy of form. One of the most esoteric articles appeared in the February 1958 issue. The subject was Russian poetry 1917–1930.

On the other hand, in some issues there was little about actual school events, with many of the societies providing no reports. In 1959 there was even an editorial complaining about the magazine, saying it was often not worth reading. There is perhaps a perennial problem for school magazine editors. Understandably, they want to demonstrate the intellectual capabilities of their contributors, but much of the material submitted will not be appreciated by the bulk of the readership. The magazine at this time contained about sixty-eight pages, so, even with full-page adverts, there was a lot to fill. One issue provided the novelty of cartoon drawings of certain members of staff.

The February 1956 issue of the *Elizabethan* made a passing reference to a recently introduced literary magazine entitled the *Scorpion* co-edited by two members of the Sixth Form. It was not referred to again. The prime mover behind the new venture was Ian Hamilton, who later achieved a degree of distinction as a writer and poet. In 2001, shortly before his death, Hamilton, was interviewed by Dan Jacobson. He told his interviewer that the *Scorpion* was intended as a scurrilous alternative to the school magazine. He claimed that, as a result of his attempts to sell it door-to-door and in coffee bars, he was deprived of his prefect's badge.

The *Scorpion* ran to two issues. Hamilton timed publication to coincide with that of the *Elizabethan* and took time from school to collect the copies from the printers. He displayed energy and initiative having, for the first issue, induced John Wain, the novelist, to write a foreword. For the second Hamilton obtained about forty or fifty responses to a questionnaire he sent to a large number of literary luminaries.

Three deaths during the decade illustrated how the links with the old independent Grammar School were disappearing. Firstly, in 1951, J.W. Malkin died, aged 91. He was believed to be the last survivor of the pupils at the Leadyard school. Then in 1955 the death of Alfred Smith, who had come to the school in 1902 and who deputised for the Headmaster during the Great War, was reported. Four years later, Antonia Wood, the daughter of Philip Wood, died at Grinton, aged 80.

In 1951 Percy Moss became Chairman of the Library, replacing Hemingway, who had served for twelve years. He also became Treasurer of the School Club. An early innovation was the provision of a lesson each week on the uses and administration of a library for the classes in the Lower School. In addition, a study area was set up. It was available for Sixth Formers even when such a lesson was in progress. The small adjacent room, which had been the library before 1938, was its office. By now, the arrears of book repairs by bookbinders were under control.

There were further reforms. The library had a stock of about 200 Penguin paperbacks, apparently lying dusty and rarely used. All were withdrawn from stock and were then reclassified, before being reissued within a separate Penguin Library. The success of the scheme was immediate, but it led to a rapid deterioration in the books, so a permanent squad of Sixth Formers on the library staff, meeting after school each Wednesday, learned how to bind Penguin books as hardbacks. Henceforth, all paperbacks acquired for the library were so bound. By 1955 there were seven librarians and four assistants in the Penguin Library, which then had 500–600 books. A careers section was added in 1952. A few years later, a Middle School Library had been formed, but it suffered from a lack of shelves.

Another reform was the reorganisation of the library staff from the beginning of 1952. The old hierarchy of Senior Librarians, Librarians, Library Assistants and (sometimes) Helpers was replaced by a simple division into Librarians and Library Assistants, with an Assistant being eligible for becoming a Librarian after two years' service. There were, initially, a Senior Librarian with a Deputy, plus thirteen Librarians and fifteen Assistants.

The level of borrowing fluctuated. During the spring term of 1955, 3,015 library books were issued but although this was an improvement, it fell well short of the record of 4,883 of several years earlier. It was now the policy to retain the dust covers on new books to brighten the appearance of the room.

Historically, pupils with overdue library books had been fined, but in 1956, in a move to reduce the number of defaulters, those with overdue books faced detention. Whether or not the change was effective is not clear, but in 1958 a new overdue books system was reportedly successful.

The library was always well stocked with periodicals and, when Percy Moss took over, was spending the not inconsiderable sum of £45 per year on them. In the late 1950s the magazines stocked ranged from *Punch* to the *Economist* and from *La France* to *Films and Filming*. At one point the Library Committee had been concerned about the dog-eared condition of magazines until Mr Moss pointed out that their condition was a sign of their being read. In 1951 there were about 5,000 books in the library, but by 1960 there were 8,000. In addition, the newly established Philip Wood Reference Library had a further thousand or so.

As at December 1952 the Old Boys' Association had about 400 members. As with the school's societies, the fortunes of its components fluctuated and at that time the badminton section was not functioning, but it was back in action within a year or so. The practice of having the Headmaster and Second Master serving on the committee continued and the indefatigable D.R. Carrick remained as a joint Hon. Secretary until at least 1956, maintaining a connection with the school going back to the 1890s. In 1958, when Percy Moss was President, there were two association football teams and two rugby teams and the badminton team was still active. In the following year a clubhouse for the rugby section opened in Victoria Road.

The Association's income for 1957–8 was, after allowing for a £12 12s 5d deficit, £303 5s 6d and of this, £171 19s 0d came from subscriptions. The main expenditure was £100 for the Rugby Club, £90 for magazines and £30 17s 6s for gratuities.

In contrast, in 1959, the income of the School Club (with an £8 deficit) was £1,693 of which £854 came from the council. The magazine produced £204, including the £90 paid by the Old Boys for their copies and £100 resulting from the magazine adverts, together with £159 from the school play, concert and gym display. The magazine cost £365 to produce and £827 was spent on sports, the library and the societies. The cost of the ground, including wages of £78, was £150. Salaries, of course, were normally met directly by the Education Authority and an annual salary of £78 would have been some kind of additional payment.

Old Boys, parents and friends were still encouraged to become Associate Members of the School Club. The minimum annual subscription was one guinea and the subscriber would receive the magazine and a personal invitation to school functions.

There were thirty-eight Associate Members in 1951–2, but this figure excludes the many retired and current masters who had also joined. In addition to its responsibility for sporting activities, societies and the library, the club was involved with school music, film shows, grounds maintenance, lectures, school excursions and the subsidising of travel and meal costs for inter-school fixtures. One of the club's least publicised functions was to meet the taxi fares home for pupils taken ill at school.

In the spring of 1951 there were actually six Housemasters. Graville was responsible for the Britons and Graham the Danes, but Allen and Thompson had shared responsibility for the Normans whilst Richardson and Moss were joint Saxon Housemasters. The involvement of Percy Moss and Thompson was short-lived, however. When Graville retired, Norman Sunderland replaced him, but, by the end of 1952, Sunderland had defected to the Danes, being replaced as Britons' Housemaster by Snook. By 1956 Joe Eccleston had replaced Snook and Len Griffiths had become the Saxons' Housemaster. Once again the Britons' House was perceived as being too small and there was a stated intention of recruiting members outside the A–C surname range, but little, if anything, appears to have happened.

In about 1951 a system of gradation had been introduced in the gym to encourage activity. The aim was to encourage boys to achieve a set standard and there were three classes, First to Third, each with its own identification. Those with a Third Class award, for instance, were permitted to wear a stripe on their shorts. For those who were keen there was a separate Gym Club, which in 1954 was claiming average attendances of thirty for Seniors and sixty to seventy for Juniors.

A popular acquisition in 1955 was a large trampoline and opportunities to use it were always appreciated. Another popular activity, usually reserved for the end of term, was a game of 'pirates'. One group would pursue another in the gym and the object, by use of wall bars, ropes and the like, was to avoid coming into contact with the floor. Gym displays continued as a regular annual event, sometimes with a hundred participants. Some included a joint country dancing display with the High School. Games of basketball and football, and rugby, athletics and cricket displays by the junior boys might be included.

There were now more sporting opportunities than ever, and during the 1957–8 season thirty-two association football matches were played by the school teams; twenty-three were won, six lost and three drawn. In rugby the numbers were thirty, eleven, fifteen and four respectively. Twenty-seven cricket matches were played with four wins, no defeats and fourteen draws. There was no explanation as to the remaining 9! Five sporting trophies were won and ten pupils, including three swimmers, were awarded county honours.

Full school colours were awarded for association football, rugby, cricket, athletics, harriers, basketball, swimming, tennis, gymnastics and chess. Seventy-nine awards were made, although a few pupils received them for more than one sport. The numbers awarded for soccer, rugby and cricket were all fewer than the numbers in a team, so selection for a team did not, of itself, guarantee an award. In the junior school thirty-four received school colours. They were awarded for the same sports except for harriers, tennis and chess.

The year 1953 can be taken as an example to illustrate the scale of the awarding of House colours. The Britons received thirty-one awards for rugby and soccer, both seniors and juniors, whilst the Danes had thirty-eight. The other two houses had similar numbers.

As to athletics, the Inter-School Sports continued to take place, usually with six local grammar schools competing, and in 1954 the school won for the fourth time running. There were also meetings further afield, for instance at York when the school competed with Holgate Grammar School and a team from Barnsley. The school also regularly competed in the County Grammar Schools' Sports and in the triangular contest with Grangefield and A.J. Dawson's Grammar Schools.

In 1954 the harriers' course had had to be modified because of a housing development at Hummersknott and became about 200 yards longer. The annual school athletics tests continued to be held in about May of each year, with each 'High' or 'Low' scored by a participant contributing points to his House total.

One of the 1954 magazines described the swimming team as then being in its third year but, by then, it was well established. Two years later, the first team won four out of seven fixtures, although the under-16s lost four out of five. In the same year six boys were selected for the Darlington Team at the Northumberland and Durham Schools Gala.

The annual hockey match against the High School continued in its traditional, less than serious, form. In 1958 the Grammar School team, which won, was reported as 'presenting a bizarre appearance, proving that brute force was preferable to tactical finesse'.

There was an assortment of new events during the decade, but none of huge moment. In 1951, at the time of the Festival of Britain, there was an exhibition of colourful beakers in the dining hall and it was claimed they had done much to improve the appearance of 'a typically depressing example of Austerity building'. The school was also redecorated, with what the magazine described as unorthodox colour schemes. They were short-lived for, by September 1954, the school had been decorated again. The previous colours were replaced with maroon and yellow.

From 19 to 22 June 1951 the school was open to all-comers to commemorate the Festival. There were various exhibitions and a Mock Parliament was held. At this time a census about the population and occupational characteristics of Darlington was organised by Sixth Form geography pupils. Four hundred forms were distributed by pupils for their parents to complete and the results were published in the magazine.

Prefects' Dances continued as an established institution, often at the Palais de Danse. The one held in December 1957 was said to have 'passed with the usual enthusiasm', but this may be an understatement for the lights were fused for one hour. Prefects' Dinners were held, but perhaps only sporadically. One was held at the Masonic Hall on 25 November 1951. Many of those attending had a late night, for 'after a postprandial session in the Green Tree Café', the diners then went on to the Odeon Cinema to await the results of the General Election.

Shortages were a thing of the past for the tuck shop and it was selling sweets and chocolates on Tuesdays and Thursdays. The junior school history trip to York, organised by Norman Sunderland, was a well-established annual event, taking place in July. The train was used and the trip normally comprised a tour of the city walls and visits to the Yorkshire Museum and the old Railway Museum, followed by tea in the Co-operative Society restaurant. A trip to Hadrian's Wall was another regular event.

In 1954 new bicycle sheds had been erected behind the dining hall, increasing the capacity for cycles. Pupils were required to lock their bikes and surprise inspections of the sheds led to in an increase in the use of locks.

There were other assorted occurrences. At the beginning of 1958, the school was hit hard by an Asian flu epidemic. The school remained open, but some classes only had about half a dozen boys attending. A year later, on 13 January 1959, Harold Macmillan, the Prime Minister, visited the school. It was a flying visit for, having arrived at 9.30 a.m., he left at precisely 10.30. Then, in the spring term, it was necessary to employ four students from Durham to ease the teacher shortage and, after forty years' service, the schools' boilers were retired on 25 March.

It might be useful to examine the class and teaching arrangements in the middle of the decade. The school was very heavily weighted towards specialisation and pupils were required, before they left the III Forms (the equivalent of Year 8), to choose between the arts and science sides. Many subjects therefore became unavailable.

At the end of 1955 there were five IV Forms. Two were designated IV Science I and Science II, with thirty-one and twenty-seven pupils respectively, and there was a separate Arts form with only seventeen in it. The other was IV General and its members, having abandoned

French after two years, shared a common course of teaching with the newly admitted boys in IV Remove. For maths and chemistry the two science forms shared sets, whilst for English and French, IV Arts were also included, so there were three teaching groups. All took history and geography and everyone, except those in the Arts form, took physics, chemistry and biology. Everyone also studied art and religious instruction. Instead of the three science subjects, the Arts form made do with general science, although Latin was also studied.

There was a similar pattern for the V Lowers, but art was now optional. The Arts pupils now had to study either Greek (6) or German (17). The pattern for General and Remove pupils was similar to that in the IV Forms, except that they now had sets with each other for many more subjects.

The School List for the V Uppers shows a few O level candidates for Latin. There were also some for general science, but this subject seems to have ceased to be available at O level shortly afterwards. German or Greek appear to have been available at A Level only, effectively debarring those who did not enter the VI Form direct via the express stream.

By 1956 the separate Science and Art forms in the IVs had disappeared and the forms were now designated IV A/B/C, with seventeen Arts pupils, still studying Latin and general science, spread amongst them. There were three sets for maths, so the Arts pupils were included, and two for physics. However, the earlier arrangements for IV General and Remove continued. The V Lower year also lost its separate Science and Art forms, but the arrangements for the General and Remove classes continued as before. Despite the rigid distinction between Arts and Science pupils there were, in both 1955 and 1956, one or two Lower VI Arts pupils with O level science subjects or Science form members with O level Latin.

Academically the school continued to do well and, by now, about thirty pupils would leave each year to go to university. Usually, several of these would be the holders of state or open scholarships. In 1958, 70 pupils were recorded as having been awarded A levels and 132 O levels, but there was no indication as to how many subjects were passed by each candidate. By way of contrast, in 1945 eighty-six had passed the School Certificate, with a mere fourteen passing the Higher Certificate.

There was, officially at least, an attempt at the end of the decade to provide a more general education for pupils. The Headmaster stressed the need to balance increased specialisation in the Sixth Form with new cultural courses, but there were examples of pupils being encouraged take general courses in subjects they were studying at A level – a pointless exercise.

In autumn 1957 the Shell forms ceased to be so called and were simply named after the form teacher, e.g. Mr Moss' Form. In practice, everyone still referred to the Shell forms and by 1960 the name 'Shell' had officially reappeared, but each form was still named after the teacher in charge of it. It is believed that when the Shells took the names of their form teachers they became mixed ability, but it has been suggested that there were large movements in and out of the forms to quickly establish streaming. This appears to be so, for, as an example, of the thirty-four pupils in Shell Mr Moss in 1960 twelve went, in the following year, into III 1, with eight going into III 2. Of the remainder, twelve passed into III 3 and two into III 4.

On the other hand, of the thirty-five boys in III 1 in 1961, no fewer than thirty-three went into IVA in 1962, suggesting that streaming was firmly in place in the III forms. Of the twelve in III 1 who had come from Shell Moss in 1961 all but one, who was untraceable, were in IVA in 1962.

For some years, pupils in Form IIID had not studied Latin, but from 1957–8 the subject was taught to all III Formers. Science teaching also became more specific, in that everyone in the year now studied physics and chemistry, in place of general science.

Pupils who elected for the Arts side now continued to study physics and chemistry in the Fourth Form in place of general science. They also continued their Latin studies, whilst those choosing the Science side started biology as a fresh subject. By now the practice in the IVs and V Lowers of teaching English, maths, geography, chemistry and physics in sets had ended.

The school's well-established societies were still popular. In 1951 the Chess Club started a junior section and it was said that pocket chess sets were greatly in evidence in the school. In September of that year, the school joined the Teesside Schools' Chess League. By 1954 the club had also entered the newly formed Darlington Chess League. Over 100 boys attended at least one meeting of the Chess Club during the year and school colours were awarded to five members and re-awarded to three. In 1956 the Chess Club's team won in the Darlington and District Chess League.

As always, the Natural History Society was popular and 'Bug' Allen was recorded as having exhibited at one meeting a young crocodile stuffed by him personally. Amongst the other regularly functioning societies were the Classical Society, the Science Society, the Stamp Club, the Astronomical Society and the Student Christian Movement. In 1958 the Play Reading Society's Secretary was worried about his society's image. In his magazine report he was concerned that it was wrongly regarded as a Sixth Form English pupils' clique and stressed that everyone was welcome.

For debating, there were still separate Junior and Senior societies. The Senior Society in 1953 managed to treble its normal attendance by having a meeting during school hours. There was a perception that when masters made a contribution to debates they altered the voting of those present, but by the end of the decade the practice of masters speaking in debates seems to have all but ended. One such speaker was W.W. Allen, who, in 1956, unsuccessfully opposed a motion favouring the abolition of hanging. During the same season, concerns were expressed about the quality of many speeches.

In 1960, when it was under the chairmanship of David Mackenzie, the Debating Society managed to obtain membership of the Public Schools' Debating Association. It provided a team for the heats at St. Peter's School, York, but was defeated by Ampleforth College.

By the late 1950s the Country Dancing Society organised barn dances for the Upper School in the school gym. The Darlington High School provided the partners and plimsolls were the required footwear. It looks as if meetings had previously alternated between the two schools. According to a magazine report in January 1955 the continued existence of the Country Dancing Society was demonstrated 'by the presence of bedraggled High School girls outside the Gym at the end of dinner hour on Mondays and by red-faced Grammar School boys walking brazenly round the High School during Thursday dinner hours'. By the summer the High School had left Cleveland Avenue for Hummersknott, so the extra distances involved would have been unwelcome.

New societies also appeared, including Le Cercle Francais in 1955. Its reports in the *Elizabethan* were invariably written in French. Whilst this might well have demonstrated the erudition of the contributor, it must have done little for the average reader. For a time it was emulated by the Classical Society, which, as 'Annales Societas Classicae', submitted its reports in Latin.

Also newly established were a Jazz Club, a Photographic Society, with competitions for Senior and Junior sections, and a Railway Society, described as being the most popular club in the school. In 1961 it was achieving average attendances of sixty at its meetings. When a classroom was converted into a pottery, the Art Society provided a Pottery Section and, initially, attendance had to be limited to a select number to maintain standards. The new offshoot also robbed the parent society of some of its support in the early days.

In 1951 the Film Society was reported as being 'dormant', yet there were proposals that next year it would make its own films. Nothing is known of any film making, but the club survived. In 1955 there were usually three meetings per term, but average attendances were under 200, compared with over 250 in the previous year. It was felt that there was a lack of Upper School support. Mr Busby, the laboratory technician, acted as projectionist in his own time. In 1959 the practice of having criticisms of newly released films posted in the main corridor started.

A New Way to Pay Old Debts was the school play in April 1951, but School Dramatic Evenings survived, with a production of *Pygmalion* in the preceding month. Also performed in April were The Junior Plays. The school magazine described them as 'amateurish by the standards of the school production, but they had lively vigour and enthusiasm'. In 1958, however, instead of a single school play, four separate productions, one by each House, were put on. They included Gilbert and Sullivan's *Trial by Jury,* and the *Ides of March,* adapted from Shakespeare's *Julius Caesar,* using modern dress. Programmes for the school play were usually 2/6d (12½p) each. For the full school plays, the practice was to use the biology lab, then under the hall, as a 'Green Room', with performers being called by a connecting telephone when needed on stage.

In May 1952, by way of a change, a marionette performance of *Alice in Wonderland* was given by the pupils and a few months later about 400 pupils from the school attended a performance of Chipperfield's Circus.

The annual school camp was still well supported during the decade, with Versailles and Copenhagen being popular destinations. The geography/geology field courses were also well established. Taking 1955 as an example, there were two geology expeditions, one to Roseberry Topping, the other to the old Gang Mines in Swaledale. Arran and the Cairngorms were also selected as destinations, sometimes with visits extending to six days. In 1956 the Geography and Geology Departments made a survey of Whitby between 25 and 27 April.

A new activity for 1955 was a House Speech Competition, held for the first time on 16 February. The School Captain presided and the school was divided into three sections for the contest.

The Final Extension

Financial constraints delayed the building of the desperately needed classroom extension and fifteen years passed from the ending of the war to its completion. However, shortly before the construction of the extension, the old cellars, which had remained substantially unaltered since 1878, were converted into a pottery. The new facility replaced Room 18, which had been used for a number of years.

By 1958 the long-awaited project was at last under way. The extension was to be built parallel to the Abbey Road boundary and would be three storeys high. Some of the old air-raid shelters had been demolished and a temporary fence stretched across the yard to delineate the building site. By this time, there were 870 pupils in the school.

The new building's style was described at its opening as 'restrained modern', so, for the first time, the school would be extended without any attempt being made to blend in the new buildings with the existing ones. The contractor was Edgar Lawson, and Eric Tornbohm, the Borough Architect, whose son was in the Sixth Form at the time of the opening, was responsible for the design.

The extension contained two biology laboratories, a junior science lab, two chemistry labs (one advanced), with a balance room which projected into the existing building. There was also provision for a geography room, a geology lab and three classrooms, with a heating chamber, a dark room and store rooms. A covered way under the building, later filled in, gave access from Abbey Road to the schoolyard. As part of the project, the verandas from the 1938 extension were removed. In the May 1960 issue of the *Elizabethan* it was claimed that the fear of damage to the new extension resulted in a ban on the carrying about of satchels or haversacks. A plethora of string bags was said to have been the result.

The provision of the new labs released the space occupied by the two existing labs under the school hall. Consequently, the kitchen, built during the war on part of the quadrangle, and the immediate post-war dining hall could be replaced by new facilities under the hall. By early 1960, before the extension was finished, the new dining hall was operating. According to one contributor to the *Elizabethan*, the better lighting 'enables diners to recognise the food before it is eaten'. The High Table and the other furniture in the dining hall, together with the beech strip panelling in the two entrances, was donated by the Old Boys' Association from its War Memorial Fund. For its part, the Queen Elizabeth Association, which had re-formed in October 1958, donated the cup case in the school's main entrance.

The new dining arrangements in turn enabled the building containing the dining hall to be converted into workshops for woodwork and metalwork. Till then the school had no facilities for teaching handicrafts. Further work, including improvements to the staff accommodation and the provision of a new music room, was also undertaken and there were extensive alterations to the heating system.

A bequest from Sir Eric Miller, who died in 1958, provided the funding for a new reference library, to be called the Philip Wood Memorial Library. It was built in the space in the court occupied by the old wartime kitchen and it also opened in 1960. It was furnished with shelves, single desks and chairs, all made of light oak. The books in the new library, which were all protected by polythene sleeves, could not be borrowed. The Memorial Library had a life of ten years only, becoming a victim of the general enlargement of the library facilities required for the new Sixth Form College.

The new arrangements led to a further change. The external stairway on the side of the hall, built in 1929, was replaced by a covered one giving access to the Abbey Road end of the hall. The opportunity was also taken to re-site the tuck shop below the new stairway.

The completion of the new buildings was the climax of Arthur Hare's twenty-six years of service to the school and, having delayed his retirement until the extension was finished, he left in the summer of 1960. Then, on the following 23 November, the new wing, although already in use, was officially opened by Dr Hare, with prayers offered by Canon Wansey, vicar of Darlington. According to the official programme, the cost of the building works was £98,745, plus £14,600 for furniture and equipment. The opening was followed by science and art exhibitions in the school, with displays of photos and documents.

At its AGM on 26 October 1960, the 100 members of the Queen Elizabeth Association present honoured Dr Hare on his retirement by unanimously electing him a Life Member. The annual subscription at that time was one guinea and it covered both husband and wife. In the following year, on 1 July 1961, Dr Hare had an honorary degree of Doctor of Civil Law conferred upon him by Durham University.

The Last Headmaster

The new Headmaster was Charles Lionel Hall, a London University graduate, who had been the Headmaster of Grangefield Grammar School at Stockton. As the possessor of a very different personality to the outgoing Headmaster, he had nothing of his predecessor's remoteness and was far more engaged with individual pupils.

Whilst it was clear by 1960 that a Labour-controlled council was likely to attempt the introduction of comprehensive education into the town, there was no certainty about either the time scale or the result. The school, with its new extension, was thriving as never before and the idea that Mr Hall would find himself devoting much of his tenure to assisting in the demise of his school would not have occurred to many at the time of his arrival. The ancient plate from the private pew at St. Cuthbert's was still attached to the door of the Headmaster's study and was seemingly safe.

There were now 863 pupils in the school, with no fewer than 200 of them in the Sixth Form. Unfortunately, class sizes were increasing, and the Sixth Form had an average of thirty-six in each of its classes. Twenty years earlier the orchestra had made its first appearance with twenty-four members. Now there were two orchestras, with almost 100 boys split between them. Staff turnover was high and between 1960 and 1964 over thirty new teachers came to the school, but owing to the continued growth in pupil numbers, slightly fewer left.

Amongst the newcomers was Robin Smith, who taught English and who became a staff member at the Sixth Form College. A returning

Old Boy was John Dodds who came – initially on a temporary basis – to teach physics. As Jack Dodds, teacher of biology and yet another Old Boy, was long established, there were, for a time, two namesakes on the staff. Following the conversion of the old dining hall, T.E. Wood was appointed as the school's first Head of Handicrafts. He was also to assist in teaching maths and English.

Keith Blood, the violin tutor, left and was temporarily replaced by Mrs V. Bisset, but his long-term successor was Mr de Frettes. At the end of 1962 Katie Cox retired. She gave eighteen years' service after being engaged on a temporary basis. Two departures in 1963 were Messrs Bradford and Wall. Bradford, who was succeeded as Senior Classics Master by Jack Pursey, was a Methodist lay preacher, whilst Wall left to train for the Methodist ministry. By this time Fred Philips was the Britons' Housemaster.

There were changes amongst the non-teaching staff too. Miss Hastie left the secretarial staff to marry, Mr Busby retired as Senior Lab Technician and Bob Wilson, the playing field warden (otherwise groundsman) since 1937, left to become a foreman with the Parks Department. Mr Farnaby was his replacement. In April 1963 David Robertson Carrick died, bringing to an end a connection with the school going back to the previous century when he had arrived as a county scholar.

Notwithstanding the building of the new reference library, the original library was not forgotten. During the autumn term of 1960 a programme of refurbishment, including the installation of new shelves, had been undertaken. Because of the growth in the availability of paperback books, the Penguin Library was also extended. It now provided for all kinds of paperbacks and, with accuracy but without originality, was renamed the Paperback Library. The result of the work, according to the *Elizabethan*, was chaos but normality was soon restored. A Book Week held in 1961 resulted in 150 books being donated by boys.

There were now no fewer than seventy Sixth Formers on the library staff, the largest number ever. To improve facilities, the reference library was opened for Sixth Formers on evenings from 6 till 9.

The expansion in pupil numbers and the resultant shortage of space resulted in the library having to be used for other purposes and by early 1963 it was felt that its standards had fallen. There was said to be a 'lack of atmosphere', and efforts of an unspecified nature were made to improve this. At the same time, the Paperback Library was again expanded. Eight hundred additional books had been acquired through the 'Bring a Paperback and Borrow a Paperback' scheme and it was hoped the total would reach two thousand. However, there were problems, apparently with the doors, which delayed bringing the scheme into operation. After modified glass doors were provided, the improved library was opened – in time for the autumn term of 1964 – by the Mayor, Alderman Alf Bird. A library survey around this time showed that *Punch* was the most popular magazine.

The success of the *Elizabethan*, which in 1964 enjoyed a circulation of 1,300, in attracting advertising continued. The demand by employers for former pupils was reflected in the number of career opportunities advertised. The May 1963 issue contained an article by J.R. Wedge. Although it was written in a facetious style, it made a serious point. He referred to the depletion of the 3rd Year VI during the school year, stating that, as a result, clubs were losing officers and forms their prefects. Wedge placed the blame on the impending disappearance of the state scholarship. He believed that, because the increased status and financial advantages over a local authority grant were now lost, boys were prepared to accept a university place based on their Upper VI results. A year later the magazine contained what appears to be the first mention of the Comprehensive proposals for Darlington. Perhaps unsurprisingly, they were attacked.

In 1964 candidates for the Magazine Committee were asked how they would improve the magazine. The principal response was that there was too much in it, because it was felt that that certain items ought to be there and too little of the content was of interest. Unfortunately, no conclusion seems to have been reached about what was interesting.

By 1964, when there were no fewer than thirty-five clubs in the school, the Senior Debating Society distinguished itself by winning the Northern Final of the Schools Debating Association at York against Ampleforth College, but it was defeated in the London Final by

Eton College, no less. Two years later, R.D. Sethna, the Saxons' House Captain, was elected National Chairman of the Association.

In 1962 the BBC presented a Literary Brains Trust at the school, organised by W.H. Smith & Son and, three years later, the school was the venue for a preliminary round of the annual debating competition for the 'Observer Mace' and its team was second to St. Peters School, York. Early in 1966 a school team participated in a Tyne Tees Television quiz held at Newcastle, but it lost in the first round. By then there was an ongoing Road Safety Quiz with other Darlington schools and the Grammar School provided both A and B teams.

Earlier in the decade, a Middle School Debating Society was formed and its first motion, which was carried, was that 'This House believes in the suppression of the working classes'! The lack of later magazine reports suggests that the society was short-lived. Another new society, the Forum, was launched. It was intended to promote intelligent discussion about matters of social, political and economic interest. Topics discussed included Cuba – allegedly with thinly disguised CND propaganda – unemployment and world starvation. It seems to have been viewed in some circles as a left-wing organisation.

There was also a Language and Dialect Society, but by late 1962 it had become dormant, as had the long-established Play Reading Society. Yet, soon afterwards, the play readings were attracting average attendances of twenty. Similarly the defunct Astronomical Society suffered three failed attempts at revival, but, in time, was functioning again. Such was the pattern for many societies.

Other newcomers were the Chemistry Society, which had, for some reason, operated for several years in a clandestine manner, and the Community Service Society, under the charge of Jack Pursey. Its purpose was to visit and help the old and handicapped in Darlington. Its members regularly visited St. Cuthbert's Hospital at Croft on Monday evenings to befriend the patients and to provide assistance.

Amongst other newcomers were a Historical Society, an Opera Society, a Fifth Upper Society and a short-lived Radio Society. Some things did not change; the Cercle Francais magazine reports were still given in French and the Natural History Society was as consistently successful as ever. Barn dances, with the music provided by a band made up of pupils and girls by the High School, went on as before.

There was, reputedly, another school activity, but no reports on it ever graced the *Elizabethan*. Rumour has it that a gambling school operated in the Tower and that it had provided itself with an electrical device which sounded a bell when someone set foot on the stairs. Understandably, its existence is not documented.

The 1960 and 1961 school camps were at Heidelberg and Avignon respectively. A party of seventy-two went to Heidelberg but, by contrast, only forty-six participated in the 1962 camp at Innsbruck. The destinations were beginning to be further afield and the 1963 and 1964 camps were held respectively at Rimini and in Switzerland.

In 1964 the first French holiday exchange took place. It seems to have operated on similar lines to the exchanges operated under the town-twinning arrangements. Nineteen French boys stayed here for three weeks, then the Grammar School pupils went back with them to France for a further three weeks. A further exchange was planned for 1965 but no information about any post-1964 exchanges has been found. There were now regular skiing trips. In 1963 Mr Lyonette took a party to Switzerland. Unfortunately, a junior pupil broke a leg, but he refused to be sent home early. During the 1965–6 year the more adventurous had the opportunity of sampling a communist regime with a canoeing and swimming holiday overland to Yugoslavia.

There were still many trips within this country. For example a Sixth Form history trip went by overnight coach to London on 16 March 1961. An afternoon was spent in the House of Commons and there were visits to the offices of *The Times*, the Science Museum and the Public Records Office. The party managed to take in a performance of *The Duchess of Malfi* at the Aldwych Theatre. Stays at Earls Orchard were still the norm for geographers and geologists and the annual trips to York, Edinburgh and Hadrian's Wall were now embedded in school tradition.

The school had a little unscheduled excitement in February 1961. A heifer escaped from the abattoir and found its way to Swinburne Road, where it encountered Harry Welding, one of the staff. He was on his bike and was knocked to the ground when the animal charged him.

It then entered the school yard and, having chased Jack Dodds and the caretaker, headed towards Woodland Road. Eventually it was shot in a garden in Elms Road.

The 1960 Old Boys' Annual Dinner, held at the Imperial Hotel, was unique in that it was attended by three of the school's four Headmasters – Mr Hall and his two predecessors, Arthur Hare and Leonard Taylor. The intention was to commemorate Mr Taylor's 80th birthday and he was accommodated at the hotel at the Association's expense. One hundred and fifty Old Boys and masters, with ages ranging from 20 to 83, attended, with many coming from distant parts of the country. A greater than usual number of former masters were also present. During this period a separate Old Boys' Dinner was usually held in London.

In 1960 subscriptions provided £182 11s 6d of the Association's total income of £230 6s 10d and the school magazine at £90 was the main item of expenditure. Fifty pounds was invested in the recently launched Premium Bonds but, because they had to be held by a person, they were registered in Percy Moss' name as a nominee.

It looks as if the subsidiary organisations were enrolling people who were not members of the Association itself, for, in January 1964, it was ruled that all members of sections, other than lady badminton players, must be members of the Association. It was, however, conceded that permission for a limited number of exceptions was possible. Indeed, on 16 September 1965 the committee resolved to allow the rugby section to increase the number of playing members who were not Old Boys. Some months earlier, the section had been permitted to form a Colts XV, deriving its members from other schools. A very real problem lay ahead for, within a few years, the fresh supply of Old Boys would cease completely.

In his history of the school Norman Sunderland referred to the school's need for another gym and for a swimming pool. Nothing seems to have been done with regard to a gym, but active steps were taken to provide a pool and it was envisaged that one would be built at the school as a commemoration of the 400th anniversary. The project having been approved by the LEA, the Old Boys' Association proposed to raise £4,000–5,000, on the basis that a similar amount would be raised by subscription. The LEA would provide the rest.

Nothing came of the proposal, and it seems reasonable to surmise that the Association's desire to assist evaporated once the local authority had decided to end the school's existence.

As well as increasing in size, the school was thriving academically. At the 1962 Speech Day, it was reported that seven state scholarships had been awarded to pupils. Of the ninety who had gained A levels, fifteen had achieved A levels with one or more distinctions in one or more subjects. O level passes had been gained by no fewer than 197 pupils.

For the year 1962–3 forty-seven boys entered university, whilst eighteen more went to colleges of advanced technology or other colleges of higher education. At that time the proportion of boys from the school entering university was double the national average for grammar schools.

The number of options available to pupils also increased. In his 1964 report to the governors, Mr Hall referred to the Upper V being organised into five forms, thus providing more options and making possible twenty courses. Economics at O level was now an extra subject available to those in the Lower VI, whilst woodwork and technical drawing were available to those in the Upper V for the first time. There are also indications that by now an increasing number of pupils were studying Latin.

The Headmaster also provided some statistics about GCE passes. In the last exams, the O level pass percentage was 65.8, with 1,250 individual subjects entered, and with 360 results in the top three grades. The Sixth Formers had 78 per cent passes, compared with 77 per cent in 1963, but it is not clear whether Hall was referring to O levels, A levels or both. Of eighty-nine VI Form leavers, forty-one entered university and eleven colleges of advanced technology, whilst thirteen went to other colleges. In contrast twenty-eight boys had gone to university in 1954. In 1964, 75 per cent of Sixth Form leavers continued in full-time education compared with 70 per cent ten years earlier. There had been a recent school inspection, and the work and calibre of the Sixth Form had particularly impressed the inspectors. A new development in 1963 was a careers evening at the school, with forty different professions and trades represented at it.

Sub-prefects were briefly reintroduced, with a handful in the Lower VI, but none are listed after 1962–3. In addition, the first School List published under the new regime set out the names of the members of staff in alphabetical order. Presumably the change was not well received by the longer-serving staff, for there was a quick reversion to the old arrangement whereby staff were listed in order of their length of service.

From 1961 the operation of the express stream was altered and the system whereby pupils in the stream did not sit O levels in the subjects to be taken by them at A level was ended. Now, they sat four or five O levels a year early whilst still in the Lower V and then sat another two or three in the Lower VI. Of the three Lower VI forms at this time, one seems to have catered for the express stream only, although eventually, in 1966, a specially designated V Lower X Form for those taking the express route appeared. In that year it contained twenty-eight pupils, including eight studying German and three Greek.

As a result of the 1961 change, comparisons of O level passes over this period become difficult, because the pupils in the express stream were now finding themselves sitting more O levels than they would have earlier.

Another feature of this period was the appearance, in 1963, of a Lower VI Remove form. In its first year there were twenty-nine in it, but the School List gives no particulars of the subjects studied by many of them. Everyone in the Remove form entered it from the Upper V and many of them passed into the Upper VI in the next academic year. Nevertheless, the majority of members of the Upper V who stayed on went into one of the other Lower VI forms, so presumably those who found themselves in the Remove were seen as needing special attention. The use of the form as a reception class for pupils entering the school from the secondary moderns came later.

Shortly before the new Remove form appeared, the two Remove forms through which boys entering the school at thirteen had passed were renamed. In 1962 V Lower Remove became V L R and IV Remove, was replaced by IV H. It took its first intake of pupils from the previous year's class III 4. Then, in the next year V L R became V Lower H.

C and D forms disappeared. Shell forms were now numbered 1 to 4, whilst the III to V Lower forms were entitled A, B, Alpha, Beta and possibly H. Most, but not all, boys in the Shells were allocated to a form by reference to the initial letter of their surname, in a manner similar to their selection for a House. As an example, boys with surnames beginning with an A, B, C or D might all find themselves in Shell 1. Clearly there was still no streaming in the first year.

The III Forms had a similar system, except that one alphabetical list of surnames was divided between the A and B forms, whilst a separate list was divided between the Alpha and Beta forms. It appears therefore that the year had two streams, each with two forms. By contrast, the allocation of surnames amongst the IV forms suggests that there were three streams, one each for the A and B forms and one common to both Alpha and Beta. Within a year or two, the practice of allocating pupils to forms in this manner seems to have ceased except for the first year. It must be stressed that there appear to have been many exceptions to the practice of placing pupils by using the alphabet.

By this time the School Lists gave no indication of pupils' examination performances or, where relevant, of their placings in class. As a result, particularly as there is little information available elsewhere, it is now difficult to work out how some forms were organised.

A staff circular from September 1964 survives and it provides an insight into the arrangements needed in a large school for the first day of the school year. The new Shell boys would be directed to the dining room under Mr Moss whilst the rest would meet with their previous year's masters in their old rooms and would then be reallocated. The assembly, later than usual at 9.30 a.m., would be as for a normal Monday. The III Forms, Upper and Lower V and Upper VI would assemble in the hall, the IVs would be with their masters in their own rooms, whilst the Lower VI would go to the lecture room. Stress was laid upon the need to quickly deliver dinner money to the office and also to indicate the numbers for school milk.

As far as sport was concerned, there appears to have been a growth in the level of activities at this time. According to the report at the 1960 Speech Day, in the previous year there had been fifty-two association football fixtures, fifty-one for rugby, twenty-five for cricket and nineteen for swimming. The level of participation was reflected in the award of county honours to two soccer players from the school, five athletes and six swimmers. Half school colours as well as the full ones were now being awarded to team members.

In 1961 school colours were awarded as follows:

Tennis	3 re-awards	1 new	4 new half colours	
Cricket	3 re-awards	1 new	5 new half colours	2 re-awards of halves
Gym			2 new half colours	
Swimming	2 re-awards	2 new		1 re-award of half
Athletics	7 re-awards	2 new	3 new half colours	1 re-award of half

The athletics calendar was also crowded. In 1964 the School Sports held at Abbey Road on 6–8 May included three new events – Senior and Junior Hammer Throwing and the Junior Mile. It was followed in turn by the Darlington Secondary Schools Athletics Championships at Longfield Road Stadium, the Durham Schools Championship at Houghton-le-Spring and the Durham Schools v. Northumberland v. Cumberland competition at Ashington. At the final event, J. Crowther and A.M. Wallace from the school had performed better than the national standard.

Then, a week after going on to win the school's pentathlon competition, Wallace was at Hendon representing Durham in the National Schools Championship. There was also an event between the school and Ashington Grammar School at Abbey Road on 8 July and the Holgate Trophy was competed for at York on 16 July. The competitors were Darlington, Barnsley, Doncaster and York. Finally, there were the IVth Block Sports [sic] on 20 July.

Despite a curtailment of their activities in 1963 because of repairs to the Baths, both the Senior and Junior Swimming Teams were undefeated during the 1964 season whilst a total of 317 gym awards were made during the year. In 1960, 318 boys had held the Third Class Award in gymnastics, with 29 having Second Class and 8 full colours. The less physical activity of chess also made its contribution in 1964, for the School Chess Team won the Darlington and District Chess League Championship for the third season in succession.

In the same year it was recorded that including the gymnastic staff, now expanded to five, no fewer than twenty staff members assisted with the various sporting and physical activities, including fell walking and country dancing. Twenty-five teams represented the school in the numerous and varied competitive events and there were 180 fixtures. The Lawn Tennis team played sixteen matches, whilst the Swimming First Team had five as against the Under-15s' eight. The country dancers took part in a BBC Home Service broadcast that also included a talk on the 'Brigands of Baydale Beck' and another on Darlington. The programme was recorded at the High School and was broadcast on 9 December 1963.

Geoff Thwaites, a 17-year-old at the school, had the distinction of competing as a swimmer in the 1964 Olympic Games in Tokyo. He missed four weeks' schooling to do so. Shortly before, he had been selected to swim for Britain against Hungary and the Soviet Union.

In 1964 there no fewer than 180 pupils on the roll of instrumental classes and, of 66 candidates for the Associated Board of Royal Schools of Music exams, 54 were successful.

June 25, 1963 was Founders' Day, but this time it was no ordinary commemoration, for it represented the 400th anniversary of the granting of the school's Charter and the school had been able to secure as its guest Queen Elizabeth the Queen Mother.

To prepare for the Royal Visit, several meetings were held, all chaired by C.N.S. Nicholson, the Town Clerk, and all boys, staff and members of the Old Boys' Association were provided with a brochure about the visit. On the day itself, after being received at Bank Top station by Lord Barnard, the Lord Lieutenant of the County, the Queen Mother went directly to a service at St. Cuthbert's, scheduled to start at 11.15 a.m. About 590 pupils were present, together with the staff and their wives. The aldermen and councillors in their robes and other dignitaries, including some Old Boys and their wives, also attended and their procession was heralded by a trumpet fanfare. The Bishop of Durham, Maurice Harland, preached the sermon.

After a ceremony at the Town Hall, then still on the end of the covered market, the visitor headed for the school, arriving in wet weather at the north entrance at about 12.45 p.m. After some presentations took place, the party moved into the school hall where a bouquet was presented to the Queen Mother. She then delivered her speech, ensuring instant popularity by requesting a day's extra holiday for the pupils. After the School Captain had responded to her, Norman Sunderland, the Senior History Master, presented the Queen Mother with a copy of his history of the school, written to commemorate the Quatercentenary. It was available to everyone else for 3/- (15p). The ceremony in the hall was relayed to other guests in the library.

The visitor then unveiled a commemorative plaque in the library and was presented with a book of photographs of the North East by Mr E.H.R. Freeman, Chairman of the Queen Elizabeth Association.

By now it was time for lunch. Both masters' rooms had been converted into dining rooms to provide buffet lunches for 150 Old Boys and their ladies, whilst the press, police and others were served with a buffet lunch in the woodwork room. The main lunch, prepared by the School Meals Service, and accompanied by toasts, took place in the dining hall. After lunch the weather was dry and, before leaving, the Queen Mother mingled with boys and parents in the playground, before signing the visitors' book on a table under the arch of the new wing. On the afternoon, the usual cricket match – Old Boys against School – took place, followed on the evening by a dance organised by the Old Boys' Association at Croft Spa Hotel.

The event was also commemorated by a Quatercentenary Dance organised by the prefects. It took place on 12 July in a school hall made up to look like a medieval castle. On the previous evening, the prefects had dined at the White Horse Hotel. Their guests were the Headmaster, the Second Master and Messrs Sunderland, Welding and Thompson. There was also a Quatercentenary Concert, which played to packed houses, on 17–18 July. The participants were the First Orchestra and the Choir.

The Royal Visit seems to have had another outcome. On 16 January 1964 a letter was sent from the Queen Mother's Treasurer at Clarence House to the Headmaster relating to the provision of photos for use in conjunction with a portrait. In a further letter the Treasurer indicated that Queen Elizabeth, as she was described, could allow about one hour from 11 a.m. on 9 June for the portrait sitting. This was the only date she could manage. Presumably the date was met, for the result was Lindsey Bird's portrait of the Queen Mother. It was unveiled in the School Library by Edgar Bonsall, an Old Boy, on 10 December 1965.

The Quatercentenary was a high point in the history of the school, for, less than three months later, the Peter Plan was unveiled. The continued existence of the Darlington Grammar School was now threatened.

The Peter Plan

The *Northern Despatch* of 28 January 1964 contained a cartoon showing two players standing on a rugby field. One is saying to the other, 'How can the system work? None of the other schools play rugby.'

The system referred to would, if adopted, totally change secondary education in Darlington. It was outlined in a report, immediately dubbed 'the Peter Plan', that had been prepared for the council by Mr David Peter, the Chief Education Officer. It had been had commissioned by the Labour-controlled council, and was unveiled on 12 September 1963. The stated intention was to seek the views of all interested parties before the council made any decision on whether to implement the report.

Peter's proposals were of enormous significance for the Grammar School, as the Chief Education Officer's brief was to prepare a scheme for the introduction of comprehensive education into Darlington. His proposals envisaged the end of both the Queen Elizabeth Grammar School and the Darlington High School for Girls.

The system for secondary education established by the Education Act of 1944 had enjoyed a general acceptance for many years but, over time, an increasing number of educationalists and politicians challenged it. There was a considerable gap in the levels of education offered in grammar schools compared with secondary modern schools, which generally had to make do with inferior facilities. As a generalisation, it was difficult for pupils selected for a secondary modern education to achieve any meaningful qualifications while at school.

Furthermore the method of selection, effectively relying upon a single examination, was seen as arbitrary. The opponents of the system of selection contended that those who did not pass the 11-plus saw themselves labelled as failures. The second chance at 13-plus, provided by some authorities including Darlington, was not seen as overcoming the objections to the system.

The opponents favoured the comprehensive system of education, whereby all pupils in a given area would, irrespective of ability, be educated in the same school. There were many local variations and there were issues such as whether pupils should be grouped according to ability for teaching. In broad terms, support for comprehensive education was stronger amongst those holding left-wing political views, although many Labour MPs, having benefited from a grammar school education, were slow to support the growing movement for change. Nevertheless, by the late 1950s an increasing number of local authorities were adopting the comprehensive system.

In Darlington, as far back as 1958 the Education Committee had attempted to alleviate the perceived arbitrariness of the 11-plus system and had modified the procedure. The modified system relied as to half upon the continuing 11-plus exams and as to half upon order of merit lists supplied by the primary schools. Neither the parents nor the pupils were given any advance warning of the examination dates. In marginal cases, or where exam results did not match the expectations for a pupil, the school record card would also be consulted.

At the same time the 13-plus exam was brought to an end and, at ages beyond 11, any transfer was dependent upon the recommendation of the secondary school Heads. Although the Heads' recommendations at both 11-plus and 13-plus were claimed to be remarkably accurate, the possibility of sole reliance upon them was not perceived as being acceptable to either staff or parents, so further reform was seen as being needed.

Then in 1959, four years before the publication of the Peter Plan, an attempt to introduce comprehensive education to Darlington was made by the controlling Labour group on the council. A new secondary school was to be built at Branksome and it was proposed that, under a pilot comprehensive scheme, the new school would take all pupils, irrespective of sex or academic ability, from the Cockerton and Pierremont areas.

There was strong parental opposition and when the plans were submitted to the Secretary of State for Education, they were rejected. The proposal was unsatisfactory in that it would have deprived those pupils who happened to live in the catchment area of the new school, but not those living elsewhere, of sitting the 11-plus and of having the opportunity of going to the grammar or high schools. When Branksome School eventually opened in 1964 it started life as a secondary modern, albeit a co-educational one.

The task given to Mr Peter was to consider the existing methods of selection for secondary education in Darlington and their adequacy. Because the plan for Branksome had been badly thought out, Peter made sure that his own proposals were the subject of careful consideration. He was aware that Ministers of Education had always objected to the closure of grammar schools on purely ideological grounds and that evidence of an improvement in the educational arrangements arising from any such closure was required.

In brief, the following proposals were put forward by him for consideration:

1. eliminate the 11-plus and send everyone to their local secondary school;

2. pupils to stay there until the minimum school-leaving age, soon to be raised to 16;

3. all secondary schools to offer GCE O level courses and, later, the new GCSE;

4. aim to have a five- or six-form entry for each school, so that they would be all of a similar size. The High School would become one of the secondary schools;

5. the Grammar School would remain on its present site and would take post-O level pupils to A or S level standard. The future name of this proposed Sixth Form School/College was left open.

It was envisaged that the comprehensive schools would have about 750 pupils each on average. There would be no single-sex schools.

The Education Officer was well aware that his proposals for the Grammar School and High School were the ones likely to give rise to problems, so he gave particular attention to the issues relating to them. He mentioned that in Darlington 22.5 per cent of pupils normally went to one of the grammar schools, a higher proportion than in most northern boroughs.

As far as the Grammar School was concerned, he had no intention of denigrating it. On the contrary, given the new role intended for it, he set out to establish the particular features that had contributed towards its prestige and consider how to attempt to preserve and, if possible, enhance them.

Peter, referring to the age of the school, stressed its many changes of character. He mentioned its admission of girls in the early nineteenth century, its existence as a boarding school and as a prep school and its one-time charging of fees. It had, he argued, undergone a continuous process of development, implying that it could now develop further.

He acknowledged that any future changes had to be for the better, with the best features of the school preserved. He picked out the importance of the size and strength of the Sixth Form. In the year 1962–3 there were 222 pupils in it, with 240 in the school aged 16 or over. Twenty subjects up to A or S level standard were offered. Both it and the High School were noteworthy for the large size of their Sixth Forms, and were therefore popular in the town.

Peter thought that, on balance, mixed schools were better than single-sex ones. He considered that delaying selection beyond eleven was not satisfactory. Selection at 13-plus only postponed the problem.

Peter asked what would be achieved by his proposals. He argued that selection should go and that all schools would provide an O level education. They would have a broader curriculum, including the study of languages, and each would serve its own area, thus saving on time and travelling costs. The existing facilities of all schools would be used and the new schools planned, such as Longfield, would fit into the overall pattern of development, so there would be a minimum of expense.

It was claimed by him that the best of the traditions of the grammar and high schools would be preserved in the 'new look' Grammar School. It was accepted that the scheme would destroy both schools in their present form, but it should be seen in the context of the revitalisation of all the secondary schools with a new sense of purpose. The staff of the two grammar schools were highly qualified, with most capable of teaching to A level, and they would be retained and concentrated. That would be more effective than having a system scattering them about. The limitation of A level teaching to one establishment would offer much greater teaching expertise and choice of subjects than if each secondary school was to provide similar facilities.

The Education Officer tried to counter the arguments in favour of the retention of the Grammar School in its existing form by observing that further extensions on the existing site were practically impossible. Future growth would therefore be a problem. In other words, if the site were to be used by Sixth Formers only, the lower numbers would avert such problems. In this respect Peter was totally wrong! The same site now accommodates more than twice the maximum number on the Grammar School roll and a huge number of additional buildings have been erected at the expense of the old school yard. In the event, reconstruction work commenced as soon as the Grammar School came to an end.

Then Peter allowed himself a little speculation. The Queen Elizabeth Grammar School in its new form would complete a Higher Education 'campus' adjoining both the Teacher Training College and the new College of Further Education. This could provide the nucleus for a flexible scheme permitting experimental and continuous development. There could be a possible sharing of facilities and a sports hall, swimming pool and playing fields were mentioned. The joint use of labs was also a possibility.

These ideas never bore fruit.

Such was the Plan. It received support from the governing bodies of three out of four of the existing secondary modern schools, but, hardly surprisingly, less from those of the two Grammar Schools. The views of the teachers' unions were sought, but the reference to the National Union of Teachers' response has been altered in the report. It originally stated that the Union 'expressed support by a narrow majority' for the retention of the 11-plus exam, with the proviso that the intake to the grammar schools should be effectively halved by limiting it to 10 per cent or 12 per cent. This had been altered to read 'expressed some support' and the reference to the size of the majority was struck out.

However, in *Going Comprehensive,* published in 1970, it is asserted that the majority of NUT members favoured 11 to 18 through schools (schools which, unlike those under the proposed Darlington system, would teach pupils from 11 to 18, assuming they stayed on beyond 16). One of the authors was Oswald O'Brien, a Labour councillor in Darlington and briefly the town's MP. According to the same book, the Chief Education Officer had previously fended off comprehensive proposals by arguing over staffing difficulties and the claimed social breadth of grammar schools.

Some interested parties considered the schemes adopted in other areas, in particular those favouring the idea of a Middle School. Others advocated schools with twice the number of pupils proposed in the plan on the basis that the range of subjects available could then be increased. Peter countered this argument by drawing attention to St. Mary's School, the local Catholic boys' secondary school. It had only a three-form entry, with a total of about 500 pupils, yet, despite its small size, it presented candidates in ten O level subjects, plus up to nine in Northern Counties exams for school leavers at fifteen. He conceded that rarer subjects like Greek, economics and divinity might have to be limited to one comprehensive school, even though they were available at the grammar and high schools. Even at those schools there was sometimes only one candidate.

Miss Stanton, the respected Principal of the Teachers' Training College, proposed her own scheme. She opposed the idea of a separate Sixth Form College and wanted each secondary school to specialise in the teaching of certain subjects only to A level. Peter considered that it would be unsatisfactory to have A level pupils scattered amongst all the town's secondary schools. They would all have weak Sixth Forms and resources as a result.

Other authorities had considered schemes with a Sixth Form College and Peter's proposals had aroused considerable interest elsewhere, but no similar scheme to his was known to have been adopted. Consequently, concerns were expressed that local pupils would be used as 'guinea pigs'.

Some respondents had expressed concerns about the secondary schools catering for individual areas, unlike the grammar schools. Peter recognised the problem but was, perhaps, being disingenuous when he expressed the hope that each school would have adequate facilities and be of a comparable standard to the others. He said they should have similar buildings, equipment and playing fields. Nothing was said about the differences in social backgrounds in various areas or about when funding would be available to provide comparable facilities for each school.

There had been queries about mixed-sex schools but no strong objections, and Peter mentioned that there was a possibility that the two Eastbourne schools would be kept as single-sex ones for parents who did not want mixed education. In the event they were merged into one co-educational school.

Not surprisingly, there was a response from those concerned with the Grammar School. It came in the form of a memorandum from the Queen Elizabeth Grammar School Association, which had a membership of about 205, mainly parents of boys of the entire age range currently at the school.

The Association recognised the problems and difficulties arising from selection at 11-plus, but considered that the facilities of the entire range of secondary schools should be improved whilst preserving the continuity leading to Sixth Form work at the Grammar School. Provision should also be made for transfer at any age.

Although its interest was confined to the Darlington Grammar School, the Association wondered whether the Education Committee had appreciated that the High School would draw the whole of its intake as a comprehensive school from the West End, creating a 'closed shop prerogative'.

The Association's view was that the Chief Education Officer was prompted by a quantitative consideration of numbers. His report did not reflect the view of the Ministry of Education that those features that had contributed to the local, regional and national prestige of the school should be preserved and, if possible, enhanced. The proposals would sacrifice those who could benefit from an academic education. The Association, in common with the rest of Darlington, had a legitimate pride in the standing of the school as one of the finest grammar schools in the country. It wanted to maintain, not sacrifice, its academic quality and to use it to uplift the quality of secondary education throughout the entire system in the town.

The memorandum expressed the view that the town was fortunate in having an admission rate into its grammar schools twice that of the national average. The result was that the school made two exceptional and distinctive contributions, not shared by other towns, to the life of Darlington. First was the opportunity for a 25 per cent cross-section of the whole town to live and work together and the second was the availability of a grammar school education to twice as many as elsewhere.

There were other factors that might not be appreciated. Education at the school was not confined to the exceptionally high standard of teaching in class. The value of the school societies from an early age was ignored in the report, as was the unique contribution of the School Orchestra.

The members of the Association were clearly fearful that the new Sixth Form establishment would be linked with, or even become, part of the College of Further Education. The memorandum went on to say that an important educational feature was the character training and acceptance of responsibility given to younger boys by the existing Sixth Form and prefectorial systems. It would not obtain it in a campus structure. The Association was, after careful consideration, unable to assess the effects on pupils in a campus society where wage earners predominated. They asked how a pupil, still of school age and status, would feel if thrust into the company of employed students with financial independence. They contended that Juniors would have no hope of such independence for years to come if a university or college education was contemplated.

A deliberate break at sixteen would discourage large numbers of potential Sixth Form students from continuing their education. The existing system encouraged boys to stay on. The implications of the report had received too little consideration. A hurried decision would be disastrous to Darlington's educational system. The memorandum ended with the quote: 'Let us not, by seeking to do better than good, end up by doing worse than bad.'

In January 1964 Darlington High School Old Girls' Association submitted its own memorandum. In part, it restated some of the objections made on behalf of the Grammar School and it also raised issues specific to the High School. The view was expressed that pupils were too young at sixteen to become a young university group. Furthermore, new industries were coming to the town and parents thinking of moving to Darlington would be influenced by the educational system available. An interesting claim was made to the effect that there had been a failure by the LEA to implement the system evolved in 1958 to replace the 13-plus entry. It was contended that fewer pupils were offered to and accepted by the High School than under the old system.

Having considered the submissions, the Education Committee approved the plan on 27 January. Coincidentally, on the same day the government announced the raising of the school-leaving age to 16 in 1970–1. One Conservative voted with Labour, whilst another made a futile attempt to defer the outcome pending a 'decision' by teachers.

The issue came before a full council meeting for ratification on 6 February 1964. Although Councillor Reg Ekins claimed that the plan depicted the views of one man alone and was 'a brilliant intellectual exercise, but not a practical proposition', the Conservatives did not oppose it outright. Alderman Frank Stephenson, a Grammar School Old Boy, proposed an amendment to refer the matter back in view of its far-reaching effects. He argued that the plan would not do away with selection – even O levels were selective. The Labour majority won the day with a vote in favour of the plan of 23 to 15. The dissenting Conservative, despite considerable pressure, again voted with Labour.

There was considerable correspondence around this time in the local press about the plan. A majority of correspondents seem to have opposed it, mainly because of the effects upon the grammar schools. Concerns included worries about there being a rat race to get into the proposed Sixth Form College and doubts were expressed about the legality of the scheme under the terms of the 1563 charter. Two Grammar School masters, Norman Sunderland and W.W. Allen, who could be described as a robust traditionalist, were amongst the correspondents, as was a Sixth Former, writing under a pseudonym, who favoured the plan. Some staff members also supported the plan. On 15 February 1964 the 350 members of the Old Boys' Association were urged by their president to write in protest, at once, to Mr A.T. Bourne-Arton, the town's Conservative MP.

Although the decision had been made, controversy kept flaring up occasionally and, at one stage, the Education Committee Chairman raised a petition in favour of the scheme and was attacked by the grammar school's staff for doing so. After some outstanding points had been resolved, the delays on the part of the Department of Education and Science remained to be addressed. Peter wrote to the Department on 9 August 1965 reminding it that the proposals had first been submitted eighteen months earlier and that the additional information requested had been supplied. The reminder worked. Acceptance of the scheme was notified within a week!

The Education Committee then resolved to start implementing the scheme in September 1967. This decision was confirmed in full council after a half-hearted attempt by the Conservatives to block the scheme, with their leader admitting that he was banging his head against a brick wall. The motion was carried 20 to 8.

The intention was that the plan would take effect in stages. Firstly, in 1967, Longfield School would open as a comprehensive school and from then all pupils would have the opportunity to take a fifth year and to sit O levels. Next, all secondary moderns would be reorganised as comprehensives with five-year courses providing a leaving age of 16 for everyone. The two Eastbourne separate-sex schools would be merged into a single-sex school and the girls' High School would become a mixed comprehensive. At the same time the Grammar School, at its existing site, would become a mixed Sixth Form College for 650 students, but ultimately would provide for 800. There would be post-GCE courses provided at what, for lack of a new title, was still called the Grammar School.

It was intended that the secondary schools would have eight form entries to cope with increased numbers. There would be no 11-plus examination in 1968 and the first unselected intake would enter the secondary schools, including the former High School, in September of that year. Year by year the proportion of unselected pupils would grow and, after five years, the schools would become fully comprehensive.

After 1967 the Grammar School would reduce in size through receiving no fresh pupils. Then, in 1970 the Sixth Form of what had been the High School would transfer to it and the new college would come into being. However, for a couple of years or so from 1970, the new college would have to cater for pupils who had entered the Grammar School before 1968 and had not reached Sixth Form age.

However, the battle for the establishment of a comprehensive system was not over. Since 1964 the Conservative Party had promised to re-examine the comprehensive proposals with a view to retaining the grammar schools if it was able to do so. Then, in May 1967, with the implementation of the Peter Plan only one year away and what had been regarded as the last 11-plus exam having taken place, the Conservatives regained control of the council.

A new battle was expected, but at the first meeting of the Education Committee the Conservatives supported a decision to spend £300,000 on alterations to the Darlington High School to implement the proposals for its future as a comprehensive school.

However, there was a by-election pending in a safe Conservative seat and the Conservative candidate's election address, published in June, referred to a new plan that would result in the survival of the grammar and high schools, albeit with a reduction in their intakes. Then at the next full council meeting, the Education Committee Chairman withdrew the minute supporting the expenditure for the alterations to the High School, saying that further consideration was needed. Inevitably the Labour Party's reaction was hostile, as was that of the *Northern Despatch*.

In September, the Conservatives published their new proposals. The grammar schools would be retained but with substantially reduced numbers and would exist in parallel with the comprehensive schools, one of which would teach to A level standard. Entry to all schools would be at twelve and selection would be based on 'a profile attainment estimation system at primary schools governed by parental choice'.

The battle lines were drawn up once again and, at a stormy meeting, the Education Committee decided by one vote to retain the

11-plus for a further year. Then, unexpectedly, the Conservative Group issued a statement to the effect that it would not continue to delay the implementation of the Plan. The reality was that, whatever the merits or otherwise of the new proposals, it was far too late to stop the implementation of Peter's proposals.

A conference about comprehensive education took place at Branksome School on 18–30 March 1968. Its purpose was to assist those concerned in making the adjustments needed, but the specific changes to individual . schools were not discussed.

It is not necessary to go into detail about the proceedings, but a succession of existing comprehensive Heads were produced to talk about their own experiences in creating mixed-sex schools, converting a grammar school into a comprehensive school and so forth. They all spoke in favourable terms about their experiences. The delegates were told how, in schools taking pupils of the other sex, there would be needs with regard to additional toilets, or for housecraft rooms for girls. There could be difficulties in integrating staff of both sections as well as pupils. Consideration needed to be given to the mode of address used in a mixed school. Boys might have been accustomed to having their surnames used, whilst girls may have been addressed by their Christian names.

All of the progressive attitudes of the 1960s were on display. Mixed-ability teaching was to be encouraged, whilst remedial classes were frowned upon, and all pupils of all abilities would be motivated and give of their best. All was optimism and there was no hint of *Waterloo Road*.

Indian Summer

In the autumn of 1965 the Secretary of State for Education had approved the scheme for secondary education in Darlington, but the impression is gained that little was said at the Grammar School about its almost certain fate. Even the Headmaster's annual reports to the governors are silent about the subject. The elephant in the schoolroom seems to have been quietly ignored, with life in the school going on as before. The die might have been cast, but initially little changed. The reality, however, was that Mr Hall would increasingly be preoccupied with the need to accommodate his school and his pupils to one change after another.

In July 1965, W.S. Richardson, now designated Deputy Headmaster rather than Second Master, retired after thirty-five years' service. He was succeeded by Norman Sunderland whilst, because of increasing numbers, R.S. Thompson became Head of Sixth Forms. Chris Bennett retired as music master and Ron Giles, Head of Economics since January 1959, also left, being replaced by Keith Willingham.

In 1965 the significant changes at Vane Terrace were yet to come, but there was a slight setback with the examination results. Durham University had ended its GCE exams in 1964 and the school had started using the Cambridge Examinations Syndicate. The A level examination entries were described by the Headmaster as 'experimental' in view of problems over standards and the consequence was a 6–10 per cent reduction in GCE passes for the year.

The 1965 school year saw a slight reduction in numbers in the school. It was seen as reflecting the end of the 'bulge' in post-war births. Entries for A level subjects might have fallen to 296 compared with 305 in 1964, but no fewer than six pupils, including Geoff Thwaites, the Olympic swimmer, gained acceptances at Cambridge. In addition, more than twenty pupils took the Associated Board of Music exams and all were successful.

In 1966 the number of O level entries was 930. The average pass rate was 1 per cent better than in the previous year, but was still below the levels achieved in the Durham Board days. At A level there were 280 subject entries, with 48 grade A or B passes achieved compared with 54 in 1965, but there was a record entry of eight pupils to Oxford or Cambridge universities. To put matters into perspective, it should be mentioned that the number of annual O level entries and pass rates for the school over a period of twelve years had doubled. It was believed at this time that about 30 per cent of pupils starting at the school were staying on to gain A level passes.

The two Upper VI Science forms had sixty pupils compared with sixty-nine in the previous year, but the Arts form had jumped in size from thirty-one to no less than forty-seven. The proportion of arts students to those studying the sciences would have been unthinkable in Doctor Hare's time, but there was apparently a national trend towards an increase in arts studies.

The Headmaster believed that it was imperative that experimentation with the school organisation continued. Such experimentation with the teaching timetable over the last two years had made it possible for boys in the Upper V to have a completely free choice of GCE subjects, although English language and literature and maths were compulsory. Formerly only certain combinations of subjects were available. Following the fashion of the time, the school also acquired a language laboratory.

The popularity of geography and geology at A Level, with over 100 candidates, was presenting a problem in that the school was having difficulty over the provision of field work. Financial help from the Education Committee was required, but whether it was forthcoming is not known.

Interestingly, Mr Hall doubted whether a further increase in Sixth Form numbers was likely. He considered that students and their parents now fully appreciated the advantages of a Sixth Form education, and that most of those likely to benefit from it were already staying on. The use of the Certificate of Secondary Education (CSE) in the secondary modern schools was making more pupils aware of their potential and any future increase in the size of the Sixth Form was likely to come from admissions from the secondary modern schools.

The school now faced external pressures, as well as those resulting from the Peter Plan. In 1966 more than 90,000 students were competing for less than 45,000 university places, so finding places for qualified pupils became increasingly difficult. There were 81 applications to university from the school under the Clearing House Scheme, plus 146 individual applications to polytechnics for degree courses. There were also ten applications to colleges of education.

A further problem was the 'quota' system. Because there was a national shortage of teachers, particularly in science subjects, an artificial limitation on the number of staff who could be employed was placed upon schools. This added to the difficulties, particularly as statistics was about to be introduced into the A level maths courses and an A level general studies course was to start.

The sweeping changes needed to establish the Sixth Form College had yet to come, but some short-term alterations in the teaching arrangements at the school were made, some relating to the admission of pupils from local secondary modern schools.

For some years able pupils had been transferred into the Grammar School Fourth Form on the recommendation of the pupil's existing Head Teacher, but now there was a change of emphasis. The secondary modern schools were attempting to broaden their curricula and to introduce the CSE exam, or possibly the O level GCE. The objective therefore was to postpone the transfer of able pupils to the Grammar School until they had completed their pre-Sixth Form education at their original secondary school.

The perception was that pupils coming from secondary modern schools at age 16 would need the facilities of a Remove form to adjust to the requirements of studying at A level standard. As has been mentioned, there was already a Lower VI Remove in existence, catering for some of the pupils progressing from the Upper V to the Sixth Form. Then, in 1966, in place of pupils already in the school, the form took responsibility for the twenty-three entrants from what the Headmaster called the Modern Schools. There was no specific entrance requirement for would-be students and each application was judged on its merits. In the Headmaster's opinion, none of the students from secondary modern schools were adequately prepared for Sixth Form science courses and, at this stage, few pupils transferring to the Grammar School had had language teaching.

In his 1966 report to the school governors the Head, having commended the performance of the former Middle School entrants from the secondary moderns, also referred to the 1965 entries to the Sixth Form, many of them possessing O Levels or high-grade CSE qualifications gained in their former schools. A year later he commented on one boy from Eastbourne who had obtained three A Levels, including two at grade A. Several pupils from secondary moderns had, by then, gone from the Grammar School to university.

Hall was also mindful that, after the V Lower year, there were slower developers who needed what he called a season in the 'Reserves'. He therefore proposed an Upper V Remove form. Its members would be entered for the CSE exam, seen at the time as the way forward by many educationalists. Sitting the GCE exam could follow, presumably one year later.

A School List for 1967–8 has been seen with an insert pasted in it showing a V Upper Remove containing ten pupils, some of whom were in the Lower VI in the following year. In that following year the V Upper Remove had gone, but there was a V Upper 4 with fourteen pupils instead. Unfortunately it is not known whether V Upper 4 had the same function as the Remove form or whether those in either form were required to sit the CSE, rather than O levels.

By this time the fate of the school was clear and a huge turnover in staff was the result. Some, like David McKenzie, who became Assistant Secretary to the Oxford Examinations Board, left or took retirement because of their opposition to comprehensive education. Others, uncertain of a position in the new college, took opportunities to find employment elsewhere, and the taking of training college lecturerships by two members prompted Osborn to mention in the *Elizabethan* that their departure was indicative of the way grammar schools were being drained of staff. Three of the long-term members who left were J.H. Green, who moved to Eastbourne School, Jack Waltham, who took a post at a college of education, and Robert Wharin, who left to become Head of Modern Languages at Branksome School.

Not surprisingly, keeping track of many of the staff over the final three years or so is difficult. Some seem to have come or gone without even a record in the school magazine. P.H. Moss retired from full-time teaching but, until 1970, continued part-time in charge of the library. Other notable retirements were those of Bug Allen, Lindsey Bird and Jim Osborn.

In 1965 Chris Bennett had retired. He came to the school from Bondgate School as a scholarship boy in 1916. Four years later, as a pupil, he had managed to form an orchestra from scratch, but a permanent orchestra had to wait till his return as a master in 1938. He was also part-time music adviser to the Education Authority. His last concert (the 25th) took place on 21 December 1964. Jack Dodds (the one who taught biology), who had joined the staff in 1954 and had been the Danes' House Captain, also left, going to the Darlington High School.

As well as two School Captains and two Vice-Captains, there were also two prefects' secretaries; previously one had sufficed. By this time the prefects were allocated by name to specific duties. There were forty-nine prefects in total and some were responsible for the tuck shop or the dining room – or the amplifiers! Most, however, were listed as form prefects. Each form had two, but many now had two form masters as well. During the final years, Harry Welding was the member of staff responsible for the organisation of prefects.

The school's uncertain future seems not to have adversely affected its societies. As always, societies declined and revived, but as the school neared its end new societies proliferated. In 1965 the Squidgers and Squoppers Society was launched, with its membership initially limited to twenty members, pending the obtaining of more playing mats. It was also thought that the Lower School would not take tiddlywinks seriously, but later a referendum on Lower School Membership took place and it was allowed, but numbers were restricted. At Christmas 1967 a marathon series of games was held in aid of the Mayor's Charity.

Another 1965 newcomer was the oddball Mythological Society. It claimed to have no president, secretary or constitution. At one meeting it reputedly had a record attendance of three and a half. It also claimed to have shown a film entitled *Arabic Shorthand*, discovering, at the end, that the film had been inserted upside down and back to front.

In about 1964 an Engineering Society started, providing visits to the Darlington Power Station and to the site of the Durham Motorway, then under construction. It hoped to build its own go-cart and parental contributions were requested, but nothing more is known of it. Then, although retaining its original title, the society subtly evolved into a motor club. In about early 1967 it held a daytime car rally, with many crews donning crash-hats and overalls. Peter Horbury, then the Club Secretary but in recent years Vice-Chairman of Design at Volvo Cars, turned up wearing a World War I German officer's helmet!

The October 1967 issue of the *Elizabethan* openly referred to The School Motor Club masquerading as the Engineering Society. It described a series of driving tests held in the school yard and reported that one driver's times became appreciably slower after it was pointed out that his mother was watching the proceedings. After one rally it was discovered that the winning team did not belong to the school, so it was not awarded the prize. Eventually the Society was brought to an end after an accident.

There were new societies catering for judo, weight training, mathematics, fell walking, speleology and aeromodelling. A Model Car Racing Club was started and the Head came along to an Open Night. He had to confess that he found driving model cars not as easy as he had expected. There was a Good Food Society, which had the ambition to compile a guidebook for local restaurants. A Public Service Vehicle Society also existed and, when it was in danger of extinction, it became the responsibility of John Hopwood, who joined the staff in 1966 and already ran the Railway Society. A merger of the two societies was mooted, but there were apparently objections from the Railway Society members.

The Film Society reached a point when it seems to have stopped showing fiction films. The range provided included such titles as *Inert Gases, Refinery at Work, Interpreting the Weather Map* and *Japan.*

The Forum had been rejuvenated and had forty-five at its first meeting, a talk on Teesside Airport by its Air Traffic Controller.

The school's first society, the Debating Society, fell into a decline after David McKenzie left, but was 'reconstructed' by Mr Darby and survived to celebrate its Golden Jubilee. Despite the Society's inauguration in 1914, the celebration was reported in the *Elizabethan* of March 1967. Most of the long-standing clubs continued, but varying fortunes were still normal. The Play Reading Society was under the charge of Arthur Trees, but he left to become a lecturer at the Training College next door. In an effort to keep him involved, the Society extended its membership to students at the college but, to balance the sexes, boys at St. Mary's Grammar School were also brought in.

A further achievement for the school had been an invitation in late 1964 to compete in the BBC's *Top of the Form* quiz. After elimination rounds, the team was chosen, comprising P.H. Mounsey, M. Spence, R.M. Lambert and R. Mitchell. Embarrassingly, the team was beaten in a practice contest with Darlington High School. Then, in the actual competition, having beaten Sheffield High School for Girls in the first round, the team was eliminated in the second by St. Malachy's College, Belfast. Tragically, Robert McDermot, the quiz-master, died in a fall on the day after the second recording.

In 1966 pressure of space was forcing the use of the main room in the library for subject teaching. The Memorial Library was made available for study use on an evening from 6 till 9 p.m., but an experimental study period in the afternoon from 4 to 6 p.m. had to be abandoned due to lack of support. Unfortunately, by the end of the year, overcrowding in the Memorial Library was necessitating the sharing of desks. An increase in the number of books also created a shortage of shelf space. A stock check in the general library at this time revealed 4,290 books, with 663 of them in the Junior section and 597 in the English section. The History and Fiction sections had 475 each.

During 1966–7 the *Elizabethan* was reduced to two issues per annum because of rising costs. The circulation had also fallen slightly to 1,200, with far more copies going to Old Boys than to pupils. In 1965 the Magazine Committee had transferred – again – to the tower, presumably because no other function could be found for it. The move appears to have been a failure. According to a report in the magazine, it was 'thwarted by a menagerie of small boys clumping up and down from the Museum. The trail of bones, machine guns and stuffed memorabilia on the stairs tells a weary tale.'

Even Sixth Formers, it seems, can have nostalgia for a supposedly better past. The May 1966 issue contained an editorial complaining of the lack of intellectuals in the school. Whilst football, pop groups and 'mod gear' were now the pupils' interests, it was implied that a few years earlier their minds were fixed on higher things. Articles on esoteric subjects still appeared; one was on lamp standards. There were new features, however, such as a French language crossword and a picture quiz. By 1967 there was a Latin crossword, but perhaps fortunately the clues were in English.

The March 1967 issue had a revamped cover. There was an E in the top-left-hand corner and the centre was filled by the image of a target surmounted by a vertical arrow. J.E. Turner was then the staff editor. The editorial in the same issue contains a rare allusion to what lay ahead, with the writer referring to a sense of passing sadness, despite his acceptance of the advantages of the comprehensive system. He sensed a general feeling of despondency around him.

The magazine's adverts included ones for the Post House Grill Room, the Darlington Co-op, the Trustee Savings Bank and Martins Bank, which asserted that it was possible to be a manager in one's thirties. However, a 16-year-old, with four O levels, had to be satisfied with a starting salary of £370 per annum.

The school was still involved in plenty of other activities. For the academic year 1966–7 onwards O level music was available as a school subject for the first time. The one-year course was open to anyone who had passed his Grade 5 Associate Board exams. Miss Gregory was at last able to retire, having been replaced as cello teacher by Mr Kirby.

A four-part choir formed by Hector Parr, who had replaced Chris Bennett, gave its first performance at Holy Trinity Church at Easter 1966. It was followed by similar performances over the next three Easters. The most ambitious project, in 1969, was the staging of Bach's *St. Matthew's Passion*. As the school was, by then, contracting and without any under-13s, help was obtained from girls at the High School. For the 1967–9 School Concerts the First Orchestra was also reinforced with players from the High School. The 1967 Concert was noteworthy for Topsy Ord's performance on the vibraphone.

The choir had its own recreational activities, including an annual holiday in the Lake District. Barn dances, Prefects' Dances, the prefects' hockey match and the annual trips to York, Edinburgh and Hadrian's Wall all continued. An official school photograph was taken on 13 May 1965. Perhaps it was the last one.

The 1966 General Election prompted a mock election in the school, with an impressive voting turnout of 92 per cent. Labour won, but there were a large number of candidates, including a representative of the League of Empire Loyalists who picked up twenty-one votes. Although those in the audience could not vote until they were twenty-one, the three real candidates for the constituency answered pupils' questions in the school library on 25 March.

An Open Day to commemorate the centenary of the town's borough status was held in 1967. The new wing, the hall, the library and the playing field were all used in various ways. School plays were still performed. In 1965 Gogol's *The Government Inspector* was the choice, followed in 1966 by Brecht's *The Caucasian Chalk Circle*. Then, staffing difficulties prevented the presentation of any more, an early sign of what was to come. Barn dances continued to feature in the school's social life and the Careers Conventions, held separately for the Upper V and VI Forms, continued, as did the annual chemistry exhibition.

At this time thirty boys went to Munsterlager in West Germany, at the invitation of the 4th Field Regiment, Royal Artillery. They spent eight days there and experienced the unit's self-propelled artillery, rode in Centurion tanks and fired the NATO rifle. The highlight was the witnessing of the firing of an 'Honest John' guided missile.

The Old Boys' Association, together with its sporting clubs, was still healthy with, for instance, 120 present at the 1966 Dinner Dance at the Croft Spa Hotel. The Annual London Dinner continued to be held and the 1965 Dinner there was attended by Chapman Pincher, who had been given the 'Reporter of the Year' award for his exclusive stories. The Headmaster was also present.

The Association's expenditure for 1965–6 was £284 5s 0d. Of this £90 was allocated for the school magazine, with £35 14s 0d for Christmas boxes, £51 13s 10d for functions and £58 7s 10d for postage. The main sources of income were subscriptions of £218 4s 6d and donations of £32 17s 0d. During the year 1966–7 the Old Boys' Association had functioning cricket, association football, rugby, badminton and basketball sections. Its three Treasurers were all members of the school staff: Messrs Moss, Green and Griffiths.

The Queen Elizabeth Association was now the Queen Elizabeth Grammar School Association and had 300 members (mostly pupils' parents and friends of the school). Most of its income came from subscriptions and despite the pending demise of the school it had increased its membership. Percy Moss and Len Griffiths also happened to be, respectively, its Secretary/Treasurer and Assistant Treasurer.

There were no significant changes to the school's sporting activities. The growth in size of the annual gym display had necessitated moving it into the Baths Hall. In 1965, 100 boys, watched by 800 spectators, performed. In the same year, in an attempt to revive an earlier tradition, the swimmers planned a water polo match (Britons and Saxons v. Danes and Normans) to conclude the Swimming Gala, but it had to be called off due to lack of time for preparation.

By now the school had no fewer than three gymnastic clubs and was giving dry skiing lessons as a preliminary to the annual skiing trip abroad. There had been a growth in the number of soccer teams and the Shells had their own soccer XI, but it sometimes had to play primary school teams. There were also separate teams for the Under-15s, Under-14s and Under-13s. According to the *Elizabethan* of February 1966, the Under-13 XI beat Haughton Secondary School 12–3.

In 1967 there were no fewer than six rugby teams, namely the First XV, Second XV, Under-15 XV, Under-14 XV, Under-13 XV and Shell XV. About twelve games per season seemed to be the norm for most teams, although the Firsts had played seventeen. In that season the tennis team won eleven games and lost three.

The school excelled at athletics. In both 1966 and 1967, with thirty-six other schools participating, the Grammar School won the Durham County Grammar Schools' Athletics Meeting. It was the eighth win for the school in the past ten years. Boys had also represented the county at football, rugby, tennis and athletics. School colours and half colours were awarded for various sports including athletics, harriers and lawn tennis.

End Game

In September 1967 when the Darlington Grammar School received its last intake of Shell Boys, the realities facing it were now very apparent. The 11-plus was now extinct in Darlington, and the new boys, the last to pass it, were destined to form the youngest year in the school for the rest of its existence. The traditional satisfaction of being able, after a year in the school, to look down upon younger boys was denied to them. The only new intake now would be into the Sixth Form of boys from elsewhere who had performed well in the GCE or CSE exams.

From September 1968 the new comprehensive schools, including the former High School, now designated Hummersknott School, took all pupils at age 11 but, despite its new status, the former High School was still frequently referred to by its old name in the Grammar School magazine.

Despite the Grammar School's falling numbers, the March 1968 issue of the *Elizabethan* complained of overcrowding. It claimed that lessons had to be held in the Lost Property Office, the librarians' office, the Sixth Form Precinct, the Fifth Form interview room and Mr Sunderland's office. It would take time for the problem to be eased by the annual reduction in pupil numbers. At the beginning of 1968 there were 850 boys on the roll, but two years later the number had fallen to 591. Many new problems would result from the loss of new pupils, including the need to reduce teaching staff. Those teaching in the junior part of the school would be hit the hardest.

Every Christmas Concert since 1941 had featured the 'Junior Singers', but the 1967 Concert saw their last appearance. The two orchestras and the Military Band were expected to survive for one or two years longer as they drew most of their members from the Middle and Upper School. The continuance of orchestral playing at Vane Terrace was seen to depend upon the ability and the will of the Education Authority to sponsor a wide increase in instrumental teaching in the comprehensive schools. The Head had little confidence in this happening, but it is not clear whether he was thinking of the few years left to his school or of the Sixth Form College. In 1968 thirty-nine candidates were successful in the Board exams, with thirteen Merits and nine Distinctions.

In 1968–9 there were thirty-nine Senior Prefects, all of whom were allocated to forms. There does not appear to have been any lesser grade but the School List for the preceding year contained a note that all members of Upper VI (even if not listed as Senior Prefects) had the status of prefects. After the admission of Shell boys ended, a decrease in the number of prefects was suggested. It was believed that eight fewer would be required in the school. An innovation in 1967 was the introduction of Form Captains. They were initially limited to the Lower School but, in the following year, all forms up to the Upper V had them.

The school endeavoured to maintain its academic standards. In 1968 there were 270 subject entries at A level with a 62 per cent pass rate, and 6 students admitted from secondary modern schools with CSE passes gained 13 A level passes. The O level pass rate was still rising and was now only 3 per cent behind the rate in the last year of the Durham Board examinations. There were good records in history, German, Latin and Nuffield Chemistry. The best VI Form mathematician sat the GCE in navigation 'as an academic excursion'.

The lure of the CSE exam continued and a small number of the Upper V block sat subjects such as art, handicrafts, history, maths, science, French and English. The results were reported as being satisfactory. An impressive 85 per cent of the previous year's V Upper block had returned to the school to continue their studies.

There were now no fewer than seven VI Form classes, but the Lower VI Remove had disappeared. There were seventeen entrants from other secondary schools and all possessed either CSEs or O level passes.

During the 1967–8 year sixty-one students applied for university through the Clearing House system, but only twenty-seven were successful. Of thirty-eight applications to polytechnics, twenty-five obtained places, whilst a further eight were accepted by colleges of education. A brochure entitled *The Education of the VI Form Student,* originally prepared three years before, had been revised and updated. More pupils were sitting the CSE exam as an alternative to O levels and in 1969 twenty-two candidates were awarded passes. From 1967 awards of prizes in metalwork and woodwork were made.

The Headmaster, trying to maintain standards whilst faced with a reduction in both staff and pupils, had the task of adapting the school to the needs of the Sixth Form College. With the exception of Hummersknott, the new comprehensive schools had no lengthy experience of preparing pupils for a Sixth Form education and Hall was particularly concerned to assess their adequacy for this task.

A study of the progress made by pupils who had entered the Sixth Form from the secondary modern schools over the last few years was therefore undertaken. Its main conclusion was that, in general, they were still handicapped by a lack of adequate preparation in sciences and modern languages, so this was an issue that would have to be addressed.

There were discussions between the Heads of the secondary schools to ensure that future demands for courses and their suitability could be assessed prior the opening of the college. To assist with the arrangements a study document was prepared to consider how best to prepare pupils in secondary schools to benefit in full from both a Sixth Form and a subsequent university or college education.

The issue of staffing also occupied Hall's mind. He was particularly concerned to retain at the Grammar School teachers whose skills would be of value to the new college. He expected that from September 1969 the Education Committee would want to reduce the number of staff at the school whilst subsequently needing to employ more at the Sixth Form College. The uncertainties about the staff's future were damaging to everyone.

Hall's desire was that attempts should be made to retain staff likely to be needed by the college, by using them temporarily and, for part of the time, in the other secondary schools, but it is not clear whether he had any great success with his object. One former master interviewed had a recollection of going to Hurworth to teach, but is not clear as to the reason. The shortages of staff during the final years, coupled with the high turnover and the need for retiring masters to stay on part-time, suggests that the Head's hopes were not realised.

The problems of overcrowding in the reference library continued into 1968 and there were also difficulties with users removing books from it.

There was, unfortunately, a wider problem for the general library. The needs of a Sixth Form College library would be different and those expected needs prevented the acquisition of new books. Much of the library's existing stock was unsuited to a modern Sixth Former and a run-down of books had already started. A stock check in the paperback library revealed that, out of 1,100 books accessed since 1957, over 300 had been withdrawn. In particular, those more suitable for younger readers were being removed. On the credit side, the absence of the Shell forms made extra periods for the Sixth Form for private study possible and tighter security reduced the defacing and unauthorised removal of periodicals.

In 1969, as a final measure, the reference library moved into the old general library whilst the old reference library became a reading room, but with the remaining old stock of the general library moved into it. By 1970, the reference library had been expanded, but there were complaints about the removal of prospectuses from the careers section. A completely new library would have to wait until the new College came.

The school did its best to maintain its sporting standards to the end. In 1968 the Headmaster was able to report that there had been a huge increase over the decade in the content of the physical education programme. For association football, rugby and cricket there were six teams each, for athletics three and for basketball four. There were now two clubs for gymnastics and the harriers and country dancing groups each had two teams. In addition, there were teams for judo, swimming, lawn tennis, golf, trampolining, weight training, fell walking, caving and potholing. The school had also undertaken a skiing tour to Hinterglemm in Austria and an adventure holiday in the South of France but, unfortunately, the annual cricket tour to Scarborough had been marred by bad weather. An athletics training week at Earls House Hostel had become an annual event.

The old traditional events, such as the School Sports, the Founders' Day Staff v. School cricket match, the Masters v. School golf competition, and the annual hockey match against Hummersknott School, which still had its old High School Sixth Formers, continued to the end. Unfortunately, cancellations because of the weather were not uncommon.

However, the difficulties facing the school led to it having no swimming team for 1968, although a scratch junior team was created for the Schools' Swimming Gala and was beaten by a single point. During two or three years up to 1970, the lack of entrants into the junior school effectively ended participation in inter-school events. The awarding of school colours, including half colours, continued. In 1968 House colours were re-awarded as well as awarded for the first time.

The school also managed to acquire a computer. The *Elizabethan* of March 1969 reported the Headmaster as saying that it had proved to be so expensive that it had been given a girl's name, DENICE. The reality was that Hector Parr, who although Head of Music was a Cambridge mathematics graduate, obtained the Head's permission to build one and the school was happy to meet the cost. The music room became an electronics workshop as pupil volunteers built up the circuitry needed. The huge computer's name was, in reality, an acronym for Darlington Numerical Indicating Computer Equipment. By modern standards it was, of course, extremely primitive and it could do no more than solve the simplest numerical problems. Many of those involved in its building were thrilled when it printed out the two-times table!

Protests and challenges to authority in the age of demonstrations such as those against the war in Vietnam, the French General Strike and the LSE sit-in were now commonplace. Whilst the school experienced no acts of mass disobedience, the school magazines of the time indicate some dissatisfaction.

The March 1968 issue of the *Elizabethan* had a new cover design, with the year '1968' printed vertically in bold type down the side. Its editorial implied the existence of censorship, saying that a comment about overcrowding in the school had been seen as a criticism of the

Head, rather than, as intended, of Whitehall. Thus was the magazine prevented from fulfilling its main purpose, which was to reflect the life and the pulse of the school, and the consequence was that boys were deterred from buying it. 'Articles, reports and notes come from a blissful cloud-world of detached insensibility, avoiding the harsh facts of school life.' The support of readers for the writer's viewpoint was needed.

In the following October issue the editor wondered whether less supervision during assembly and at lunchtime and breaks might be justified. He also hoped that one or two out of the four extra rooms now available might be allocated for VI Form use, regretting that most prefects were not allowed to use the Prefects' Room. He expected to be disappointed, however.

School uniforms were the next target. It was a fault of the system that there was an insistence upon having both them and regulations as to hairstyles. The concept of uniformity was now unfashionable and there should merely be a requirement for neat appearance, a term not defined by the writer. Finally, the Sixth Form needed more freedom. 'The keynote of its development must be not discipline, not conformity to a system, but freedom of thought, of speech and behaviour.' A later issue of the magazine did concede that Mr Hall, in his attempts to restrict the length of hair, was fighting against the fashions of the time. As the unidentified writer put it, 'not even a headmaster can prevail against Georgie Best, TV personalities and – *miserabile* [sic] *dictu* – his own staff!'

The voicing of concerns continued. By March 1969 there were editorial worries about the magazine's future as it was seen as not appealing to large sections of the Upper School. There was a widespread feeling in the VI Forms that if an article is submitted which, in any way, criticises the school, it will not be published, so contributions tend to be confined to articles with ideas not relevant to many people.

As if to symbolise changing times the October issue appeared in a new style, with more pages than its predecessor, but it was cheaper-looking with a typewriter-style font. It was also renamed the *New Elizabethan*. A questionnaire about the magazine was said to have revealed anti-establishment views amongst readers, with 'everyone' expressing a wish to ban censorship. Most also wanted to abandon the society reports and the '*Salvete*' and '*Valete*' features, which listed the pupils arriving at or leaving the school. Nothing was said about suggested replacements.

The magazine itself contained letters complaining about games being compulsory, the lack of facilities for drinks and the lack of communication in the school about its future and the intended building alterations. Because of the transitional arrangements, many pupils would, of course, still be attending after the college had opened and the building operations started.

The last magazine for the school was published in April 1970. Only 750 copies were printed, but all were sold. It had been submitted for review to the *Evening Despatch* and the *Darlington and Stockton Times* and was received favourably. Comment was made in the magazine about the criticism of the overabundance of society reports, but it was argued that they were necessary. There was a letter complaining about the quality of school meals, contrasting them with the much better fare supposedly supplied to the masters. In the letter the writer said that he had assumed it would be censored. Someone else complained about the lack of accommodation for coats in the school.

The results of a survey conducted in the Lower and Upper VI were set out. Of the respondents, 65 per cent were against comprehensive education, but 27 per cent were in favour of the Darlington scheme. However, 75 per cent thought that the scheme had not affected their education and a further 10 per cent thought that it had had a favourable effect.

The range of articles in the school magazine was perhaps wider than it had been previously. The October 1969 issue contained two articles, written from totally opposite viewpoints, about the Investiture of the Prince of Wales. The hostile article contrasted the expenditure with the sufferings in Biafra after its attempted breakaway from Nigeria.

A Third Former interviewed Mr Jennings, who had been school caretaker for 18 years. His two most memorable experiences were being filmed for television when he was pursued by a heifer in the school yard and when he had to cope with a phosphorous fire in six separate locations in the lab technician's room. Using chemicals was clearly a hazardous activity. Eighteen months earlier the magazine had reported that the chemistry department had, in the last term, suffered three fires and three explosions, with two people sent to hospital.

A new departure for the magazine was the first in a series about classic cars and there were also record reviews. The discs featured were by Diana Ross and the World of Blues Power. Classified ads appeared. Someone wanted £10 for a five-string banjo, whilst someone else had some potholing boots for sale. The trade advertisements were also more wide ranging and included ones for Joe Cleminson's cycle shop, the Art Shop (then in Duke Street) and the Kart House for motor bikes. By the time of the October 1969 issue the Magazine Committee was installed in the librarians' office. It apparently had four moves in as many editions.

Even in momentous times, trivialities are permitted. On 19 July 1968 two members of the Magazine Committee found time to count the panes of glass in the school. There were, we are told, 5,219, including 1,539 of stained glass in the hall and 1,078 in the new wing.

There had been another questionnaire. This one was about the staff's favourite television programme. The staff, or so the school magazine claimed, had opted for *The Magic Roundabout*, followed by the BBC News. It was mentioned that the Rev. Tibbo, a staff member, had not chosen *The Epilogue*, but it was alleged that one admirer had pointed out that it was on past his bedtime. For the boys in IVA the favourite was *Tom & Jerry*, followed by *Top of the Pops*, whilst for IVB the preference was *The Champions* followed by *Match of the Day*.

In the closing days of the school, what was described as exotic artwork appeared in the prefects' room, but it was quickly removed at Mr Thompson's request. Once, no doubt, a peremptory demand would have been made. Now Mr Thompson contented himself with saying that whilst he had no personal objection, he was concerned about how the cleaners might react.

A noteworthy retirement at Christmas 1968 was that of W.W. Allen, who came to the school from London in 1928. He had been involved with the School Cadet Corps and the school camps and, for over a quarter of a century, was the Normans' Housemaster. A. Hird was his successor in the post. Although Bug officially retired in December he agreed to stay part-time for a couple of terms because of the staffing difficulties. In the following summer he was to return to London. The 1968–9 School List shows Jim Osborn and Percy Moss near the foot of the listing of staff, despite their long service, presumably as a reflection of their also working part-time.

In 1969, one year after Miss Jewsbury left after many years as Headmistress of the doomed Darlington High School, Mr Hall retired. No successor was appointed and Norman Sunderland found himself in temporary charge of the school for the time left to it. The *New Elizabethan* said that a few years earlier when 'to some of us scruffiness in personal appearance, loutishness in behaviour and debasement in levels of honesty seemed far too marked amongst young people, Mr Hall strove to maintain decent standards. A close look at the School today reveals how well he succeeded. In particular, his insistence upon courtesy and consideration for others seems to have produced good results.'

He undoubtedly found himself in a difficult position once the Peter Plan started to be implemented. The school lost its annual intake of new pupils, finding and retaining staff became a nightmare and funding was allocated for the benefit of the new college. In addition he found himself in an anti-authoritarian era. Despite these obstacles Hall strove to maintain the school's educational standards and its discipline and he seems to have largely succeeded. One of his greatest achievements must have been the flexible arrangements made by him for admitting pupils from the secondary modern schools into the Sixth Form.

No fewer than seven other teachers, some of whom had been at the school for one year only, left at the same time as the Headmaster. The staff shortages persisted after his departure.

It was now customary to hold an end of term service. Churches used included Holy Trinity, St. Cuthbert's and Bondgate Methodist Church, the venue of Mr Hall's last service on 16 July 1969. The end of term service in March of that year was held at St. Cuthbert's and for the first time 'in living memory' the boys needed to find their hymn books, as there were no printed service sheets.

Old traditions, such as the wearing of gowns by graduate masters, continued to the end, as did long-established school activities and excursions, such as the annual trip to Hadrian's Wall. So, by and large, did the school's societies. As ever, some prospered, whilst others, amongst them the Middle School Debating Society and the Fell Walking Society, fell quietly by the wayside. Even at this late stage, new ones still appeared, including the Bridge Club, the Ships Society and the Subbuteo Table Soccer Club. The 1968 school camp consisted of a canoeing holiday in the South of France.

There were still firsts and there were still achievements. The Prefects' Dance held in the school hall in July1968 had, for the first time, a 'beat group'. During the same month, the school took part in a Science Fair Exhibition at Middlesbrough, but unfortunately the two exhibits were damaged in transit. In 1968, Nigel Watson and Bill Edmunds, with Carol Welding and Joan Pringle, danced at the Albert Hall at the International Folk Dance Festival and the school was second in the semi-final of the English Schools Debating Association competition held at the school.

One by one, the traditional events of the school took place for the last time. The final Speech Day was held in the Baths Hall on 18 November 1969, followed by the ultimate School Concert on 12 December, held at the College of Technology rather than at the Baths Hall. A last Prefects' Christmas Dinner took place on 23 December. The last Old Boys' Day and Founders Day events were held simultaneously on July 3 1970, with victory in the last of the traditional cricket matches going to the Old Boys. Presentations were then made to veteran masters Percy Moss, Norman Sunderland, Jim Osborn and R.S. Thompson.

The end was a much quieter affair than the beginnings at Vane Terrace.

Aftermath

The new Queen Elizabeth Sixth Form College of September 1970 was in a transitional state. The first new intake consisted of students from the comprehensive schools, plus pupils from the defunct Grammar School, all intending to study for the first year of the A level course. With the possible odd exception, the only students in the second Sixth Form year were Grammar School pupils from the Lower VI of the previous year. Although it was now a comprehensive school, Hummersknott had retained a separate Upper VI Form as an interim measure for 1970–1 only, so avoiding the need for former High School girls to transfer to Vane Terrace for the one year.

Because of the necessary transitional arrangements, the college had a large number of younger pupils on its books in the form of the final two annual entries to the old Grammar School. They provided the college with the entire V Lower and Upper years of the old Grammar School, so the college would not be clear of pre-VI Form students until the summer of 1972. Although students from comprehensive schools were entering the college from 1970 onwards, they had, apart from girls at the High School, started their secondary education at secondary modern schools. The first entry of students who had started at age 11 in a comprehensive school would not occur until 1973.

No work to adapt the old premises to their new needs had been previously carried out, so those at the college had to suffer the disruption of building work. Although there were significantly fewer students in the second VI Form year than would be normal, the college had the added burden of the two V Form years. Not surprisingly there were problems. The shortage of space compelled the college to use the Drill Hall in Larchfield Street for some lectures, so time was lost while students passed between the two sites. Music Department instrumental teachers had to use the boys' cloakroom and later the tower, just below the clock mechanism. Because there were no fixed hours at the college, it was difficult to get students together in their own time.

On one Monday morning, the male staff turned up to find that their toilets no longer existed. The new principal told the lecturers that they must use the toilets in Stanhope Park until the building work was completed. The consequence was a threatened strike. Within a week a row of WC pans, without any partitions between them, had been hastily installed in a room at the college.

The building work involved two main projects. One was the construction of a new library occupying the whole of the old court. It opened in March 1971. The other required the demolition of the north wing, the old site of the Headmaster's house, so the round turret that had been a feature of the school for so long went. The replacement wing, costing an estimated £135,000, provided an administration block with staff and student common rooms. Three windows from the old building were re-used to blend the old and the new

The archway behind the now filled-in court, dating back to the 1930s, became a pottery. The metalwork and woodwork rooms also went and the caretaker's house was demolished around this time. The air-raid shelters that had stood at the front of the school had been removed two or three years before. In 1971 a chapel was dedicated in the Tower, but the lack of a fire escape presented problems, so it became used for storage only.

There was a gradual realisation amongst those familiar with the old school that the new establishment would be a very different beast. It was to be a college, not a school. There were complaints of apathy in the college's social life, and it was said that only three or four societies had survived from the Grammar School, but the reality was that the all-embracing school social life had gone. As there were no fixed hours at the college it was difficult to gather students together for meetings or events. As far as any musical life at the college was concerned, it was believed that no choir or orchestra would thrive.

The practice of addressing boys by their surnames outlived the end of the Grammar School, presumably through habit. It was anomalous, because the girls attending the college were addressed by their Christian names and it appears that this practice soon extended to the boys as well.

The old prefectorial system died with the Grammar School, being replaced by a student council. There were problems of an unknown nature, however, and the first council was soon disbanded and replaced by a second one. To represent the interests of the remaining Grammar School pupils below VI Form level, a Lower School Committee was formed. In the first year there was to be one member from each of the nine forms on the committee and the Head of the Lower School would act as chairman.

The school magazine became the college magazine, retaining, for a few years at least, the name *New Elizabethan,* and it was the claim of the first editor that there would be no censorship, except as was imposed by the law of the land. The first post-1970 copies leave the impression that the magazine reflected a Darlington Grammar School viewpoint, but that is probably unsurprising as the first editor, if an Upper VI member, would have come from the school. A significant proportion of the staff had also come from the Grammar School.

Around this time some of the staff who had not been engaged long term by the college left. Amongst them were 'Rusty' Thompson, J. Dodds, an Old Boy who went to teach physics at St. Mary's School, John Hopwood and Harry Welding, who both went to Hummersknott. In the short term, the college had needed staff to teach the rump of non-VI Formers at the college.

The Old Boys' Association did not survive the school for long. The last Old Boys' Day was celebrated on 3 July 1970 and then, on 8 December, the committee met for the last time. The disbandment of the Association, founded fifty-one years earlier, was the outcome. Although there would be Old Boys around for many more years, the existing officers were anxious to retire and there were no obvious successors. The Association had always devoted much of its efforts to supporting the school, so much of the justification for its existence was lost.

Different considerations applied to the Association's sporting teams and they survived for some time longer. In an effort to preserve as much as possible of the history of the school, Percy Moss sent a list of relevant items to the Chief Education Officer with the recommendation that the collection be suitably housed in Darlington.

In 1978 St. Cuthbert's Church accepted the gift of a chalice (still in regular use) from the Old Boys' Fund. The Old Boys had supported the church in the past, having, for instance, provided benches in the churchyard. It looks as if the gift represented an attempt, nearly eight years after the Association was dissolved, to utilise its residual funds.

Teething troubles are a feature of infancy, so those of the Sixth Form College soon ended and over the years it has increased in size and influence. Almost the whole of the once vast schoolyard has been built on and the college now caters for numbers unimaginable forty-five years ago. It claims an academic record second to none.

Norman Sunderland stressed that his book was not 'the history of a school with a glorious and exciting past and with a host of distinguished old boys', blaming the relative poverty of the north-east. That may be so, but for most, if not for all of its time at Vane Terrace, and despite its faults, the Queen Elizabeth Grammar School succeeded in what it was intended to do.

Changing times ensured that many of the school's expectations and objectives in 1878 were considerably different from those of ninety or so years later, and, as we have seen, when he presented his plan for comprehensive education in Darlington, David Peter remarked upon the Grammar School's ability to re-invent itself. He went on to argue that its conversion into a Sixth Form College was merely a continuation of the same process. Whether it was or not may be open to argument, but the ability of the school, often in the face of difficulties, to maintain its standards is surely unanswerable. A facade of tradition, sometimes a little spurious, enabled the school to cloak the extent to which it changed over the years.

Appendix I – The School Prayer and Hymn

The School Prayer

Let us thankfully commemorate before Almighty God
His servants Elizabeth, who was pleased to grant the
foundation charter of this ancient grammar school,
Robert Marshall, our first benefactor, Henry Neville,
Earl of Westmorland, and James Pilkington, Prince
Bishop of Durham whose zeal, fervour and wisdom
revived the light of learning in this town.
Let us also remember those whose eminent labours
have advanced our knowledge and assisted our Faith
such as were the priests of the Collegiate Church
of Cuthbert in early times and those who followed after.
We pray that the torch of learning and the flame of
true religion may never be quenched in our midst;
that brotherly love and Christian charity may abound;
and that we, who enjoy the fruits of so many labours,
may not be unworthy of our heritage.
Amen

*****

The School Hymn

We build our school on Thee O Lord:
To Thee we bring our common need,
The loving heart, the helpful word;
The tender thought, the kindly deed –
With these we pray
Thy Spirit may
Enrich and bless our School alway. [sic]

We work together in Thy sight,
We live together in Thy love;
Guide Thou our faltering steps aright,
And lift our thoughts to heaven above;
Dear Lord we pray
Thy Spirit may
Be present in our School alway.
We change but Thou art still the same –
The same good Master, Teacher, Friend,
We change; but Lord we bear Thy name,
To journey with it to the end;
And so we pray
Thy Spirit may
Be present in our School alway.

Appendix II – Staff

Alphabetical list of known teaching staff

Name	Years	Comments
W.W. 'Bug' Allen	1928–68, then part-time	Head of Biology
W.C. Anderson	1879–1890	English
J.H. Appleyard	1968–70?	Head of Art
A. Ashman	1955?–66	Chemistry. Later at Durham University
J.I. Ashworth	1965–6	Biology. Replaced J. Dodds
E.C. Axford	1936–40	Head of English
E.B. Baker	c.1906–08	
Bannerman	1889–93	Maths master. Replaced by Widdowson
T.W. Barker	1878–88 (gone by 85?)	
Miss Barnes	1940–?	Wartime replacement for Snook
F.W. Bartlett	1959/60–2	
J.P. Bateman	1965–9	Head of English Language
C.W. Bell	1892–4?	Gone by December 1894
C. Bennett	1938–65	Music. Old Boy

J.H.B. Bennett	1954 (1 term)	Modern Languages. Old Boy
J.K. Benneworth	1944	Temporary
R.M. Best	1968–*c.*70	Geography
J.L. Bird ('Dicky')	pre-1951–68	Art.
Mrs V. Bisset	1961/2	Violin. Temporary replacement for K. Blood
W. Blain	1894–1915	Maths, woodwork. Died 1939
J.S. Blamire	pre-1951–70?	
D.W. Bliss	1956–60	History
K. Blood ('Captain')	1951–61	Violin.
Miss K. Blythe	1940–3/4	Temporary
J. Board	1958–61, 1962–70?	PE
Boland	1947–9 (or early 1950)	
Mrs Bowlby	1939	Lower III Form Mistress
E.G. Bowley	1932–44	From Central Secondary School
E. Bowman	1882 (one term)	First Form Master
J.M. Bradford	1960–3	Head of Classics
C. Bride	1914–15	Temporary replacement of Turner
W.E. Brown	1921	Woodwork. Part-time?
J. Bruce?	1932–pre-51	
J.C. Brydon	1933–45	From Central Secondary School
W. Buchanan	1929–30	Left to return to college
G.H. Burdon?	1932–pre51	
R.A. Burniston	1919–58	Maths. Non-graduate. Lost leg 1944

H. Buxton	post-1960–67	
W.R. Calcott	1956–7?	Temporary
J.M. Camburn	1955–pre-64	PE. County cricketer
J.R. Canney	1922–9	History (probably replaced Todd)
David R. Carrick	1903–46	Chemistry, later Second Master. Old Boy
Miss B. Chalker	c.1944–?	Temporary
Miss P. Challis	1960	English. Temporary
G.T.L. Chapman	1948–58	Head of Geography. Replaced Golland
Mrs H.R. Chetwynd	c.1944–5	Temporary
Miss J.E. Clapton	c.1940–3	N. Sunderland's wartime replacement
Miss B.E.K. Clarke	1943? Gone by July '44	Temporary
G.L. Clarke	1966–?	Biology
Miss J.E. Clarke	1940–?	Miss Henson's replacement
J. Clarke-Shaw	1892–4	Replaced Fernsby
T.J. Cleeve-Warne	1879–89	Darlington FC founder member
Coleman	1890–1	Replaced by Bell
Miss M. Collier	c.1944	Temporary
Miss Connolly	1943? Gone by July '44	Temporary
P. Copley	1964–9	
Miss K.F. Cox ('Katie')	c.1944–62	French. Originally temporary.
H.O. Crane ('Hoc')	1932–49	From Central Secondary School.

D.C. Craven	1915/6–?	Temporary
D.B. Crompton	1965–?	Chemistry
N.E.? Dangerfield	1896–7	Replaced Finn
D.S. Darby	1962–6	English
Mrs E. Davison	1959/60–61	
C.W. Dawson	1905	Replaced Ferguson
Colin Dean	1965–70	Geography, geology. Old Boy
G.P. Dodds	1898–1903	Chemistry. Replaced Knott
John (Jack) Dodds	1954–65	Biology, careers. To DHS. Old Boy
John Dodds	1962–70	Physics. Old Boy
Doran	?–1968	English
R. D. Douglas	1962–5	History
G. Drake	1908	Replaced Baker?
A.B. Dresser	1895–1929	Drawing (part-time)
N.S. Dunthorne	1958–Dec '60	History
J. Eccleston ('Joe') AFC	pre-1951–7/8	History
Miss Ellam	pre-1938–9	Preparatory Dept.
H.B. Ellis	1955–8	Head of Modern Languages
Samuel Elton	1878 (2 terms)	Drawing
Miss Emerson	1926–38	Preparatory Dept.
R.H.C. Fairbairn	pre-1951–8	English. 'Dickie'
J.S. Ferguson	1895–1905	French, woodwork
A.R. Fernsby	1892	Resigned to train for Holy Orders
A. Finn	1895–6	Replaced Clarke-Shaw
G.H. Fisher	1929–49	Taught maths, but had Arts degree
P. Fothergill	1924–1943	Modern languages. One arm and one eye

B. de Frettes	1961/2–70?	Violin
J. E. Gale	1956	English. Temporary
C.W. Garrard	1878–9	English. Health breakdown
R. Giles	1958–65	Head of Economics
Gus Golland	1920–48	Geography. Non-graduate. Old Boy
Mrs Anna Gomez	1938–50/1	Violin. Replaced by K. Blood
W.F. Graham ('Cosh')	1949–58	Geography. Old Boy (School Captain)
W.W. Graville	1932–51	From Central Secondary School. Non-graduate
J.H. Green ('Jasper')	1949–68	Chemistry. Old Boy
Gregoire	1885–9	Replaced Pryce
Miss L. Gregory	1938–67	Cello. Part-time after 1961
L.W. Griffiths ('Len')	1950–70?	PE, maths
Miss E.M. Guy	c.1944	Temporary
Charles L. Hall	1960–9	Fourth Headmaster
H.A. Hall	1915–?	Temporary. Replaced Mitchell
R.W. Hamilton	1923–6	Helped with 1920s Orchestra
J.L. Hancock?	1932–pre-51	
W.M. Hancock	1945–70?	French. Originally temporary
Arthur Hare ('Doc')	1934–60	Third Headmaster.
F.W. Hastie ('Seth')	1945–70?	Maths. Old Boy
J. Haworth	1936 (2 terms)	Temporary. English
Miss S. Hawthorn	c.1944–46	Temporary
J. Hemingway	1933–50	From Central Secondary School
J. Henderson	1916–?	Temporary
T. Henderson	1896–c.1914, 1921–9	Music, singing. Part-time

Miss Margaret Henson	1921?–40*	Preparatory Dept.
A.J. Hermitage	1959/60–62	
J.M. Hindson	1953–4	Replaced Lidgey. Old Boy
A. Hird	1959/60–70?	
S.W. Hobson	1933–47	Modern Languages. Army service WWII
Miss W. Hobson	1943	Temporary
M.W. Hodgson	1966–*c.*70	Maths, physics
A.J. Hogg	1892–8	Chemistry. Replaced Staines
F. Hopper	1962/3–70?	PE. Careers master from 1966
John A. Hopwood	1966–70	Chemistry
C.A. Hovington	1964–9	English? Originally temporary. Old Boy
H.R. Hughes	1915–43	French, German. Replaced Storry
S.W. Hughes	1919–1922	Geography
Hurst	*c.*1949	
W.E. Inchbold	1878 (2 terms)	Classics
H.A. Ives	1920–47	Physics
Dr H.W. Izzard	1945–54	Modern Languages.
E.E. Jackson	post-1960–6	
Miss M. James	*c.*1944	Temporary
E. Jeavons	1962/3–5	Modern languages. Old Boy
G.R. Jenkins	1919–1920	Replaced by H.A. Ives
J.R. Jewitt	1958–60	
J. Kelleher	1966–7	On exchange from California
D.G. Kent	1966–?	Maths
Rev. R. Kent	1961–5	Part-time. Divinity
V. Kirby	1966/7–?	Cello
A.S. Kirbyshire	1914–8	Chemistry. Replaced J. Milner

J.H. Knaggs	*c.*1920?–Pre21	Old Boy
G.H. Knott (Nott?)	1898	Science master. Replaced Hogg
J. Lambert	1925/6–9	Replaced Hamilton
Miss Sarah Lawrence	1887–1905	Preparatory Class
J.P. Leighton	1924–50	Science
H.G. Lidgey	1949–53	Replaced Pickering
M.J. Lock	1965–8	Metalwork
J. Lovell	1946?–9	Biology
Lowe	*c.*1880	English
M.G. Lumsdon	1949–70?	RI, Ancient Greek
J. Lunn	1965–8	History
D. Lyonette	1961–4	PE
Rev. J. Mack	1965–6	Replaced R. Kent
J.R. Madell	1957	Temporary
J. Magoon	?–1952	English. Replaced by Owen
J.J.S. Malkin	1954–5	Chemistry. Old Boy
Marne	*c.*1900	Maths
J.W. Marshall	1878–96	Music. Part-time
D.H. Martin	1930–8	Involved with Orchestra
A. Massingham ('Massey')	1879–1910	Classics. Senior assistant master
W.F. Maurice	1960–70?	Head of History
R. Maw	1933–5	From Central Secondary School
R.S. McArthur	1930–*c.*1933	Art. Replaced Buchanan
J. McGregor	1948–9	
D. McKenzie	1959–66	Maths. Old Boy
A.T. Milne	1930–1	History. Replaced by N. Sunderland

J. Milner	1911–14	Science. Killed in action 1916. Old Boy
Dr J.W. Milner	1960–1	Physics
Rev. J.R. Missen	1917–?	Temporary. Chemistry
C.J. Mitchell	1914–15	Temporary replacement for Mutimer
R.H. Moar	1919–36	Senior English Master
Molyneux	1961–6	Head of Geography
Jacob A. Morgan	1913	Temporary maths master. Old Boy
Mrs D.I. Morris	1958–*c*.60	
P. Moss	1939?-68	Maths, Head of Library. Non-graduate. Old Boy
Dr Muller	1878–90	French, German. Part-time
R. Mutimer	1908/9–*c*.17	Geography. Killed in action
W.J. Nesbitt	1958–60	English. *Northen Echo* literary critic
E. Newcomb	1963–5	English
Newman	*c*.1885–1894	
R.E. Newton	1915–post-38/pre-51	Maths. Replaced Blain
Mrs Noble	1963–4	Chemistry
G.H. Nott, *see* G.H. Knott		
Fred W. Ord	1913–28	Elder brother of L.C. Ord. Non-graduate
L.C. Ord	1915–43	Maths. Non-graduate
Miss T.M. Ord ('Topsy')	*c*.1944–70?	Latin. Originally temporary.
P.J. Osborn	1930–68	Head of English
J.W. Owen ('Jesse')	1952–55	English.
H.C. Parr	1965–70	Head of Music. Old Boy

Geo. Peacock	1921	Woodwork. Part-time?
T.G. Pearson	1947–59	Physics. Old Boy
J.R.L. Perry	1903	Chemistry. Temporary
F. Phillips	1952–70?	PE. Old Boy
W.E. Pickering	1948 (Jan–Dec)	English, Latin, Scripture
N.A. Pooler	1964–c.70	Chemistry, physics
E.W.Y. Pratt ('Ike')	1949–c.70	Chemistry. Old Boy
J. Pryce	1882–4	French, German
Jack W. Pursey	1963–70	Head of Classics
D. Quinn ('Albert')	1949–70?	Maths
J.D. Ramsdale	1960–64	Modern languages
Mrs M. Raymond	1967–?	French
K.W.W. Redpath	1905–?	Woodwork. Part-time
Mrs Reed	1942–50	Temporary until Nov. 1943
L.G. Reedman	1955–60	Head of Classics
W.S. Richardson	1930–65	Second Master in succession to Carrick
E.L. Robson	?–1951/2	PE. Replaced by Phillips
Fred Robson	1948–54	PE. Replaced by Camburn. Old boy
Rogerson	1885–8	First Form Master
C.R. Rowland	1962–5	English. Replaced by Bateman
Miss Ruecroft	1921–5/6	Preparatory Department Graduate. Left to marry
T.N. Rutherford	pre-1951–56	
W.H. Ryder	1929	
J. Scaife	1967–?	PE
M. Scarr	1945–7	Old Boy
Shaw	1945–8	Geography. Old Boy
Shiell	c.1947–50	Physics

A. Shillington	1905–6	Modern languages. Replaced Dawson
A.J. Smith	1902–1938	Senior Classics Master. Acting Head 1916–19
D.L. Smith	1964–9	PE
F.M. Smith	1911–14	Classics assistant. Replaced by J. Todd
G.L. Smith	During WWI– Pre-1921	
Robin E. Smith	1960–70	English
W.M. Smith	1884 (1886?)–8	First Form Master
R.G. Snaith	1968–9	Metalwork
W.M. Snook	1938–1954	Head of Classics. Textbook author
H.J. Staines	1893	First chemistry master. Lasted two terms
J.A. Stanley	1959–70	French
B. Stephenson	1963–4	Head of Metalwork
C.R.B. Storry	1906–15	French
N. Sunderland	1931–70	Head of History. Deputy Head from 1965
R.L. Swinden	1933	Temporary replacement for McArthur
Miss Taylor	1915–?	Temporary
A.R. Taylor	1939–pre-54	English
Leonard W. Taylor	1913–34	Second Headmaster
R. Taylor	1950?–?	Same as A.R. Taylor?
W.H. Teasdale	1967–9	English
C.E. Thompson	1967–8	English
R.S. Thompson ('Rusty')	1945–70	Head of Physics
Rev. G. K. Tibbo	1966–?	Divinity. Part-time

H. Tiplady	1910–1	Science assistant. Old Boy. Died 1914
J. Todd	1914–21/2	History, Latin. Old Boy
A.C. Tofts	1880–*c*.84	Played for Darlington Football Club
Arthur W. Trees	1965–66	English literature
E.S. Turner	1907–16	Classics assistant. Killed in action 1916
J.E. Turner ('Jet')	1950–70	Latin
F. Walker	1933–49	From Central Secondary School
J.H. Wall	1959/60–3	Left for Methodist ministry.
J.E. Waltham	1951–68	Geography
P.J. Ward	1967–8	Latin
T.J.C. Warne, *see* T.J. Cleeve-Warne		
Watson	*c*.1890	
W. Watson	*c*.1958/9	Temporary
W.H. Welding	1950–70	Maths. Old Boy
J. Welford	1956–8	Chemistry?
R. Wharin	pre-1951–67	French/German. 'Fat Sam'
J. Wheway	1958–61	
F.J. Widdowson	1893–1902	Junior maths master and Housemaster,
Ada Williams	1905–18	Preparatory Dept.
A.R. Williams	?–1964	Left to join HM Forces.
J. Williams	1915–6/7	Chemistry. Left for munitions work.
R.T. Williams	1962–?	Geology
K.E.W. Willingham	1965–70	Head of Economics
K. Willmore	1922–4	First tuck shop master

Miss Wilmott	1914/8–1931	French, German
Mrs Mary Wilson	1958–69	Art
R. Wilson	1958–60	
J.N. Winn	1968–?	History, economics
Philip Wood	1878–1912	First Headmaster
T.E. Wood	1961–70?	Head of Handicrafts. Also English, maths
D.W. Woodcock	pre-1951–55	
Miss E. Woodfine	1964–?	Modern languages
Woollam	1883 only?	First Form Master

* Miss Henson undoubtedly retired in 1940, dying shortly afterwards, but her starting date is a puzzle. One source suggests that she came to the school in 1928, but she is also referred to as being on the staff in 1921. However, according to the governors' minutes she started in 1915, but in the School Lists both Newton and Burniston who came in 1915 and 1919 respectively are shown as being senior to her. To add confusion, the school magazine recording her retirement said that she had given 15 years' service. It may be that Miss Henson was employed on a temporary basis in 1915 and was then re-engaged post-war.

Some dates are impossible to verify because only passing references to the member of staff have been found. In other cases the starting date might be slightly inaccurate. Sources do not always distinguish between the employee's date of engagement and the date when teaching started. The list does not include foreign assistants or peripatetic music teachers.

The following were taken on part-time or temporarily during 1966–7: Mrs Raymond, W.H. Teasdale, C.E. Thompson, P.J. Ward, Father Park.

In the autumn term 1938 there were, in addition to Dr Hare and D.R. Carrick, the Second Master, twenty-five assistant masters. They were in order of their arrival at the school: L.C. Ord,* H.R. Hughes, R.E. Newton, R.A. Burniston,* H.A. Ives, A.R. Golland,* J.P. Leighton, F.S. Fothergill, W.W. Allen, C.H. Fisher, W.S. Richardson, P.J. Osborn, R.S. McArthur, N. Sunderland, W.W. Graville,* H.O. Crane,

S.W. Hodgson, E.G. Bowley, J.C. Brydon, J. Hemingway, R. Maw, F. Walker,* E.C. Axford, C. Bennett,* W.M. Snook. In addition there were Miss Henson and Miss Ellam in the Preparatory Department.

An asterisk after a name indicates a non-graduate. The proportion was higher than in post-war years because of the intake of staff from the Central Secondary School.

In January 1946 there were thirty-four teachers including the Head and W.S. Richardson. The others were Burniston, Ives, Golland, Leighton, Allen, Fisher, Osborn, Sunderland, Graville, Crane, Hobson, Hemingway, Walker, Bennett, Snook, Moss, Miss Ord, Mrs Reed, Miss Cox, Izzard, Hastie, Scarr, Shaw, Thompson, Hancock, Bird, Blamire, Eccleston, Fairbairn, J. Lovell, Mrs Gomez, and Miss Gregory.

The eleven listed from Izzard to Lovell had all come since the previous September!

By 1966 there were fifty-one assistant masters or mistresses and they are listed below as set out in the school list. They are shown in their order of starting at the school and Heads of Department have their department indicated in brackets after their name. The then Housemasters were Phillips (Britons), Green (Danes), Allen (Normans) and Griffiths (Saxons).

W.W. Allen (biology), P.J. Osborn (English), P.H. Moss (libraries), Miss Ord, W. Hastie (maths), R.S. Thompson (physics/geology), W.M. Hancock (German), J. Blamire (applied maths), Miss L. Gregory, L. Bird (art), R. Wharin, M. Lumsdon (divinity), D. Quinn, J.H. Green, L. Griffiths (PE), E. Pratt (chemistry), J.E. Turner, H. Welding, J. Waltham (geography), F. Philips, Mrs Wilson, R. Hird, J. Stanley (modern languages), W.F. Maurice (history), R.E. Smith, T.E. Wood (handicrafts), J. Board, D.S. Darby, B. de Frettes, J. Dodds, F. Hopper DPE (careers master), J. Pursey (classics), P. Copley, C.A. Hovington, N.A. Pooler, D.L. Smith, E. Woodfine, C. Dean, K. Willingham (economics), J.P. Bateman (English language/general studies), D.B. Crompton, M.J. Lock, J. Lunn, H.C. Parr (music), A.W. Trees, G.L. Clarke, J.A. Hopwood, D.G. Kent, M.W. Hodgson, J. Kelleher, Rev. G.K. Tibbo.